Reana Bezić

Juvenile Delinquency in

Research Series of the Max Planck Institute
for Foreign and International Criminal Law

Publications of the Max Planck
Partner Group for Balkan Criminology

Edited by Hans-Jörg Albrecht
& Anna-Maria Getoš Kalac

Volume BC 6

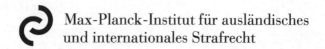

Max-Planck-Institut für ausländisches
und internationales Strafrecht

Reana Bezić

Juvenile Delinquency in the Balkans

A Regional Comparative Analysis
Based on the ISRD3 Study Findings

Duncker & Humblot · Berlin

Bibliographic information published by the Deutsche Nationalbibliothek

The Deutsche Nationalbibliothek lists this publication in the Deutsche Nationalbibliografie; detailed bibliographic data are available on the in-ternet at http://dnb.d-nb.de

© 2020 Max Planck Society for the Advancement of Science e.V.
c/o Max Planck Institute for Foreign and International Criminal Law
Günterstalstr. 73, 79100 Freiburg i.Br., Germany
www.mpicc.de
Sales and distribution together with Duncker & Humblot GmbH, Berlin, Germany
www.duncker-humblot.de
University of Zagreb – Faculty of Law, Trg Republike Hrvatske 14, 10000 Zagreb, Croatia
www.pravo.unizg.hr

International Review:
Prof. Dr. Marcelo Aebi, University of Lausanne, Switzerland

Cover picture: Nezavisni Kalesijski Portal www.PNK.ba
Portrait picture: Foto Vilić

Text editing and typesetting: Peter Welk (Lektorat Freiburg)
Printing: Stückle Druck und Verlag, Stücklestr. 1, 77955 Ettenheim, Germany
Printed in Germany

ISSN 2199-658X
ISBN 978-3-86113-281-3 (Max Planck Institute)
ISBN 978-3-428-15995-6 (Duncker & Humblot)
ISBN 978-953-270-141-8 (Zagreb Faculty of Law)
DOI: https://doi.org/10.30709/978-3-86113-281-3
CC-Lizenz by-nc-nd/3.0

For my parents Sanja and Toni with deep love and respect

Foreword

The report on "Juvenile Delinquency in the Balkans: A Comparative Analysis based on the ISRD3 Study Findings" for the first time provides a comprehensive analysis of juvenile crime in Balkan countries. The research benefits from data collected in the third wave of the International Self-Report Delinquency Study for various countries of the Western Balkan.

The study ties in with surveys on self-reported delinquency that have been one of the focal points of theoretical and empirical criminological research on juvenile delinquency since the early 20th century, but have so far been essentially limited to North America and Western Europe. The Balkan region, like Eastern Europe and the former Soviet Union, initially remained largely excluded from these developments even after the social, economic, and political transformation process that began in the late 1980s. The lack of research is certainly partly due to the disintegration of the former Yugoslavia and the civil wars that accompanied it. However, the still rather weak position of an empirically oriented criminology in the Balkan countries also contributes to this. In this respect, beyond adding to the specific area of juvenile crime studies, *Reana Bezić's* comparative research contributes to building up a theoretically guided empirical criminology and a criminological network in the Balkan region.

The availability of empirical data on juvenile delinquency in the Balkan region, which in the past was limited and restricted to official police and judicial statistics, has only changed with the implementation of the third wave of the International Self-Report Delinquency Study (ISRD3). Coordinated by an international research consortium and designed to collect comparable data, this study for the first time systematically integrated the Balkan region into self-report surveys on juvenile delinquency. In this process, as a member of the Max Planck Partner Group for Balkan Criminology and the Faculty of Law at the University of Zagreb, *Reana Bezić* was actively involved in the consortium in adapting the survey instruments to local conditions and in collecting the data in her home country Croatia. For the present work, in addition to the Croatian data, she also had at her disposal the data sets for Bosnia and Herzegovina, Kosovo, Northern Macedonia, and Serbia. As yet, this is the first comparative regional study based on the latest ISRD data.

However, the aim of the study is not a mere replication of self-report studies previously conducted in other (world) regions. Rather, it is about a precise recording and comparative analysis of juvenile delinquency in a region that differs from other European regions in central determinants of juvenile delinquency. The starting point of the study is the classification of the Balkan region as a distinct political, historical, sociological, and criminological setting to which the explanations that were generated in earlier Western European and American studies under different framework conditions are not or not directly transferable. This is because – unlike the countries of North America and Western Europe, which are affected by an increasing individualization – the countries of the Balkan region are still quite strongly characterized by a type of social integration in which the family as well as other conventional social instances of socialization and control play a significant role. Last but not least, religion and religious affiliation have a special significance in this context. In this respect, the author succeeds in elaborating such particulars of the social context that distinguish juvenile delinquency in the Balkans from that in Western European countries.

The Balkan-specific developments identified on this basis and their explanation make a significant contribution to the general understanding of youth-specific delinquency as well as to the further development of a theory of juvenile delinquency that takes systems of informal social control as its starting point. The related analyses and theoretical elaborations make this study an innovative undertaking that represents a remarkable step in the development of an empirical criminology for the Balkan region, significantly expands international knowledge on juvenile delinquency, and holds a wealth of suggestions for further research.

Freiburg, February 2021   *Professor Hans-Jörg Albrecht*

Acknowledgements

I can still vividly remember preparing for my first academic presentation in English in Dubrovnik eight years ago. Back then I was just finalising my law studies and was about to continue my professional path as a lawyer. It never had crossed my mind to engage in a PhD project, let alone pursue an academic career. However, a couple of months later I found myself in the middle of the just emerging Max Planck Partner Group for Balkan Criminology (MPPG) at the Zagreb Law Faculty and had already got heavily engaged in criminological research. One of the research projects I was taking part in was the Croatian component of the ISRD3, which also became the topic of my master thesis. A long story cut short – one thing led to another, and here I am today, not only having earned my PhD, but also having been fully accepted at my Law Faculty's Department for Criminal Law. None of this would have been possible without Assoc. Prof. Dr. *Anna-Maria Getoš Kalac's* kind support and early-on recognition of my scientific and professional potential. The inclusion in the MPPG she supervised provided me with an opportunity to conduct my doctoral research project in an international environment at the Max Planck Institute for Foreign and International Criminal Law (MPI), surrounded by top experts in the field of Criminology and Criminal Law.

Despite my PhD project being quite challenging at times, admittedly even overwhelming occasionally, thanks to the commitment and enthusiasm of my supervisors, Prof. Dr. Dr. d.c. mult. *Hans-Jörg Albrecht* and Assoc. Prof. Dr. *Anna-Maria Getoš Kalac*, it finally came to life. Their energy, outstanding work ethics and brilliant criminological thinking became a driving force and an inspiration to step outside mainstream scientific pathways. I am forever grateful to both of them for believing in me and supporting my work throughout the past years, just as I am thankful to Prof. Dr. *Davor Derenčinović* for endorsing my academic present and future in criminology at the Law Faculty.

My deep appreciation and gratitude go to Dr. *Michael Kilchling*, Dr. *Volker Grundies* and Prof. Dr. *Marcelo Aebi*, whose scientific excellence, support and encouragement guided me through the ups and downs of my PhD research. I would also like to thank my colleagues at the Department for their collegial support, in particular Assist. Prof. Dr. *Marta Dragičević Prtenjača* and Assist. Prof. Dr. *Sunčana Roksandić*, who were always happy to share their experiences.

For our inspiring conversations and their honest criticism, I wholeheartedly thank my dearest friends and colleagues from the MPI, particularly Dr. *Anina Schwarzenbach*, Dr. *Clara Rigoni* and *Salvatore Scotto Rosato*, as well as my friends and colleagues from the MPPG office, particularly *Petra Šprem* and *Karlo Ressler*. This core group of my peers shared all the challenges and successes I encountered on the scientific journey towards and throughout my PhD project.

Last but not least, my deepest gratitude goes to my beloved partner *Marko*, my parents *Sanja* and *Toni*, and to my closest family, who all unconditionally stood by my side on every step of the way.

The book at hand, as well as the PhD thesis it is based on, marks both my personal and professional life. I have learned many lessons along the way. The most important and my favourite one can be boiled down to this:

> "You can go as far as your mind lets you. What you believe, remember, you can achieve." (*Mary Kay Ash*)

Zagreb, December 2020   *Reana Bezić*

Table of Contents

List of Figures and Charts

List of Tables

Chapter 1

Introduction

This study analyses juvenile crime in the Balkans. It is based on self-report surveys carried out in several Balkan countries. It thus adopts a comparative perspective on studying juvenile crime and its variation in the Balkan countries. It furthermore contrasts the results with what we know from juvenile crime research in North American and Western European countries.

Research on juvenile delinquency has a long history. It is argued that juveniles represent the most important human capital on which societies have to rely in order to achieve sustainable progress and social change. Juvenile delinquency is a complex issue and one of the most challenging criminological and social problems. Throughout the 20th century, criminology has produced numerous studies focused on aetiological factors and phenomenological characteristics of juvenile delinquency. But the vast majority of these studies were conducted in the United States, Canada and selected Western European countries.[1] In contrast, juvenile crime research in the Balkans has remained limited. Only few empirical studies have been carried out in this region. Most of the juvenile crime literature emphasizes legal and normative issues. This has resulted in an 'empirical black hole' in the Balkans, which in turn makes cross-national and comparative criminological research on juvenile crime by far overdue.[2]

Until now, criminological research on juvenile crime conducted in the Balkan region was based on official crime and court statistics.[3] However, in some Balkan countries, not even official statistics are available for conducting criminological research. Until recently, in Bosnia and Herzegovina, there was no institution that collects data about crime and criminal justice on the state level.[4] When it comes to police statistics in Bosnia and Herzegovina, the data were collected based on their internal rules and procedures with a modified methodological approach, and the authorities do not present standardized information on processed crime reports to the public.[5] A look at prosecution and court statistics reveals further problems as these are based on the

---

1   *Hartjen & Priyadarsini* 2003; *Junger-Tas, Terlouw & Klein* 1994; *Li* 1999.

2   *Getoš* 2014.

3   See *Getoš Kalac, Albrecht & Kilchling* 2014.

4   *Maljević & Muratbegović* 2014, 105.

5   *Maljević & Muratbegović* 2014, 105.

application of various criminal codes;[6] furthermore, data are not collected on the national level. Similarly, in North Macedonia, a uniformed methodology for collecting and entering statistical data is absent,[7] which makes conducting criminal research based on official statistics a challenging enterprise. However, other countries in the Balkans – for example Croatia – allow for systematic accounts of juvenile crime on the basis of official statistics. In Croatia, the data most commonly used for criminological research are usually either police data or those from the annual reports of the Croatian Bureau of Statistics. These data sources also account for registered juvenile crime and suspects.[8] Research based on official statistics in Croatia demonstrates a slight decrease in the number of convicted juveniles, and the offence which clearly dominates the juvenile crime structure concerns property crime (approximately 70% of all juvenile crime reported and juveniles accused in 2013). A decrease in juvenile crime and a dominance of property crime can be noted for almost all Balkan countries.[9] Based on available data, when looking at the period 2000–2012, juvenile delinquency in North Macedonia is decreasing, and the offence juveniles were mostly convicted for was also property crime (78% of all juvenile convictions).[10] Based on available data in Kosovo, although reported crime committed by juveniles has increased, uncertainty remains on whether this is due to a widening of criminal law or whether this stands for a real increase of criminality.[11] Since 2000, Serbia has exhibited a stable number of juvenile delinquents known to police, and juvenile crime has been overwhelmingly related to property offences (approximately 90% of all reported crime for each year).[12]

Therefore, not only are there methodological problems – or even a complete lack of available official statistics in some Balkan countries –, there is also a universal limitation of official statistics by not covering crime that is not reported or, if so, is not officially recorded. Perhaps the most serious disadvantage of police-based crime accounts is that they do not cover the so-called 'dark number of crime' or 'dark figure' (Dunkelziffer). This encompasses the crimes that are committed but never reported or cleared up by the police and the justice system. Official statistics are often said to

---

6   As a state, Bosnia and Herzegovina is composed of two entities: the Federation of Bosnia and Herzegovina (FBiH) and the Republika Srpska (RS) as well as one district, the Brčko District of Bosnia and Herzegovina (BDBiH). Each level of government has its own legislative, administrative and judicial institutions. The criminal justice system follows this constitutional structure. Therefore, there is the Criminal Code of BiH, but each entity also has its own criminal code (the Criminal Code of the FBiH, the Criminal Code of the RS and the Criminal Code of the BDBiH).

7   *Bužarovska* 2014, 249.

8   *Getoš Kalac & Bezić* 2017, 246.

9   *Getoš Kalac & Bezić* 2017.

10   *Bužarovska* 2014, 249.

11   *Helmken* 2010, 806.

12   *Škulić* 2010, 1200–1202.

reflect just the 'tip of the iceberg' of the true volume of crime.[13] Therefore, this research will be based on a self-report study, as this approach is the true treasure trove of insights into delinquency.[14] The main purpose of this approach is to uncover the full extent of juvenile crime in the Balkans, but also to overcome the problems related to the official statistics in the region.

In most Balkan countries, the International Self-report Delinquency Study (ISRD3) was the first self-report study carried out to investigate juvenile crime, mainly focusing on delinquency. This thesis will provide a first comprehensive description of the prevalence and incidence of juvenile crime in the Balkans, based on self-reports in the juvenile populations of five countries of the region. This will provide a basis to study the extent of the phenomenon of juvenile crime and allow for an analysis of its structures. Furthermore, this study will also go into a cross-national comparison of the prevalence and incidence rates of juvenile crime in five Balkan countries: Bosnia and Herzegovina, Croatia, Kosovo, North Macedonia and Serbia. The analyses will focus on differences and similarities among the countries. Based on these differences and similarities in prevalence and incidence rates, further analyses will focus on indicators which may have an impact on the development of juvenile crime. In general, this study will focus on theory-testing and the search for mechanisms that explain juvenile crime in the region. The main theory that will be tested is the social control theory (as elaborated by *Hirschi* 1969), with a focus on family, school and religion and their potential to provide bonds which in turn prevent crime. *Hirschi* (1969) was not interested in answering the question why individuals commit crimes but focused on crime-preventing factors.

Summarizing the scope and goal of this study, the extent of juvenile crime and its relation to other factors in the context of the Balkan region will be prominent issues. The aim is to present basic data on juvenile crime in the Balkans by first addressing the prevalence of juvenile crime and then analysing the influence of family, school and religion. This will also provide useful information for establishing and developing national prevention programmes as well as for investigating the possibility of transferring internationally endorsed intervention programmes in order to reduce juvenile crime in the Balkans. Furthermore, this research aims at promoting the use of scientific evidence in planning public policy and practice that would result in evidence-based policies in the Balkan region.

---

13   *Van Dijk* 2010.
14   *Junger-Tas & Marshall* 2012, 4.

Chapter 2

Self-Reported (Juvenile) Delinquency –
A Research Summary

Self-report surveys are nowadays a well-established research method in criminology. They are one of the three major ways of measuring delinquency and crime. The development and widespread use of the self-report method for collecting data on delinquent and criminal behaviour was one of the major innovations in criminological research in the 20th century. The roots of self-report surveys can be traced back to the 1930s when they were used for measuring essential attitudes.[15] A remote predecessor would be a questionnaire ordered by *Charlemagne*, the Holy Roman Emperor, in the year 811, which was actually a crime survey[16] for local magistrates and magnates.[17] This chapter provides a general overview of the historical development of the self-report method and its role in criminological research.

2.1   Self-Report Research

2.1.1   The evolution and use of self-report delinquency research

In criminological research, the long discussion on the dark figure of crime, accompanied by the mistrust in police-recorded crime statistics, resulted in attempts to find an alternative way of revealing the true prevalence and incidence of crime. The problem of unrecorded crime and the desire to overcome the official control barrier of crime measurement haunted moral statisticians (the ancestors of the criminologists) since the 1820s and well into the 1930s.[18] One of the outcomes of this self-critical

---

15   *Junger-Tas & Marshall* 1999, 291; *Kivivuori, Salmi, & Walser* 2013.

16   The second question in the survey questionnaire asked why there were so many civil unrests and disorders, while the third question referred to causes of theft, which was widespread (*Kivivuori* 2011, 1). The results of *Charlemagne's* survey is largely lost – only one brief summary remains about the causes of theft connected to problems of authority, poverty and family structure (*Petersen et al.* 2004, 744).

17   *Kivivuori* 2011, 1.

18   *Kivivuori* 2014, 2309.

overview of moral statistics was the concept of a "dark figure" coined by the Japanese lawyer *Shigema Oba* in 1908.[19] *Thorsten Sellin* summarized the mistrust in official criminal statistics with his now famous dictum, which later became known as Sellin's law, stating that "[d]ue to a number of variable elements represented by changes in administrative policies and efficiency, the value of a crime rate for index purposes decreases as the distance from the crime itself in terms of procedure increases".[20] This means that there is an increasing lack of accuracy throughout each level of the criminal justice system.

Self-report surveys were first tested by the sociologist *Edwin H. Sutherland* in 1934, who was also trying to find a way out of the impasse caused by the poorly developed criminal statistics and empirical evidence on crime based on official statistics.[21] In her book "Can Delinquency Be Measured", *Sophia M. Robinson* mentioned *Edwin H. Sutherland* as a researcher who had already conducted experiments on the basis of self-report questionnaires.[22] It appears that *Sutherland* did so among his students during the 1930s, but he did not publish the results.[23] During his speech in front of the Milwaukee police in 1936, he presented some of the results from his experiment as follows:

> Of a class of forty, ten did not hand in papers, and since I did not have signature, I could not tell whether they were lily whites or had so many and so serious thefts that they refused to tell. Of those who did hand in reports, only one insisted that he could remember no thefts.[24]

He aimed at developing statistics with respect to criminals who are not recorded in official statistics in order to compensate for the bias in official crime statistics.[25] At that time, it was also argued that, as not so many 'criminals' were recorded, it would be unfair to punish harshly those who were caught.[26] Many other scholars at that time recognized the shortcomings of using official data as a measure of crimes committed, or as a way to identify those who had committed a crime.[27] Self-report surveys or hidden-crime surveys grew up as surveys that could solve the above-mentioned problems.[28] In 1943, *Austin L. Porterfield*, a professor of sociology at the

---

19   *Kivivuori* 2014, 2310; *Oba* 1908.

20   *Sellin* 1931, 346.

21   "Specialized statistical studies are still in a primitive stage, the units are not adequately defined and they are confined to the characteristics at a particular time and have little value in showing the process by which crime develops" (*Sutherland* 1934, 40).

22   *Robinson* 1936, 43.

23   *Kivivuori* 2011, 79.

24   *Kivivuori* 2014, 2312.

25   *Krohn et al.* 2010, 509.

26   *Kivivuori* 2011, 4.

27   *Krohn et al.* 2010, 509.

28   *Kivivuori* 2011, 4.

Texas Christian University, published a paper titled "Delinquency and Its Outcome in Court and College" in the "American Journal of Sociology", which is seen as the first paper that used self-report surveys to study delinquency among college students.[29] His scientific vision was presented, in full light, in his monography "Youth in Trouble" in 1946.[30] *Porterfield* analysed the juvenile court files of 2,049 delinquents from Texas, with the aim to identify the total number of offences they had finally been adjudicated for. He found 55 different offences. Then he conducted a survey among 200 male and 137 female college students in Texas in order to determine whether they had committed any of these 55 offences, and, if that was the case, at which frequency. One of his findings was that there was a high prevalence (which he called "ubiquity") of past delinquency among male and female college students.[31] In the sample of 200 pre-college male students, 22 % reported drunk driving, 8.5 % a false fire alarm, 13 % setting a fire in buildings (arson), 58.5 % gambling, 10 % shoplifting, 7.5 % burglary and 6 % attempted rape.[32] One male student even reported a murder, and another one reported having committed a negligent homicide, but *Porterfield* did not discuss these issues in his findings.[33] His main outcome was that delinquency is normal, and he argued that delinquents are not fundamentally different from law-abiding citizens.[34] The methodology of the study was unsophisticated in terms of the sampling, the delinquency scale used as well as the reliability and validity of the delinquency items. However, this was a landmark study in the history of the self-report methodology for two reasons: first, it warned criminologists of the existence of extensive hidden crime; and second, it introduced a method of measuring, at least partially, the dark figure of crime. Reviewers of *Porterfield's* book, however, did not immediately recognize it as turning point in criminology. This came later, in the 1950s, when he became known as the founder of the self-report delinquency survey.

The self-report technique was improved during the 1950s, and its true potential was then recognized in a self-report survey carried out by *Nye* and *Short*[35] and published in 1957. They paid special attention to methodological issues, such as scale construction,[36] reliability, validity, and sampling; their focus was not only on the distribution of delinquency but also on its aetiology and the relationship between social class and

29 *Porterfield* 1943; *Kivivuori* 2011.
30 *Kivivuori* 2011, 83.
31 *Porterfield* 1946, 38.
32 *Porterfield* 1946, 40–41.
33 *Porterfield* 1946.
34 *Porterfield* 1946, 45.
35 *Nye* 1958; *Nye, Short & Olson* 1958; *Short* 1957.
36 They used the Guttman scale which was a technical innovation in that time that allowed a relatively cheap and quick way of improving the quality of the analyses. They made a break away from the simple dichotomies between delinquents and non-delinquents in criminological research (*Aebi* 2009).

delinquent behaviour.[37] They made a list of 21 criminal and delinquent acts, but in their analyses, they mostly employed a scale composed of a subset of only seven items. They did not find a relationship between social class and delinquency, and the results of their study served to question the existing theories.[38] Soon after that, self-report questionnaires became a widespread method for criminological research. In the 1960s, a number of studies further examined the relationship between social status and delinquency.[39] They were very advanced in using the self-report method, and they used it among a more ethnically diverse population,[40] paid attention to validity as well as reliability[41] and put the focus on measuring the seriousness and frequency of the offence.[42]

2.1.2   Impact of self-report studies on crime theory

The development of self-report surveys played an important role in the evolution of criminological theory.[43] Some of the results challenged previous theories. The self-report methodology challenged the theoretical field in two major ways. First, self-report data offered the possibility to question previous knowledge about the relationship between social class and crime as well as a biased policing strategy. Previous theories had been based on the assumption that the typical offender comes from lower classes. This was challenged by some self-report findings, mostly inspired by *Short* and *Nye's* work. As they did not find a relationship between social status and delinquency, they suggested that the juvenile justice system is using extra-legal factors for making decisions. Limits and biases of official statistics were supported by the labelling theory. In particular, assumptions put forward by the labelling theory provoked interest in the mechanisms, which resulted in official registration (and the consequences of encounters with police and courts) as well as the selection processes, which produced suspects and ultimately convicted and sentenced criminals. Second, the self-report methodology provided the opportunity to collect data on the individual level and to measure social processes and interactions that may have had an influence on the causes of crime. During the 1960s, researchers extended the use of the self-report methodology by including questions regarding a juvenile's background with a delinquency scale in the same questionnaire.[44]

---

37   *Thornberry & Krohn* 2003.

38   *Nye, Short & Olson* 1958.

39   *Akers* 1964; *Clark & Wenninger* 1962; *Dentler & Monroe* 1961; *Empey & Erickson* 1966; *Erickson & Empey* 1963; *Gold* 1966; *Slocum & Stone* 1963; *Vaz* 1966; *Voss* 1966.

40   *Voss* 1966.

41   *Gold* 1966.

42   *Gold* 1966.

43   *Aebi* 2009, 28.

44   *Thornberry & Krohn* 2000.

This gave them the chance to explore etiological issues. Researchers were focusing on questions about family,[45] peers[46] and school.[47] This enabled them to test their hypotheses outside the official crime statistics. The most renowned example of using the self-report methodology in examining etiological theories can be found in "Causes of delinquency" by *Travis Hirschi* (1969). *Williams* and *McShane* state that *Hirschi's* social control theory was "the first one to be expressly rooted in the self-report tradition" and "gave criminologists theoretical puzzles to solve with the new methodology".[48] *Hirschi's* well-known hypothesis that the weakening of social bonds will allow for a higher probability of deviant behaviour, as well as his elements of the social bond (attachment, commitment, involvement and belief), are best tested and measured by asking respondents about their social background, interactions, activities and attitudes.

During the 1970s, several studies took the same direction as *Hirschi's* social control theory and were evaluated by using self-report surveys.[49] There are also other varieties of control theories, such as the self-concept theory[50] and the self-control theory[51], which were developed thanks to the progress of the self-report method. Furthermore, there are some other theoretical perspectives that are particularly beholden to the self-report methodology: the social learning theory,[52] the self-concept theory[53], and the deterrence theory[54] were routinely tested by self-report surveys.[55] Early research on the deterrence theory was based on official data with the aim to examine the severity of punishment, the probability of receiving punishment and the relationship between punishment and official national crime rates.[56] The predictor of this theory is that people make rational decisions. Therefore, so as to be able to test this predictor, researchers need to be able to determine what people assume to be the penalties and the probability of punishment. Official data do not allow for collecting this kind of information, but the self-report methodology does.

---

45   *Nye, Short & Olson* 1958; *Dentler & Monroe* 1961; *Voss* 1964; *Stanfield* 1966; *Gold* 1970.

46   *Short* 1957; *Voss* 1964; *Reiss & Rhodes* 1964; *Matthews* 1968; *Erickson & Empey* 1963; *Gold* 1970.

47   *Reiss & Rhodes* 1964; *Kelly* 1974; *Polk* 1969; *Gold* 1970.

48   *Williams & McShane* 2010, 150.

49   *Conger* 1976; *Hepburn* 1976; *Hindelang* 1973.

50   *Wells* 1978.

51   *Gottfredson & Hirschi* 1990.

52   *Akers et al.* 1979.

53   *Jensen* 1973; *Kaplan* 1972.

54   *Waldo & Chiricos* 1972; *Silberman* 1976; *Jensen, Erickson & Gibbs* 1978; *Anderson, Chiricos & Waldo* 1977.

55   *Thornberry & Krohn* 2000, 38.

56   *Krohn et al.* 2010, 519.

Its improvement led to examinations of related issues such as the experimental effect,[57] informal deterrence[58] and the extended rational choice model.[59]

In conclusion, the self-report methodology had and still has an important impact not
only on how crime is studied but also on the theoretical orientations through which
criminal behaviour is explained.

2.1.3   Introduction of self-report research in Europe

Only a few years after the *Nye* and *Short* survey, self-report research was introduced
in Europe.[60] In Scandinavian countries, the first self-report survey started with the
Nordic Draftee Research (NDR) programme. The fieldwork was conducted first in
Sweden in 1959 and then in Finland in 1962, followed by Norway and Denmark.[61]
The original NDR researchers focused on the moral idea that crime is normal, an
idea that was based on the self-report findings which demonstrated that petty crime
was quite prevalent among juvenile delinquency.[62] They also wanted to know to
what extent crime statistics reflected the real extent of crime and that, if crime statistics had proven unreliable, each nation should conduct a self-report survey annu-
ally.[63] The NDR research ended with the monograph by *Stangeland* and *Hauge*
(1974) which contained a chapter about comparative research, but a full international
report never appeared.

Among all Scandinavian countries, Denmark was the only one to regularly conduct
surveys from 1979 onwards. *Flemming Balvig* and *Britta Kyvsgaard* conducted self-
report delinquency surveys in Copenhagen suburbs in 1979, 1989, 1999 and 2005,
yielding very interesting trend results and triggering the Scandinavian discussion on
the polarization of delinquency.[64] These Danish findings probably helped stir up interest in self-report delinquency research in other Scandinavian countries. Their influence on Finnish developments of self-report surveys in the early 1990s was strong.
There is a second national representative self-report survey in Sweden called CAN,
but it only measures juvenile consumption of alcohol, narcotics, and tobacco and has
been conducted every year since 1971.[65] In Sweden, except for two national self-
report surveys, the Ninth Grade Survey and the CAN, the most common self-report
surveys are local or regional report studies. Some of them are mainly measuring

---

57   *Saltzman et al.* 1982.
58   *Paternoster & Piquero* 1995; *Layton MacKenzie & De Li* 2002.
59   *Krohn et al.* 2010, 519; *Pogarsky* 2009.
60   *Aebi* 2009, 27.
61   *Aebi* 2009, 27.
62   *Kivivuori* 2009, 78.
63   *Kivivuori* 2007, 3.
64   *Kivivuori* 2009, 79.
65   *Andersson* 2009, 221.

health, youths' ways of living, living conditions and job opportunities, and they have only a small number of questions regarding delinquency and crime. Few local self-report studies are conducted by outside researchers, starting with the Örebro Project in which the self-report survey is only one part of the project together with register studies and qualitative research conducted in the city of Örebro.[66] It was carried out as a pilot study in 1965 and published in 1971, while a second round was held in 1974, the replication of which was published in 1998.[67] The Stockholm Project investigated crime in an urban environment in Sweden, with a focus on the capital, and the self-report survey was only one part of this project.[68] However, in Finland, some self-report studies have also been conducted the main topic of which was not only crime and/or delinquency. The European School Survey Project on Alcohol and other Drugs (ESPAD) started in eight countries in the 1980s; the last round was conducted in 35 countries in 2015.[69] This survey was based on anonymous self-reports about drug and alcohol use. The ESPAD results are used in cross-validating ISRD data. In the period from the mid-1970s to the 1990s, the self-report technique was more seldom used in Scandinavian countries.

In Germany, the first self-report surveys were conducted with local or regional samples in the late 1960s and at the beginning of the 1970s.[70] Here, unlike in the Balkan region, they had been conducted since the end of the 1960s. The first wave was inspired by the idea that juvenile crime is widespread and ubiquitous. The focus was therefore put on the selection process (who goes out of the dark field and into courts, prisons?).[71] A survey by *Villmow* and *Stephan* (under the supervision of *Harald Arnold*) was carried out in the early 1970s and included a combination of self-reported crime and victimization items. This can still be found in most self-report surveys carried out today. One interesting finding of this study was the connection between reported serious offences and victimization. Those juveniles who reported heavy participation in crime were also among those who reported a high degree of victimization. The main conclusion was that victims and offenders cannot be clearly separated from each other, i.e. offender and victim roles overlap. In the United Kingdom and Ireland, the first self-report surveys were conducted in the 1960s, and since then, thirty major self-report delinquency studies have been carried out there, collecting data from more than 140,000 individuals.[72] They were inspired by the American self-report studies, mostly after the publication by *Nye* and *Short* (1957).[73] The first

---

66   *Andersson* 2009, 224.
67   *Andersson* 2009, 224.
68   *Andersson* 2009, 225.
69   *Kraus* 2015.
70   *Görgen & Rabold* 2009.
71   See, e.g., *Villmow & Stephan* 1983.
72   *McVie* 2009.
73   *McVie* 2009, 156.

major self-report delinquency study in England was the Cambridge Study in Delinquent Development. It is perhaps the most long-lasting longitudinal study of offending worldwide and has had a strong impact on the field of developmental and life-course criminology.[74] The second period of self-report research development in Europe, from the mid-1970s to the end of the 1980s, was a period in which self-report measurement was seldom used and quantitative analyses were relatively difficult and time-consuming. In this period, only few surveys were conducted in the United Kingdom: in Sheffield (1975), England and Wales (1983), and Scotland (1989).[75]

Since the 1990s, after the period of stagnation, Scandinavian countries have resorted to conducting regular self-report studies. Finland was the only Scandinavian country to participate in the first round of ISRD, which was conducted in 1992 in thirteen countries. In 1995, Finland launched the Finnish Self-Report Delinquency (FSRD) study in schools among 9th grade students, which is still periodically ongoing.[76] A similar national survey, called The Ninth Grade Survey, was conducted in Sweden in 1995 and has been run every second year since 1999.[77] It is the only national representative self-report survey in Sweden measuring general delinquency from a national perspective. The questionnaire of this survey was inspired by the one of ISRD1.[78] Analyses from 1995 to 2005 show decreasing crime trends, a result that also comes up if looking at the findings from the NDR survey. It is important to notice that both studies have paid a lot of attention to methodological issues by running different reliability and validity tests, observations during fieldwork, tests of different versions of the questionnaire, and follow-up interviews. The FSRD and the Ninth Grade Survey both targeted students in the ninth grade because this is the last time when a full age cohort can be reached in a single institution. The second round of the International Self-Report Delinquency Survey (ISRD2) was a big comeback regarding the cross-national comparison of data among all Scandinavian countries. In 2002–2003, the Mare Balticum youth victimization survey was conducted in Estonia, Finland, Germany, Lithuania, Poland and Sweden. It focused on crime victimization but also included a self-report delinquency scale.[79]

Since 1998, the Hanover-based Criminological Research Institute of Lower Saxony (*Kriminologisches Forschungsinstitut Niedersachsen*, KFN) has been conducting a series of self-report delinquency surveys in the cities of Hamburg, Leipzig, Munich, and Stuttgart, among others.[80] The KFN surveys were based on large samples and a

---

74   *Farrington* 1995.
75   *McVie* 2009.
76   *Salmi* 2009.
77   *Aebi* 2009, 15.
78   *Andersson* 2009.
79   *Dünkel, Gebauer & Kestermann* 2005.
80   *Wilmers* 2002.

questionnaire which covered twelve types of violent and property offences.[81] In 2007, a very large self-report survey funded by the German Ministry of the Interior was conducted among 9th- and 4th-grade students; the final sample size was 53,000 juveniles.[82] *Brettfeld* and *Wetzels* conducted a self-report study mainly focusing on attitudes of young Muslims living in Germany, but also containing some questions about delinquency.[83] This study was conducted among 9th- and 10th-grade students in the cities of Hamburg, Cologne and Augsburg.[84] As mentioned before, in the years 2002–2003, a survey on "Juveniles as victims and offenders of violence in the countries of the Baltic Sea region" (Mare Balticum Youth Survey) was conducted in Germany and five other European countries.[85] Germany has participated in the first round of the ISRD study as well as in ISRD2 and ISRD3. Many more self-report studies have been conducted in Germany on a local or regional level. Most of them focused on adolescence. However, since 1980, the German General Social Survey (ALLBUS), an ongoing survey at the national level, has been conducted among adults every two years.[86] From the 1990s onwards, the ALLABUS survey has included four items regarding delinquency (shoplifting, fare dodging, driving under the influence of alcohol and tax evasion).[87] As presented above, Germany has a long tradition of conducting self-report delinquency studies. The self-report surveys did not have a strong impact on criminal policies yet, but they are references in the Periodic Security Report published by the German government.[88]

In the UK, among the self-report surveys launched in the 1990s were Young People and Crime, The Youth Lifestyles Survey, "Understanding Offending amongst Young People" and ISRD1. Young People and Crime was conducted by *Graham* and *Bowling* in 1992 and 1993. The target group were males and females between 14 and 25 years of age in England and Wales, with an overall sample of 2,529 young people.[89] The survey was conducted through face-to-face interviews by using a pencil and paper questionnaire which was based on the ISRD1 questionnaire.[90] The Youth Lifestyles Survey was a follow-up survey of Young People and Crime conducted in England and Wales among 4,848 males and females aged 12–30.[91] "Understanding Offending amongst Young People" explored the choices young people make with

81   *Wilmers* 2002.
82   *Görgen & Rabold* 2009.
83   *Brettfeld & Wetzels* 2007.
84   *Brettfeld & Wetzels* 2007.
85   *Dünkel, Gebauer & Kestermann* 2005.
86   *Görgen & Rabold* 2009.
87   *Görgen & Rabold* 2009.
88   *Aebi* 2009, 17.
89   *Graham, Bowling & Smith* 1996.
90   *McVie* 2009.
91   *McVie* 2009.

respect to their involvement in offending and, in particular, young people's decisions to resist, desist from and persist in offending behaviour.[92] It consisted of a survey of 1,274 3rd- and 4th-year secondary school pupils from two Scottish towns, interviews with 276 young people in three age groups (14–15, 18–19 and 22–25 years) and interviews with a small sample of police officers, teachers and social workers.[93] In 1992, ISRD1 was conducted in England and Wales by interviewing 2,533 young people of 14–25 years of age in their homes.[94] The project had three main components: to describe the nature of offending among young people, to contribute to a comparative international study and to provide (for the first time in the UK) comparative data among young people from different ethnic groups.[95]

The Peterborough Adolescent and Young Adult Development Study (PADS+) is a study about the social lives and crimes of 700 adolescents and young adults in Peterborough, UK.[96] The aim of the study was to explore young people's exposure to their social environment and its interaction with their personal characteristics and experiences, as well as to predict their crime involvement by introducing modern research design and new methodologies.[97] The United Kingdom also conducts self-report surveys supported by some of its institutions, such as: Offending Crime and Justice Survey in England and Wales; and the Northern Ireland Crime and Justice Survey in Northern Ireland.[98] The United Kingdom did not participate in ISRD2, but did so in ISRD3 (with surveys in England and Scotland). There are also some local and regional studies, but naming all of them would be beyond the scope of this thesis. The increase in the number of self-report studies was supported by the Central Government's funding practices, the main provider of financial support, and the political willingness to develop juvenile justice policies through "evidence-based" approaches with the help of self-report surveys on juvenile delinquency.[99]

The first self-report study in Belgium was conducted in 1976, followed by two other surveys in the 1980s.[100] In the 1990s, there were no systematic Belgian self-report survey, and in the 2000s, only two surveys were conducted in the Flemish region and in Brussels.[101] Therefore, self-report surveys do not play an important role in developing criminal policies regarding juveniles in Belgium.

---

92   *Jamieson, McIvor & Murray* 1999.
93   *Jamieson, McIvor & Murray* 1999.
94   *Bowling, Graham & Ross* 1994.
95   *Bowling, Graham & Ross* 1994.
96   *Wikström, Oberwittler, Treiber & Hardie* 2012, 44.
97   *Wikström, Oberwittler, Treiber & Hardie* 2012, 44.
98   *Aebi* 2009, 16.
99   *Aebi* 2009, 16.
100 *Aebi* 2009, 18.
101 *Aebi* 2009, 18.

Among the Western European countries, France was the last one to introduce self-report studies. The first one was conducted in 1999, with a sample of two cities.[102] As much as in Belgium, self-report studies do not play a role here in the development of juvenile crime policies.

2.1.4 Cross-national research based on the self-report method

Throughout recent history, many attempts have been made to use the self-report methodology in international comparative research. In the last decade, the interest in comparative and cross-national research has been growing. Globalization and the increase of international contacts among policy-makers and scientists create a need for more comparative studies on crime and criminal justice. The United Nations initiated a worldwide comparison between nations on the basis of police and criminal justice statistics.[103] However, this comparison was made based on official crime statistics. These data have their limitations because countries differ widely in the organization of their police and criminal justice systems, the definition of offences as well as the rules and the way they collect and present their statistics.[104] The Council of Europe is also undertaking efforts to improve the accuracy and usefulness of international crime statistics and to tackle the drawbacks of underreporting and nonstandard indicators with the the European Sourcebook project.[105] A big impact on the development of cross-national self-report studies was made by the International Crime Victimization Survey (ICVS). This investigation collected victimization data from a large number of countries.[106] It was conducted for the first time in 1989 among 14 industrialized countries. A second round was carried out between 1992 and 1994 – this time not only in industrialized but also in Central, Eastern European and developing countries. A third sweep was conducted in 1996 and included eleven industrialized countries, 13 developing countries and twenty countries in transition.[107] In 1996, the countries which participated in the ICVS for the first time were Albania, Bolivia, Croatia, Kyrgyzstan, Latvia, Macedonia, Mongolia, Paraguay, Romania, Yugoslavia, and Zimbabwe.[108]

The major step in cross-national comparative research with a focus on juvenile delinquency was done with the International Self-Report Study (ISRD). The idea to conduct an ISRD – a cross-national study focusing on juvenile delinquency and victimization – was the outcome of the NATO Advanced Research Workshop held in

---

102 *Aebi* 2009, 18.
103 See *Vetere & Newman* 1977; *Pease & Hukkula* 1990.
104 *Junger-Tas* 2010, 72.
105 Council of Europe 1996, 2003, 2006 & 2014.
106 *Van Dijk et al.* 2007.
107 *Zvekić* 1998.
108 *Zvekić* 1996.

Noordwijkerhout in the Netherlands in 1988.[109] The first sweep of this study was launched in 1992 by the Dutch Research and Documentation Centre (WODC).[110] The study was conducted in 13 developed countries: three Anglo-Saxon countries (Northern Ireland, England/Wales, and Nebraska/USA), five countries from North-western Europe (the Netherlands, Germany, Belgium, Switzerland, and Finland), and three countries from Southern Europe (Italy, Spain, and Portugal). The objectives of the ISRD1 project were to examine the cross-national variability in patterns of self-reported delinquent behaviour so as to measure the prevalence rates of juvenile delinquency and to improve the self-report methodology. The most important lesson learned from ISRD1 was that a standardization of the methodology should be improved in order to have better possibilities for data comparison.[111] Although the instrument was tested and used a reliable and valid questionnaire,[112] some researchers introduced individual modifications to it by not including all of the questions, by using different wording and different categories of responses. As a result, it was challenging to merge different datasets and produce a cross-national comparison of the data.[113] When implementing a new method, it is important not only to test the instrument but also to instruct researchers on how to apply it.

Based on the lessons learned in the ISRD1, a second round of the study was conducted in 30 countries in 2006.[114] It should be noticed that two countries from the Balkan region participated, too: Slovenia and Bosnia and Herzegovina. This time, much more attention was devoted to the methodology. A steering committee was established at the Annual Conference of the European Society of Criminology in Helsinki in 2003.[115] They developed an ISRD survey protocol with the aim to employ a standardization of the comparative design and methodology, such as a standardized questionnaire and sampling process, precisely defined coding rules, and data entry as well as an agreement to integrate national databases into an international one.[116] The ISRD2 opted for city-based samples, rather than national random samples, because the main purpose of the study was to examine the theoretical correlates of juvenile delinquency.[117] A core sample was a school-based one of at least 2,000 students per participating country. The sample design required a minimum of five

109 *Junger-Tas et al.* 1994.
110 *Junger-Tas et al.* 1994.
111 *Aebi* 2009.
112 *Zhang, Benson & Deng* 2000.
113 *Junger-Tas* 2010.
114 Armenia, Aruba, Austria, Belgium, Bosnia and Herzegovina, Canada, Cyprus, Czech Republic, Denmark, Estonia, Germany, Hungary, Iceland, Ireland, Italy, Lithuania, the Netherlands, the Netherlands Antilles, Northern Ireland, Norway, Poland, Portugal, Russia, Scotland, Slovenia, Surinam, Sweden, Switzerland, the United States of America, and Venezuela.
115 *Aebi* 2009.
116 *Junger-Tas et al.* 2012.
117 *Junger-Tas* 2010, 74.

cities, including a metropolitan area, a medium-sized city, and three small rural towns. Most of the countries used a paper-and-pencil version of the questionnaire; however, some used the online version. The main theoretical framework was the social bonding theory. Nevertheless, the questionnaire included the Grasmick self-control scale that allows for testing the general theory of delinquency and/or the self-control theory (*Gottfredson* and *Hirschi* 1990), as well as questions related to the social learning theory and lifestyle variables that allowed for testing the opportunity-based theory.[118] After the end of ISRD2, it was clear that it would be followed by an ISRD3 project[119]– as one of the main ideas of the ISRD project was to achieve a research cycle to be repeated at certain time intervals. It is important to notice that this was the first time for most of the Balkan countries to participate in a self-report study with a focus on juvenile delinquency. Some of the results of this ISRD3 project will be presented in this doctoral research.

2.1.5 Self-report methodology in longitudinal studies

After having conducted numerous national self-report studies, there was a clear need for expanding their scope by following original respondents from their teenage years up to their adulthood in a longitudinal penal design. Longitudinal research in criminology is focusing on the development of criminal careers and on the influence of risk or protective factors and life events on the development of offending.[120] The first major self-report delinquency study in England was the Cambridge Study in Delinquent Development. It is perhaps the longest-lasting longitudinal study of offending worldwide and continues to have a strong impact in the field of developmental and life-course criminology. The Cambridge Study was conducted for the first time in 1961 among 411 males, all of whom were living in a deprived working-class inner-city area of South London. It was focused on their criminal careers up to the age of 50 and looked at their officially recorded convictions, self-reported offending and life success up to the age of 48. The main aims of the study were to investigate the development of offending and antisocial behaviour from the age of 10 to the age of 50 as well as the adult life adjustment of 'persisters', 'desisters' and 'late-onset' offenders at the age of 48. The Cambridge Study had a strong impact on criminological research because of the data that were collected from a wide range of sources, the quality of the collected information and the long time range of the study. Since the 1990s, self-report research has increased in the UK so that many new longitudinal studies have been conducted. Thus, new longitudinal surveys were introduced, such as the Peterborough Adolescent and the Young Adult Development Study, the Edinburgh Study of Youth Transitions to Crime and the Belfast Youth Development

---

118 *Aebi* 2009.

119 For more information about the ISRD3 study, see *Chapter 4*.

120 *Farrington* 2015b.

Study. The Edinburgh Study of Youth Transitions to Crime is a longitudinal study of 4,300 young people who started secondary school in 1998 in the city of Edinburgh. It aims at furthering our understanding of criminal offending in young people by studying the physical and social structure of neighbourhoods, the individual's development over their life course, and interactions with the official apparatus of social work and law enforcement. Already in its early sweeps, the study showed that juvenile delinquency is very strongly correlated with measures of parental supervision, but less strongly with measures of parental attachment. It suggests that at a young age, it is more important that parents focus more on supervision and direct control of children than on the quality of their attachment. Self-report studies conducted in the United Kingdom investigated the distribution and causes of crime as well as the development and testing of criminological theories. The Belfast Youth Development Study (BYDS) is one of the recent longitudinal adolescence studies on drug use in UK. The first phase of the study (2000–2005) concentrated on the school years between ages 11 and 16, while the second phase (2006–2010) examined how the participants experienced their development into late adolescence and early adulthood between the ages of 16 and 22.

It is important to notice that Germany, together with the UK, is one of the few countries in Europe where longitudinal studies based on self-report delinquency surveys are being conducted. There are two types of longitudinal research in Germany: first, those conducted on the local level; and second, those that aim at comparing the self-report data with official statistics.[121] Although most of them started in the 2000s, one study ranged from 1977 until 1996, following a group of children from the age of 13 until they were 25 years old.[122] It was conducted by the Department of Child and Adolescent Psychiatry at the Central Institute of Mental Health in Mannheim.[123] The main finding was that the prevalence of persistent offending is underestimated by police and court data in case of early adulthood juveniles.[124] In the 2000s, many self-report surveys with a longitudinal approach started in Germany, such as the school-based surveys in Münster and Duisburg.[125] Findings show a slight decrease in self-reported delinquency over time.[126] A longitudinal study conducted in Bremen found that decisions made by the criminal justice system were influenced by young people's education and work status.[127] Other longitudinal studies in Germany encompass "Wege aus schwerer Jugendkriminalität" by *Lösel*, *Bliesener* and *Bender*.[128]

---

121 *Aebi* 2009, 17.
122 *Görgen & Rabold* 2009, 131.
123 *Görgen & Rabold* 2009, 132.
124 *Görgen & Rabold* 2009, 132.
125 *Boers & Reinecke* 2007.
126 *Görgen & Rabold* 2009, 131.
127 *Schumann* 2007.
128 *Görgen & Rabold* 2009.

Among the most prominent longitudinal self-report surveys on juvenile delinquency in the USA are the Pittsburgh Youth Study and the Rochester Youth Development Study. Limitations of previous surveys of this kind were the main reason for conducting the Pittsburgh Youth Study.[129] Its focus is on the development of juvenile offending, mental health problems, drug use, and their risk factors. The survey started in the 1980s with three different samples of boys, which are followed up at frequent intervals in order to test to what extent the results are replicable.[130] The Rochester Youth Development Study (RYDS) began in 1986 and has a longitudinal research design to follow a group of juveniles from their early teenage years through to their early adulthood.[131] The purpose of the RYDS is to investigate the causes and consequences of adolescent delinquency, with a focus on serious chronic offenders.[132]

2.2 Main Findings of Self-Report Research

As presented in the previous chapter, the self-report methodology has a long history of researching juvenile delinquency. Research on the dark figure of crime and mistrust in police-recorded crime statistics has shown that most young people commit a criminal offence at least once in their lifetime. Most of the crimes committed by young people do not come to the attention of the police or courts. Most of these offences are petty ones. Self-report delinquency studies have shown that petty crime among juveniles is a normal part of adolescence, with a peak around the age of 16. Thus, research has shown that serious crime and chronic offending is rather rare among juveniles. Most young people stop offending after transiting into adult life. It is important to notice that long-term self-report analyses have shown that juvenile delinquency is decreasing across Europe.

The self-report studies presented below support the above-mentioned findings as well as some aetiology factors of juvenile delinquency. Based on self-report surveys, some of the risk factors of delinquency are a low social status of one's family, restricted educational opportunities, a negative family climate, strained child-parental relationships, parental violence and violent video games. Theoretical approaches used in most of the self-report studies in Europe concern social control (*Hirschi* 1969), the self-control theory (*Gottfredson* and *Hirschi* 1990), and the development theory (*Sampson* and *Laub* 1993).

Most of these findings were established and/or confirmed by the Cambridge Study. This was the first major self-report delinquency study in England; it was not designed

---

129 *Loeber et al.* 2003.
130 *Loeber et al.* 2003.
131 *Thornberry et al.* 2003.
132 *Thornberry et al.* 2003.

to test any particular theory of delinquency, but to test different hypotheses about the causes of delinquency and different risk factors which influence juvenile delinquency. The results showed that the cumulative prevalence of self-reported offending was very high: up to 32.96 % of urban working-class males admitted having committed at least one crime that could, in theory, have led to a criminal conviction.[133] Commonly, they reported less serious offences, such as burglary (only 22 % admitted burglary, and only 14 % were convicted for this offence).[134] Repeated self-report surveys have shown that the most common crimes of shoplifting, theft of and from vehicles, and vandalism declined in prevalence from the teenage years to the twenties and thirties, while theft from work, assault, drug abuse, and fraud were not declining over time.[135] This study produced six categories of predictors for later offending at ages 8–10: antisocial child behaviour, impulsivity, low intelligent and low school achievement, family criminality, family poverty, and poor parental child-rearing (including poor parental supervision, parental conflicts and separation from parents).[136] Many of these findings have been confirmed by research in other countries.

Findings from the Young People and Crime survey showed that the prevalence of male participation in offending increases with age, from 24 % to 31 %, but the frequency declines, and the type of offending changes in the same way as reported in the Cambridge Study: the older males are more likely to commit fraud and theft at the workplace and are less likely to engage in violent and property offences.[137] The study reported that predictors for later offending for both genders were contact with delinquent peers, truancy and low parental supervision.[138] The results of the Young People and Crime Survey were similar to ones of the Cambridge Study.

The KFN survey conducted in 2000 in Germany showed that 69 % of respondents reported participation in crime. The range of self-reported criminal offences also included petty offences such as fare-dodging. Like in Scandinavian countries, delinquency represents a rather normal behaviour in adolescence. Serious offences were reported only by a small number of respondents, varying between 1 % and 4 %. Different types of crime, violent offences and vandalism, as well as severe forms of theft were reported much more frequently by boys than by girls, but when it comes to shoplifting, there are no gender differences. Results show different levels of violence among ethnic groups. This was explained through a "culture of honour" with a particular influence among juveniles of Turkish and Yugoslavian origin. One of the findings from the *Brettfeld* and *Wetzels* survey was that for non-Muslim juveniles, there is a negative correlation between religiosity and self-reported violence (43 %

133 *Farrington* 2003, 146.
134 *Farrington* 1989.
135 *Farrington* 1989.
136 *Farrington* 2003.
137 *Graham, Bowling & Smith* 1996.
138 *Graham, Bowling & Smith* 1996.

of those declaring themselves to be not at all religious report violence, as opposed to 18.5 % of very religious juveniles), but for Muslim juveniles, such a correlation was not found (29.2 % of not at all religious vs. 28.6 % of very religious juveniles). In a survey conducted in Freiburg and Cologne among juveniles from 9th grade in 1999, 11.5 % of female and 28.9 % of male respondents reported having committed at least one violent act during the past twelve months, and theft was the most widespread crime among both females and males. The German ISRD2 study was conducted in small towns, medium-sized cities and large cities among juveniles from 7th to 9th grade. The results showed that 31 % of the juveniles reported having committed at least one offence during the previous year. The most common offences were less serious: vandalism (13.4 %), group fights (12.1 %), carrying a weapon (10 %) and shoplifting (7.9 %). More serious offences were reported by less than 5 % of respondents, and in this category, the most common offences were assault (4.7 %) and selling drugs (3.3 %). A significant factor which comes up in multivariate analyses is the lifestyle of juveniles. It affects delinquent behaviour indirectly through characteristics of the family (parental supervision and attachment) and neighbourhoods. However, low self-control, risky leisure time behaviour, and delinquent peers are also strong predictors for less serious violent and property offences.

In 1992–1993, the Norwegian Research Council's Centre for Youth Research conducted the self-report survey "Young in Norway" among students between 12 and 16 years of age.[139] Among all 15 delinquent behaviours, truancy (54.3 %), cursing at a teacher (45.1 %), and refraining from paying on the bus (40.9 %) were most frequently reported.[140] These are all petty crimes, while reported serious crimes were between 2 % to 5 %.[141]

With regard to juvenile crime, the analysis of delinquency trends has been greatly facilitated by the re-emergence of self-report delinquency studies. By a lucky coincidence, both Sweden and Finland launched national self-report delinquency surveys in 1995, whereas the Danes had already initiated a series of surveys as early as 1979. The Finnish Self-Report Delinquency (FSRD) study and the above-mentioned Swedish national self-report delinquency survey are a series of nationally representative self-report surveys of juvenile delinquency in the mentioned countries. The first round was conducted in 1995 and the most recent one in 2008. In its 6th round, the FSRD study shows a decrease of reported property-related crimes as well as a stable situation regarding the reported prevalence of violence offences and the use of toxic substances.[142] The trend is rather similar for both genders, although the declining trend is steeper among males. In the 1990s, participation in property offences was more prevalent among boys, but in 2008, male prevalence was similar to female

---

139 *Pedersen & Wichstroem* 1995.
140 *Storvoll, Wichstrøm, Kolstad & Pape* 2002.
141 *Storvoll, Wichstrøm, Kolstad & Pape* 2002.
142 *Salmi* 2009, 208–210.

prevalence.[143] Participation in violence is still more prevalent among boys than girls. However, using intoxicants has been somewhat more common among girls than among boys in all six sweeps. One of the major trends recorded during the FSRD has been an increasing number of "completely law-abiding" juveniles.[144] In the 2008 sweep, however, this trend seems to have come to an end. Delinquency trends are more or less similar in all Scandinavian countries; especially Finland and Sweden have nearly identical trends regarding juvenile delinquency, but also in the number of "completely law-abiding" juveniles.[145] Danish criminologists conducted self-report delinquency surveys in a suburb in Copenhagen in 1979, 1989, 1999, and 2005; they found that adolescents participated less in crime and have become increasingly law-abiding. The rise of law-abidingness largely reflects the decrease of property offences, such as theft and vandalism.[146] In Norway, two large-scale youth surveys with self-report delinquency questions were conducted in 1992 and 2002, and as opposed to Finland and Sweden, the prevalence of vandalism destruction increased here, while the prevalence of violent behaviour decreased.[147] Adolescent participation in shoplifting decreased in Finland and Sweden after the mid-1990s, but has levelled off in recent years. A long-term analysis suggests that juvenile crime increased in the Scandinavian countries from the Second World War until the 1970s when the trend reversed.[148]

The main findings of the ISRD1 results were published by *Junger-Tas, Marshall,* and *Ribeaud* in 2003, among which the following were prominent: lifetime prevalence rates are similar across countries, but there are cross-national disparities; property offences are highest in the most developed countries, which was explained by the opportunity theory; the Netherlands (which has the most tolerant policy on the possession and use of soft drugs) is in the middle of the drug-use scale rates; the peak age of delinquency is 15 in the Anglo-Saxon cluster and 16 in other clusters; the prevalence and frequency of offending are lower for females than for males, but gender disparity is smaller for property offending and drug use while it is larger for violent and serious offences; relationships with parents are not connected with overall delinquency but related to serious delinquency and drug use. In the ISRD1 study, rates of lifetime offending presented that three-quarters of the sample reported having committed a delinquent act in their life, and nearly half had done so in the last year.[149] This finding confirmed the hypothesis of that time that juvenile delinquency is much more widespread than official statistics make believe. They also reported

---

143 *Salmi* 2009, 208–210.
144 *Salmi* 2009, 208–210.
145 *Kivivuori* 2009, 88.
146 *Kivivuori & Bernburg* 2011.
147 *Kivivuori & Bernburg* 2011.
148 *Kivivuori & Bernburg* 2011.
149 *Bowling, Graham & Ross* 1994, 82.

that juvenile delinquency increases during childhood, with its peak at the age of 20 (17 for females and 20 for males).[150] Males were also 2 times more likely to report having offended in the last year than females.[151]

Some of the findings from the ISRD2 survey were published by *Junger-Tas, Marshall, Enzmann, Killias, Steketee*, and *Gruszczynska* in 2012, including the following: lifetime as well as last-year delinquency rates were highest in Anglo-Saxon and West European countries, while the lowest were found in post-socialist countries; there were big differences between countries in rates of property offences (in Anglo-Saxon, Western European and Northern European countries, they were especially high); property crime is high in the very prosperous countries cluster with a mobile juveniles population which is hard to control; delinquency is lower among females than males; the age of onset does not differ among countries, it ranges between 12 and 14 years; young people generally operate in groups – vandalism, car theft and breaking into buildings are more likely to be committed in groups, while shoplifting is also done alone quite frequently; migrant youths, mostly originating from Turkey as well as Central and Eastern Europe, commit more violent offences.

The ISRD2 survey focused on testing four theoretical perspectives: the social bonding/social control theory, the self-control theory, the routine activities/opportunity theory, and the social disorganization theory. They found support for all four theoretical perspectives: the social control theory was supported mostly through school-related variables, followed by parental supervision; the self-control theory and interaction between self-control and opportunities were supported by juvenile's lifestyle, while the routine activities theory was tested through lifestyle and delinquent friends; and the social disorganization theory was correlated through neighbourhood disorganization.[152]

Salmi and *Kivivuori* (2006) conducted a survey on risk factors of delinquent behaviour by using cross-sectional data collected in Finland. They found that when self-control and school achievement were controlled, the direct effect of social control (including parental and teacher support) on delinquency eroded but remained robust. Swedish researchers have criticized the way parental control is measured in criminological research, mostly because they argue that parental knowledge depends on a child's spontaneous disclosure of information.[153]

In their book "Breaking Rules", *Wikström, Oberwittler, Treiber*, and *Hardie* tested the new Situational Action Theory (SAT) which aims at explaining the role of the person-environment interaction in crime causation based on the PADS+ project,

---

150 *Bowling, Graham & Ross* 1994, 82.

151 *Bowling, Graham & Ross* 1994, 51.

152 *Junger-Tas et al.* 2012, 349.

153 *Hikan & Kerr* 2000.

which was designed to test key propositions of SAT.[154] They proposed effective ways to change young people's involvement in crime through certain measures. These measures are supposed to have an influence on the development of juvenile's morality and the ability to exercise self-control.[155]

All of these studies were mostly conducted in Western Europe and the USA. Theories which were drawn from these studies were based on the results from highly developed countries with a specific cultural, historical and economic background. This is also one of the reasons why this doctoral thesis is based only on data from Balkan countries. Its aim is to empirically test whether the same theories which were applied and tested in Western European countries and the USA are also valid in the Balkan region.

2.3   Self-Report Research in the Balkans

As *Sundhaussen* states, "the Balkans are complicated like hardly any other European region",[156] and this is not only true when talking about defining its boarders but also when discussing its past political, historical, sociological, and criminological setting.[157] When dealing with criminological research in the Balkans, it is important to notice, as *Getoš Kalac* states, that the "Balkans are, besides being a unique historical, cultural, religious and legal region, also a criminological region *sui generis*".[158] Given the lack of national criminological research going on in the region, comparative European surveys, especially quantitative ones, have so far, at best, covered only part of the region.[159] This has created an 'empirical black hole' in the very centre of the Balkans, therefore making a cross-national research with a Balkan approach far overdue.[160] Some of the international comparative research (almost) does not include Central and Eastern European countries, which is also one of the reasons for creating an 'empirical black hole' in the Balkans.[161] This lack of criminological research from and on the Balkans has had an effect not only on research and education but also on policy-making.[162] This kind of policy-making is not a product of modern

---

154 *Wikström, Oberwittler, Treiber & Hardie* 2012, 405.
155 *Wikström, Oberwittler, Treiber & Hardie* 2012, 409.
156 See *Sundhaussen* 2014.
157 *Getoš Kalac* 2014, 24–25.
158 *Getoš Kalac* 2014, 25.
159 *Winterdyk & Kilchling* 2014.
160 *Getoš Kalac* 2014, 9.
161 See *Albrecht & Kilchling* 2002.
162 *Winterdyk & Kilchling* 2014.

evidence-based policy models.[163] Looking at European criminology, one can conclude that no other region has received as little attention as the Balkans,[164] and the same is valid for self-report research. Reasons could lie in the region's complex historical, economic, and cultural situation, but also in the lack of a solid network of professionals and institutions, which was overcome by establishing the Max Planck partner group for Balkan Criminology (MPPG)[165] as a joint venture of the Max Planck Institute for Foreign and International Criminal Law in Freiburg (MPI) and the Faculty of Law at the University of Zagreb (PFZ).

In the Balkans, the first self-report research with a main focus on juvenile delinquency started with the second sweep of the International Self-Report Delinquency study (ISRD2). It was conducted between 2005 and 2007 in 31 countries and has led to a better knowledge about the causes of delinquency in these countries, which were divided into clusters.[166] It was tried to expand the survey to countries that belong to Central and Eastern Europe.[167] This cluster is of interest for this thesis, although unfortunately, only three countries participated in the end: Bosnia and Herzegovina, Hungary and Slovenia, which were part of the post-socialist countries cluster. Therefore, among the countries analysed in this thesis, Bosnia and Herzegovina was the first country to conduct the international self-report study focused on juvenile delinquency.[168] The most frequently reported delinquent acts in Bosnia and Herzegovina were group fights, carrying a weapon, vandalism and shoplifting (not taking into consideration illegal downloading, which was the most reported delinquent act in the survey).[169] When comparing the data on a cross-national level, Bosnia and Herzegovina was among the countries (most of which were new EU members as well as non-member countries) with the lowest last-year prevalence rate of minor and serious property offences. One of the explanations by the researchers (who came from developed countries) was that in these countries, there is a general lack of big self-service shops[170] and thus of opportunities for theft; therefore, countries with smaller shops have a higher degree of social control.[171] Another explanation was that in these countries, a higher level of informal social control is exercised on young people.[172] A first explanation could be because of a lack of researchers from lesser developed countries in terms of knowing the economic and social situation in these countries. Most studies and analyses in the Balkans have been conducted by researchers from

---

163 *Winterdyk & Kilchling* 2014.
164 *Getoš Kalac* 2014.
165 See http://balkan-criminology.eu/en/ [19/10/2018].
166 *Junger-Tas & Marshall* 2012, 5.
167 *Junger-Tas & Marshall* 2012, 5.
168 *Maljević* 2006, 416.
169 *Budimlić et al.* 2010, 349–350.
170 *Junger-Tas* 2012a, 71.
171 *Junger-Tas* 2012a, 71.
172 *Junger-Tas* 2012a, 71.

outside, with a lack of local language proficiency and different cultural mentalities, which was risky with regard to the research outcomes.[173] Gathering a network of researchers from the Balkan region with an ability to share their specific knowledge about their respective home country is also one of the goals of the MPPG, which adds value to every criminological research. The second explanation is part of the research questions in this thesis: to test if informal social control plays a role in the decreasing delinquency acts in the Balkans. In ISRD2, a comparison was made between all clusters on the first level – and between countries within the post-socialist cluster on a second level.[174] Together with the countries from the Latin American cluster, the post-socialist ones showed the lowest rate of "last-year" and "lifetime" juvenile delinquency.[175] The clusters hardly differed when measuring the age of onset, which is between 12 and 14.[176] As was expected, boys have higher rates of delinquent behaviour than girls.[177] A test regarding the theory on social control was made based on ISRD2 data, with the results supporting that theory.[178] A strong correlation was found between family bonding and family control, suggesting that one factor cannot have an impact on behaviour without the other, and frequent leisure time was found to be highly correlated to attachment to father and mother as well as parental control.[179] As a conclusion, it was proposed to consider family integration as a whole, not as two separate dimensions in the variables family control and family attachment.[180] It is important to notice that these findings were based on the overall sample – i.e., not on cluster analyses. Therefore, it would be of interest to check if, based on the overall sample (including countries from all over the world), the same findings would unfold in the Balkan region.

Major progress regarding self-report research on juvenile delinquency in the Balkans was achieved with the third sweep of the International Self-Report Delinquency study (ISRD3). It was expanded to Southeastern European and thus to most of the countries in the Balkans. In Croatia,[181] Serbia,[182] North Macedonia,[183] and Kosovo,[184] this was the first time a self-report juvenile delinquency survey has been conducted.

---

173 *Getoš Kalac* 2012b.

174 The post-socialist cluster contained the following countries: Estonia, Lithuania, Poland, Czech Republic, Hungary, Slovenia, Bosnia and Herzegovina, Russia, and Armenia.

175 *Junger-Tas* 2012a, 91.

176 *Junger-Tas* 2012a, 91.

177 *Junger-Tas* 2012a, 84.

178 *Junger-Tas* 2012b.

179 *Junger-Tas* 2012b, 205.

180 *Junger-Tas* 2012b, 206.

181 See *Getoš Kalac & Karlović* 2014, 150.

182 See *Nikolić-Ristanović & Stevković* 2015.

183 See *Bužarovska* 2014.

184 *Krasniqi* 2014.

As mentioned before, there is a lack of self-report studies on juvenile delinquency in the Balkans. However, some self-report studies have been conducted on the national level. The Balkan Epidemiological Study on Child Abuse and Neglect (BECAN) was a cross-sectional research project of lifetime and past-year prevalence of exposure to violence among children 11 to 16 years old.[185] The BECAN study was primarily a victim survey and did not focus on juvenile delinquency. The self-report questionnaire aimed at investigating the problem of children's violence exposure in nine Balkan countries. The study was conducted from 2009 until 2012 in the following countries: Albania, Bosnia and Herzegovina, Bulgaria, Croatia, Greece, North Macedonia, Romania, Serbia, and Turkey.[186] It utilized the ICAST-C questionnaire which measures self-reported exposure to various types of violence (by all potential perpetrators), its items being structured in different sub-scales corresponding to children's exposure to physical, psychological, and sexual violence and neglect.[187] BECAN was the first study to examine past-year and lifetime prevalence in multiple countries in the region as well as the first one to use a comparable cross-country methodology based on self-report surveys. Findings from the BECAN study show that the rates of physical violence exposure were high in almost every second child reporting past-year exposure and in more than every second child reporting lifetime victimization.[188] Physical violence exposure varied between 50.6 % (North Macedonia) and 76.3 % (Greece) for lifetime and 42.5 % (North Macedonia) and 51.0 % (Bosnia and Herzegovina) for past-year prevalence.[189] While exposure to sexual violence is typically more often associated with female victimization, in this study, self-reported experiences of males were found to exceed or equal those of females.[190] In particular, males in Albania, Bosnia and Herzegovina, North Macedonia, Greece, Romania, and Serbia reported higher levels of exposure to sexual violence than girls.[191] No differences were observed between males and females across countries in relation to lifetime exposure to psychological violence .[192]

The European School Survey Project on Alcohol and Other Drugs (ESPAD) was another one of the few self-report method studies conducted on an international level and including Balkan countries. The main purpose of ESPAD was to collect comparable data on substance use among 15-to-16-year-old students in order to monitor trends within as well as between countries.[193] Between 1995 and 2015, six surveys

185 *Nikolaidis et al.* 2018.
186 *Ajduković et al.* 2013.
187 *Nikolaidis et al.* 2018, 3.
188 *Nikolaidis et al.* 2018, 12.
189 *Nikolaidis et al.* 2018, 12.
190 *Nikolaidis et al.* 2018, 12.
191 *Nikolaidis et al.* 2018, 12.
192 *Nikolaidis et al.* 2018, 9.
193 ESPAD Group 2016.

were conducted in 48 European countries.[194] Croatia participated in all six sweeps, North Macedonia in three sweeps, Bosnia and Herzegovina and Serbia in two sweeps, and Kosovo participated in the fifth sweep only. Most of the Balkan countries participated in the fifth round,[195] and the results presented in this thesis are based on that report. Consumption of alcoholic beverages in bars, discos etc. (on-premise) during the last 30 days was highest in Croatia (65 %) and lowest in Montenegro (33 %), as well as the frequency of lifetime use of any alcoholic beverages: 93 % in Croatia and 77 % in Montenegro. Frequency of use of marijuana or hashish during the last year was again highest in Croatia (13 %) and lowest in Bosnia and Herzegovina (3 %). According to the 2105 ESPAD report,[196] high-prevalence countries for cigarette use in the past 30 days include Bulgaria, Croatia, the Czech Republic, France, Latvia, Monaco, and Slovakia (at around 40 %), while the low-prevalence countries are Albania, Iceland, Montenegro, and Norway (at around 12 %).

One of the problems regarding criminological research in the Balkans concerns the lack of a coherent criminological research strategy on the national level, which is mainly measuring issues of abuse of children, health, and ways of living, with a small number of questions regarding juvenile delinquency, and the research setting is usually divided between academic and/or research institutions, various governmental bodies and NGOs.[197] Self-report research on juveniles is mostly done on the local and regional level instead of being part of a national strategy or international research. In Croatia, only one longitudinal research project was conducted from 1970 until 1989;[198] its basic objective was to determine which significance delinquency at an early age has for later life.[199] The first questionnaire for self-reported delinquency among juveniles in Croatia was constructed in 1982, when it was still part of Yugoslavia.[200] It was called "Questionnaire of self-reported risk and delinquent behaviour";[201] in a revised form, it was also used for a study conducted with 1,422 students in Zagreb and Osijek, in order to test it.[202] In Bosnia and Herzegovina, the recent project "Behaviour and knowledge of children on the internet: attitudes of children, parents and IT teachers" has been conducted. The aim of this research was to describe and uncover online behaviour and habits of children, as well as to create social protection programmes against the risk to become victims or perpetrators of socially

---

194 *Capak* 2016.
195 *Hibell et al.* 2012.
196 ESPAD Group 2016.
197 *Getoš Kalac* 2014, 43.
198 *Ručević* 2008, 423.
199 There is very limited data about it, and no findings are available.
200 *Ručević, Ajduković & Šincek* 2009, 3.
201 Upitnik samoiskaza rizičnog i delinkventnog ponašanja (SRDP – 2007).
202 *Ručević, Ajduković & Šincek* 2009.

unacceptable behaviour.[203] Thus, children aged 9 to 17 from primary and secondary schools showed their own perception of their online behaviour and habits. Attitudes about the online behaviour and habits of children were also explained by parents of children of the same age group, as well as by IT teachers in selected schools.[204]

The Survey on the Position and Needs of Youth in the Republic of Serbia, conducted by the Ninamedia Research Agency in 2015, shows that in the past 12-month period, 8.6 % of youngsters between 15 and 19 years of age were subjected to verbal or physical violence committed by their peers and that 2.7 % were subjected to digital violence, while 16.2 % witnessed violence or intolerance among peers.[205] A total of 75 % subjected to violence did not report these events to the competent authorities, and more than one-fifth of all youth did not know whom they ought to report them to. Only 15.6 % of respondents in this age group had actually participated in a programme promoting the principles of tolerance, mutual understanding, and anti-discrimination in the previous 12-month period.[206]

The Centre for Education, Research and Development conducted a self-report survey which included a sample of 1,000 third-year students from 40 secondary schools. It presented that 23.7 % of students had been involved in a fight at least once during the past 12-month period. It also showed that 16 % of male students got drunk more than three times a month, while 14 % of students had consumed marihuana or other drugs in the past 12-month period.[207]

Criminological research in the Balkans is in its initial phase, which is now changing with the establishment of MPPG and the Balkan Criminology Network. As mentioned above, self-report research on juvenile delinquency in the Balkans started in the 2000s and is expanding to more and more countries in the region. With the hitherto lack of research, there is not much to conclude about juvenile delinquency in the Balkans, but to test theories produced on the findings from Western Europe and the USA in the Balkan setting with the aim to have an impact on criminal policies in the respective countries.

In summary, there is a lack of self-report research in the Balkans. The ISRD3 study represents the first research project of this kind covering several Balkan countries with a main focus on juvenile delinquency. For the first time, it provides a possibility for cross-national analyses and the capacity to examine the aetiology of crime and delinquency in the region. We do not know much from the previous research. ISRD2 covered only three countries from the region, and its results suggest that the rate of

---

203 *Muratbegović & Vujović* 2016.
204 *Muratbegović & Vujović* 2016.
205 Ninamedia Research 2015.
206 Ninamedia Research 2015.
207 *Simeunović-Patić, Meško & Ignjatović* 2016.

juvenile crime is rather low. Surprisingly, the results showed that Bosnia and Herze-govina is among the countries with the lowest past-year prevalence rate of minor and serious property offences. Being a victim survey, the BECAN study is the first one to examine past-year and lifetime prevalences in multiple countries in the region as well as to use a cross-country comparison methodology based on the self-report survey. Results show that the rates of physical violence exposure are high, with almost every second child reporting past-year exposure and more than every second child reporting lifetime victimization. The ESPAD study also included several countries from the region, with a focus on substance use among 15-to-16-year-old students. Students in Croatia reported the highest rate of both alcohol consumption and the use of marihuana and hashish among all participating Balkan countries. There are also several self-report studies conducted only in one Balkan country, but they were mainly conceptualized as victim surveys or with a focus only on violence among children and without a possibility for cross-national comparisons. Therefore, this thesis is the first one to provide a comprehensive overview of juvenile crime in the region. It also examines, for the first time, the aetiology of juvenile crime in the Balkans with a focus on the informal control theory.

Chapter 3

Research Questions

3.1 Phenomenology: Differences in the Extent and Nature of Juvenile Crime in the Balkans

Measuring criminal behaviour can be carried out in three ways. One method concerns the use of official data collected by criminal justice institutions, such as data on reported suspects as well as on accused and convicted offenders.[208] The other two measures are based on self-reported crime and surveys of victimization.[209] Self-reported delinquency surveys are studies in which mostly juveniles reveal information about their delinquency. In this study, *delinquency* is used as broader term and includes various types of antisocial or deviant behaviour, even if these delinquency acts are not defined as offences in criminal law, such as truancy and running away from home.

As discussed in the previous chapter, it can be concluded that there is a lack of empirical research on juvenile delinquency in the Balkans.[210] The only available data in most of the countries are official statistics. Most offences committed by juveniles are never reported to the authorities, and some of the juveniles involved in illegal acts are never arrested or prosecuted in a juvenile court.[211] In some countries in the Balkans, like e.g. Bosnia and Herzegovina, not even official statistics were available on a national level until recently.[212]

The first research question aims at exploring the extent of offences among juveniles in five Balkan countries: Bosnia and Herzegovina, Croatia, Kosovo, North Macedonia, and Serbia. This self-report research is supposed to establish prevalence and incidence rates of crime and delinquency of juveniles that have a higher validity than official delinquency measures. The main idea is to focus on the self-reported juvenile

---

208 *Thornberry & Krohn* 2003.
209 *Thornberry & Krohn* 2003.
210 For details, see *Chapter 2*.
211 *Burfeind & Bartusch* 2016, 84.
212 For details, see the *Introduction*; *Maljević & Muratbegović* 2014.

delinquency scale produced from the offending module of the ISRD3 question-naire.[213] It contains twelve different delinquency acts, covering a wide range of be-haviours from serious to less serious crimes.[214] This scale will be presented in a way to disclose juvenile crime in the Balkan region, but also to compare it between five countries of the region in order to test to what extent it constitutes a problem and to analyse if there are regional differences regarding the prevalence and type of com-mitted offences. By exploring the extent of juvenile crime in the Balkans, answers to the following questions will be provided: what is the prevalence rate of crime among juveniles involved in delinquency acts? How frequently are juveniles in-volved in crime? Which types of delinquent offences occur most often? Are there differences between the Balkan countries? If so, what are these differences? The fo-cus of this research is not put on individual offenders and offending but on juveniles as a group, in order to obtain a general understanding of delinquency in the Balkans.

The Second round of the ISRD survey (ISRD2) was launched in 31 countries with the idea to expand it to Central and Eastern Europe, but only Bosnia and Herzegovina ended up participating. Therefore, a comparison of ISRD2 and ISRD3 data, aiming at monitoring possible trends, can only be done for Bosnia and Herzegovina. There-fore, this research omits these trends since no data is available for the other four investigated countries from the Balkan cluster.

Cross-national research has a long history, and the globalization of economies – along with the growing interdependence of countries in Europe and worldwide – has created a need for more comparative studies of crime and criminal justice.[215] Most of these comparisons are based on official measures and therefore have certain lim-itations – first of all, they underestimate the true volume of crime,[216] and there are differences among countries regarding the definition of crime, its counting units, methodologies, etc.[217] Of course, self-report studies are not without challenges or restrictions either. Self-report indicators of offending are plagued by a number of problems. One of them concerns the substantial over- or under-reporting of criminal incidents.[218] Thus, in the Balkans, the ISRD2 study came up with partially contra-dictory results. For the Balkan countries, high levels of victimization were reported while at the same time, low levels of self-reported delinquency were observed.[219]

---

213 The ISRD3 questionnaire consists of ten modules: demographic background; family; school; victimization; leisure and peers; morality, self-control and neighbourhood; offending; substance use; Institutional Anomie theory; procedural justice questions. See *Enzmann et al.* 2018, 15.

214 For more details about the self-report delinquency scale, see *Chapter 4.*

215 *Junger-Tas & Marshall* 1999.

216 *Kirk* 2006.

217 *Albrecht* 1988.

218 *Kirk* 2006.

219 *Junger-Tas et al.* (eds.) 2012.

An explanation is possibly found in the willingness to report one's deviant behaviour, which may also vary among countries.[220] Because of that, the results from the ISRD3 study's crosswise model[221] will be presented as a way of statistically correcting the systematic response bias[222] in order to analyse the validity of the data.

3.2 Aetiology: Causes of Juvenile Delinquency in the Balkans

The ISRD3 survey provides data suited for testing various theoretical orientations about the causes of delinquency. The main theoretical approach used in this doctoral research is the informal social control theory, which is based on the social control theory by *Hirschi* (1969). This is one of the most frequently tested theories in criminology.[223] *Hirschi's* theory begins with the main proposal that "delinquent acts result when an individual's bond to society is weak or broken".[224] He argues that delinquency can occur when the juvenile is alienated from society. According to *Hirschi*, this alienation takes place from certain social bonds. These are represented by four major elements: attachment to significant others, such as parents, teachers, family, friends; commitment to act, which leads to achieving one's personal goals; involvement in conforming to conventional social activities; and belief in the general social and moral norms as well as values of the society.[225] The stronger the bonds are, the less probable involvement in juvenile crime becomes. As part of *Hirschi's* social control theory, the informal control theory perceives bonds to society through the social institutions of family, school, and religion. In the following, the theoretical background of each variable will be presented, as well as the manner in which the variables were analysed within this research.

In this research, the focus is on the informal control theory, and therefore, one part of the analysis deals with the models concerning family, such as family attachment and family control. *Hirschi* claims that juveniles who have strong bonds with their parents – concerning the factors family attachment and family control – accept their parents' norms and values. They behave in a way that they do not break society norms because they do not want to disappoint their parents.[226] The models contain two variables regarding family, with the aim to test whether family control plays a

---

220 *Enzmann et al.* 2018, 15.

221 *Yu, Tian & Tang* 2008; *Zhang, Benson & Deng* 2000.

222 More details about the crosswise model methodology will be presented in *Chapter 4*.

223 *Ellis & Walsh* 1999, 1.

224 *Hirschi* 1969, 16.

225 *Hirschi* 1969.

226 *Hirschi* 1969.

bigger role in post-socialist countries than attachment to parents. Previous cross-national studies have suggested that the family can play a different role in relation to juvenile delinquency between different cultures.[227] Some studies have shown that family control has a bigger impact on juvenile delinquency than family attachment.[228] The test for this study was made in the Balkan region as a whole – as well as among five Balkan countries in order to look at their similarities and differences. Theories drawn from these studies were based on the results from developed countries with a specific cultural, historical, and economic background. The idea was to empirically test whether the same theories that were applied and tested in Western European countries and the USA also have explanatory power in the Balkan region.

Along with the family, school is one of the main environments in which young people develop.[229] In youth socialization, the school plays an important role, not least as they spend a considerable amount of time there.[230] In *Hirschi's* social control theory, attachment to school is also seen as a bond which impacts juvenile delinquency. In his self-report study, attitudes toward school correlated with self-reported and official delinquent acts. The results showed that 49 % of the boys who disliked school had committed two or more delinquent acts in the previous year, compared to only 9 % of those who did like attending school. Another correlation regarding school attachment and juvenile delinquency was based on the question "Do you care what your teacher thinks about you?". *Hirschi* concluded that the less a boy cares about what teachers think about him, the more likely he is to have committed a delinquent act. ISRD2 findings were similar to those found by *Hirschi*. Individuals with a close bond to school are less likely to commit delinquent act because they care more about their teachers' expectations and will respect and adopt their norms and values.[231] Based on the ISRD2 questionnaire, the ISRD3 questionnaire was in line with *Hirschi's* social control theory, so the same analyses can be made for the Balkans to see if the same theory is functioning in the same way in these different societies.

Hirschi's social control theory does not consider the macro-structure of a society, nor does it take into consideration that juveniles were born and raised in different societies and in different economic and social contexts, which could have an impact on their parents' socializing skills and ways of parenting.[232]

In this research, the first test is made for the informal social control perspective by measuring the influence of family attachment, family control, and school on juvenile delinquency, so as to be in line with a prime importance of the theory. However, the study also includes other elements of the macro-structure of the society. The first

---

227   *Minkov & Hofstede* 2012.
228   *Schreck & Hirschi* 2009.
229   *Egli, Lucia & Berchtold* 2012.
230   *Lucia, Killias & Junger-Tas* 2012, 211.
231   *Lucia, Killias & Junger-Tas* 2012, 232.
232   *Sampson & Laub* 1993.

main element is the socio-economic status, tested through variables such as unemployment of mother and/or father or the financial deprivation of family and juveniles. Some of the previous studies found an influence of socio-economic advantages and economic depression on juvenile delinquency through family factors by showing an impact on family control.[233] The hypothesis is that parental unemployment has an impact on decreasing juvenile delinquency through stronger family control and monitoring.

The next part will focus on the influence of religion on juvenile delinquency. The Balkan region has a complex religion structure. Since the Early Modern Era, the population has split up into three major faiths: Orthodox, Muslim, and Catholic.[234] This makes it a good region to examine the influence of different religions on juvenile delinquency. Previous studies have also focused on the question to what extent and in what manner religion has an influence on delinquency.[235] This study analyses the relationship between religion and juvenile delinquency with a distinction between two aspects of religion that may affect delinquency, namely belonging to a particular religious organization and juvenile religiosity.[236] These two aspects are connected with both external and internal mechanisms of sanctions.[237] External sanctioning occurs when people are part of a social or religious group and are punished by this group when deviating from a social norm.[238] Internal sanctioning is not connected to belonging to a certain social group; instead, it is expected that peoples' religiosity has an impact on their perception of norms, which then shapes a person's own conviction that certain conduct is not appropriate.[239]

In this study, the analysis will focus on religion and religiosity. The first correlation tests whether belonging to a different religion plays a role in juvenile delinquency. This test is followed by the correlation between religiosity and juvenile crime. The hypothesis is that belonging to a certain religion does not necessarily imply that individuals have internalized their respective group's norms. Additionally, for a compliance with certain rules, the process of internalization is more important than formally belonging to a certain religion. If norms are internalized, their violation will lead to internal sanctions such as feelings of guilt and shame.[240]

---

233 See *Nye, Short & Olson* 1958; *Rutter & Giller* 1983, 136–137.

234 *Sundhaussen* 2014.

235 See *Hirschi & Stark* 1969; *Sloane & Potvin* 1986; *Pettersson* 1991.

236 *Robertson* 1970.

237 *Koster, Goudriaan & van der Schans* 2009, 482–483.

238 *Koster, Goudriaan & van der Schans* 2009, 482.

239 *Koster, Goudriaan & van der Schans* 2009, 483.

240 *Coleman* 1990.

3.3   Cross-National Comparison between Countries from the Balkans and Western Europe

Cross-national comparative studies in criminology and criminal justice are important but relatively uncommon.[241] The main justification for cross-national comparisons is to test criminological theories and to explore the conditions under which they can or cannot be confirmed. It is too ambitious to search for universal findings that can be replicated in different contexts, times, and places. Therefore, the main challenge of this cross-national research is to identify and explain the differences and similarities in juvenile delinquency between countries in the Balkans, but also between the Balkans and Western Europe. The aim is to explain them by putting delinquency in the respective social, cultural, historical, economic, legal, or criminal justice context. That is why the research mainly focuses on Balkans countries; but it will then expand to the cluster level so as to analyse whether there are any differences between the Balkans and Western Europe – and if so, what these differences refer to.

As presented in *Chapter 2.3*, there is a lack of empirical research, including cross-national research. In ISRD2, the highest level of delinquency was found in the wealthiest countries of Western Europe, while lower levels were found in post-socialist countries, including Bosnia and Herzegovina.[242] In this cluster, girls were found to commit less delinquent acts than boys, but (unlike in Western Europe) the disparity between the sexes increased with age. It was suggested that the reason for that may be found in the influence of different cultural and social-economic conditions in the respective countries.[243] The ISRD2 findings showed that family attachment does not differ significantly between the countries, but there were significant differences in the effects of parental control.[244] This was the strongest factor to explain truancy and the most serious delinquency in all clusters of the ISRD2 study, followed by visiting a disorganized school and certain animosities toward school.[245]

The value of a cross-national comparison lies not only in testing criminological theories and their explanations but also in finding out whether some prevalences and frequencies of offending differ between countries and why they stand out. On a conceptual level, it makes sense to compare the prevalence and frequency rates from different countries. This comparison should then serve as a base for a proper determination of the value, as well as for a content examination of the received results. For example, if results show that there is significantly more group fighting in country A than in country B, the explanation may be found in policy-making decisions and programmes. This finding may serve as an indicator of the efficiency of a certain

---

241 *Farrington* 2015a.

242 *Junger-Tas, Enzmann, Steketee & Marshall* 2012, 329.

243 *Junger-Tas, Enzmann, Steketee & Marshall* 2012.

244 *Junger-Tas, Enzmann, Steketee & Marshall* 2012, 339.

245 *Junger-Tas, Enzmann, Steketee & Marshall* 2012. 332.

crime policy, which might potentially then be implemented in other countries depending on their differences and similarities. Overall, this kind of cross-national comparison makes more sense among countries with a similar social, cultural, historical, economic, legal, or criminal justice background, since it is more likely that different programmes will not function in the same way in, for example, both highly developed and less developed countries.

To conclude, the main focus of this research was to find differences and similarities between different countries in the Balkan region and to provide plausible explanations for them by respecting the contexts of the respective countries. These explanations will be presented in the following in two directions: the first part will show phenomenology similarities and differences in juvenile delinquency in the investigated countries, including possible reasoning. The second part will deal with the aetiology of juvenile delinquency in the Balkans through testing informal control, therefore also providing possible solutions for their cause.

Chapter 4

Methodology

The primary purpose of this chapter is to discuss selected methodological issues and therefore to offer a better understanding of the following substantive chapters (in that sense, it aims at providing a sort of technical guide). It also provides the context of the study which has shaped the ISRD research process in the Balkan region.

The chapter is organized as follows: the first part discusses the logic of the comparative research method with an exclusive focus on the Balkan countries that participated in the ISRD3 study. The second part describes the sampling procedure with a focus on the most significant sampling-related issues. This is followed by a discussion on instruments, measurements, and validity of the data. The last part gives an overview of the statistical models used in the following chapters.

4.1 Comparative Research Methodology

The focus of this research is on juvenile delinquency in a selection of Balkan countries, namely Bosnia and Herzegovina, Croatia, Kosovo, North Macedonia, and Serbia. The analyses will be based on ISRD3 study findings. As a comparative study of youth crime and victimization, ISRD3 has two distinguishing features: (1) the large cultural diversity between the participating countries; and (2) the explicitly comparative design.[246] At the time of writing, 27 countries from around the world had finished data collection and data entry, with another six countries still being in the phase of conducting fieldwork.

A cross-national survey dealing with such a large and varied sample of research sites across the globe poses serious challenges and causes major problems, methodologically and logistically.[247] One of the challenges which dominate the discourse about the logic of comparative research is the selection of countries.[248] *Durkheim* distinguished three applications of the comparative method with regard to the selection of

---

246 *Enzmann et al.* 2018, 7.

247 *Enzmann et al.* 2018, 7.

248 For more details, see *Allardt* 1990; *Armer & Grimshaw* 1973; *Bennett* 2009; *Elder* 1976; *Enzmann et al.* 2018; *Newman & Pridemore* 2000; *Kohn* 1987; *Karstedt* 2001; *Marshall & Marshall* 1983; *Nelken* 2009; *Nelken* 2010; *Prezworski & Teune* 1970; *Ragin* 1987; *Rokkan* 1968; *van de Vijver & Tanzer* 2004.

nations: the first one was the analysis within one society at a given moment; the second one was the comparison of relatively similar societies differing, however, in some aspects; and the last one was the comparison of different societies which share some features, or the comparison between different periods within one society that show radical changes.[249] In this research project, the focus is on the second method proposed by *Durkheim*.

Comparative research usually starts with the assumption that no national differences exist in the variables of interest.[250] If any differences are found, they are interpreted through variations among the compared countries.[251] Since the countries in the ISRD3 study differ in many aspects, it is very difficult to point out which factor should exactly be used to interpret the found differences. Therefore, in this research, countries were selected that show similarities (but still differ in some aspects). A comparison among countries with more similarities than differences has the additional advantage of reducing cultural variability and allows for a more advanced specification of the theoretical propositions.[252] Thus, the countries in this analysis are all located in the Balkan region: Bosnia and Herzegovina, Croatia, Kosovo, North Macedonia, and Serbia. This region is an integral yet unique part of Europe, and despite its rich and diverse past, these countries share a common culture, political, historical, and structural traits.[253] However, at the same time, they feature differences that are the result of social and cultural evolution, national constructionism, and relative instability, for example in countries like Kosovo and Bosnia and Herzegovina.[254] As *Sundhaussen* states: "Despite several particularities and differences, an empirically sound cluster of common characteristics can be identified that gives the Balkan a distinctive, fascinating and sometimes scary profile."[255] It should be noted that the countries in this analysis were all part of the former Yugoslavia and that the region is currently characterized by a divide between EU members and non-members. Croatia joined the European Union in July 2014, while North Macedonia and Serbia are candidate countries; Bosnia and Herzegovina as well as Kosovo are only potential candidates.[256]

249 *Durkheim* 1982.
250 *Marshall Hean & Enzmann* 2012, 23.
251 *Marsh* 1967.
252 *Marshall Hean & Enzmann* 2012, 25.
253 *Winterdyk & Kilchling* 2014, 63.
254 *Winterdyk & Kilchling* 2014, 63.
255 See *Sundhaussen* 1999; *Getoš Kalac* 2012a; *Winterdyk & Kilchling* 2014.
256 For a complete list of when particular countries became EU members, candidates and potential candidates, see European Union: Candidate countries and potential candidates, http://ec.europa.eu/environment/enlarg/candidates.htm [01.08.2018].

Joining the EU requires a country to meet three key criteria. These were defined at the European Council in Copenhagen in 1993 and are hence referred to as the "Copenhagen criteria":[257]

- *Political:* stable institutions guaranteeing democracy, the rule of law, human rights, and respect for as well as protection of minorities;
- *Economic:* a functioning market economy and the capacity to cope with competition and market forces in the EU;
- *Acceptance of the community acquis:* the ability to take on and implement effectively the obligations of membership, including adherence to the aims of the political, economic, and monetary union.

Many of these issues are closely connected to crime and crime control and should therefore be taken into consideration for further analysis.[258]

Another reason for focusing on the analysis of the Balkan region was its lack of empirical research.[259] ISRD1 was launched in 1990 by the Dutch Research and Documentation Centre (WODC), with the aim to create a comparative picture of the nature and extent of delinquency in Europe and the USA.[260] However, none of the countries in the Balkan region participated. However, ISRD1 produced interesting outcomes.[261] Therefore, between 2006 and 2008, ISRD2 was conducted in 31 countries. This second round tried to expand the survey to Southeastern European countries. However, only Slovenia and Bosnia and Herzegovina participated, becoming part of the post-socialist cluster in the data analysis.[262] ISRD3 is thus the first internationally standardized survey with a focus on juvenile delinquency that covers more countries from the Balkan region.

4.2 Sampling

This section is based on the paper "International Self-Report Delinquency Questionnaire 3 (ISRD-3): Background paper to explain ISRD2-ISRD3 changes".[263] The

---

257 For more details, see European Union: Conditions for membership, https://ec.europa.eu/neighb ourhood-enlargement/policy/conditions-membership_en [01.08.2018].

258 *Winterdyk & Kilchling* 2014, 64.

259 More details about the current state of empirical research on juvenile delinquency in the Balkan region are available in *Chapter 2.2.*

260 For details, see *Junger-Tas, Terlouw & Klein* 1994.

261 *Enzmann et al.* 2018, 2–3.

262 *Smit, Marshall & van Gammeren* 2008.

263 This is a modified and expanded version of the paper prepared by the ISRD3 Steering Committee for discussion at the ISRD3 workshop, 22 September 2011, ESC Meeting, Vilnius, Lithuania. The current version includes the final decisions made since the 2011 meeting. For more details, see *Marshall et al.* 2013.

ISRD3[264] design is complex, with analytic units at different levels: countries, cities and towns, schools, classrooms, and respondents (i.e., juveniles). Most of these units will be presented in the following part of this thesis.

4.2.1   City-based and national sampling design

The ISRD3 study has different goals, one of which is to describe the scope of crime during a certain period of time and in a certain region. For this purpose, the best methodological way would be to get a nationally representative sample. However, the description of the prevalence of juvenile delinquent behavior is only one of the goals of ISRD3, while its major goal is the explanation of offending. In this research, the national representativeness of the sample is less important because the focus lies primarily on testing the correlations of offending and to a lesser extent on the potential to precisely measure the full extent of delinquency within a country. In the ISRD study, city-based random samples are preferred to national sampling because of the following reasons:[265] the first reason is that the effects of youth policies and youth programmes are easier to evaluate at the city level than at the national level. Therefore, differences between countries in the correlation of delinquency prevalence based on the city level may be explained by local structural differences (e.g. unemployment rate, youth policies, youth programmes), such as in the case of graffiti.[266] The second reason is that when examining correlates of juvenile delinquency derived from criminological theories, the representativeness of the sample is not highly important.[267] Lastly, it is very costly, time-consuming, and in some countries simply impossible to draw a nationally representative random sample of juveniles, particularly in large countries, or economically weak ones that lack the necessary research funding.

According to the ISRD3 research protocol, in the Balkan countries, samples were to be city-based, covering students from grades 7–9, i.e., corresponding to the age categories 12–14, 13–15, and 14–16. The time frame of the fieldwork varied between countries. Fieldwork was postponed in some countries because at the beginning of research, some city authorities were not willing to cooperate, such as in the case of Zagreb, Croatia. Other reasons for postponing fieldwork were natural disasters. In Bosnia and Herzegovina, large floods happened at the time of conducting fieldwork, therefore it was postponed to the following year. Each Balkan country had its own

---

264 The ISRD is an international study coordinated by the Steering Committee. It is chaired by *Ineke Haen Marshall* (Northeastern University, USA). The other members include *Dirk Enzmann* (Hamburg University), *Mike Hough* (Birkbeck College, University of London), *Martin Killias* (University of St. Gallen, Switzerland), *Janne Kivivuori* (National Research Institute of Legal Policy, Finland) and *Majone Steketee* (Verwey-Jonker Institute, the Netherlands).
265 *Junger-Tas et al.* 2010, 6–8.
266 For details, see *Chapter 2.2*.
267 *Junger-Tas et al.* 2010; *Maxfield & Babbie* 2001.

research group in the field. A short summary about the research teams and the selection of cities for each Balkan country is presented in the next paragraphs. Data collection patterns of the ISRD3 project are summarized in *Table 1*.

During 2013, the ISRD3 study was conducted in Croatia for the first time by the Max Planck Partner Group for "Balkan Criminology" (MPPG).[268] The main problem was that common funding was not provided. The Faculty of Law of the University of Zagreb and the local government of the city of Varaždin helped by providing material and organization. Fieldwork was conducted with the help of student volunteers and MPPG members under the leadership of Assoc. Prof. *Anna-Maria Getoš Kalac* and the author of this thesis. Data collection was carried out in spring 2013 and winter 2014.[269] It was decided to use a city-based sampling strategy. The survey was conducted in the city of Zagreb, the capital, and in the city of Varaždin, a medium-sized city in Croatia.

Fieldwork in Bosnia and Herzegovina was conducted under the leadership of Assoc. Prof. *Almir Maljević* in 2014 and 2015. Data collection started after obtaining approvals from the ministries of education at all levels. Research was conducted in 28 cities and towns,[270] except in the Brčko District in Bosnia and Herzegovina, because their government considered the instrument not to be suitable for local children.

In Serbia, ISRD3 data were collected in Belgrade and Novi Sad, two of the biggest cities in the country, in 2013 and 2014. The Ministry of Education, Science and Technological Development gave its general approval for conducting the survey. Here, ISRD3 was conducted under the leadership of Prof. *Vesna Nikolić-Ristanović*. In charge of data collection was Mrs. *Ljiljana Stevković*, which happened in cooperation with the Faculty of Special Education and Rehabilitation as well as the Victimological Society of Serbia.[271] The funds for data collection were provided by the Swiss Federal Office of Migration.

---

268 For details, see http://balkan-criminology.eu/en/projects/isrd3/ [29/10/2018].
269 The Code of Ethics in Research involving Children was used. Approval was obtained from the Ministry of Science on 26 March 2013. Consent of the school principals, parents, and participants was sought. The interviews were conducted by student volunteers from the Social Work Study Centre under the leadership of Ms. *Tea Antolčić* and Ms. *Reana Bezić*. Assoc. Prof. *Anna-Maria Getoš Kalac* held several seminars with training sessions before fieldwork was carried out. Student volunteers were trained in filling out the Data Collection checklist and instructed about the Sampling Protocol. Research volunteers prepared the accurate time slots for conducting the survey in the classrooms and constituted contact persons who were responsible for conducting research in the respective schools. Assoc. Prof. *Anna-Maria Getoš Kalac*, Ms. *Tea Antolčić*, and the author organized all the administration work, established contact with local governments, principals, and teachers regarding the time slots for the research, as well as ensuring that all interviews were carried out in the same way.
270 The ISRD3 survey in Bosnia and Herzegovina was conducted in the following cities and towns: Zenica, Zavidovići, Cazin, Odžak, Tuzla, Gradačac, Donji Vakuf, Travnik, Mostar, Konjic, Čitluk, Goražde, Ilovača, Prača, Sarajevo, Livno, Široki Brijeg, Novi Grad, Teslić, Prijedor, Bijeljina, Srebrenica, Zvornik, Nevesinje, Uvac, Bratunac, Trebinje, and Banja Luka.
271 *Stevković & Nikolić-Ristanović* 2016.

In Kosovo, the ISRD3 survey was conducted in the two biggest cities, Pristina and Prizren, during the autumn semester of 2013/14. Fieldwork was conducted here under the leadership of Dr. *Mensut Ademi*.

North Macedonia approved a survey under the leadership of Dr. *Natasha Jovanova* in the capital, Skopje, and the middle-sized city of Kumanovo. The suburbs of these cities were also included. Fieldwork took place in 2014.

Most of these Balkan countries participated in an international self-report delinquency study for the first time, except for Bosnia and Herzegovina, which had been part of the ISRD2 study in 2005/06. Therefore, it is not surprising that the research teams in most participating countries faced problems with getting the approval of state and local institutions, as they did not have protocols for such research.

4.2.2   School-based survey

The standard sampling unit is the school class. Schools can be used as sampling units if class-based sampling is impossible. In both cases, a probability was used that was proportional to size sampling. As mentioned before, ISRD3 has a target population of 7th-, 8th- and 9th-graders. However, in the Balkan region, there are some differences in the educational system. In Croatia and Serbia, elementary school starts at the age of six/seven and ends with the 8th grade. In Bosnia and Herzegovina and North Macedonia, elementary school ends with the 9th grade. Kosovo has a different educational system from the above-mentioned countries. According to the law, it is divided into primary and secondary education, both mandatory and free of charge in the publicly funded educational institutions. Primary school starts at the age of six and ends with the 5th grade. The lower secondary education includes classes from 6 to 9, i.e. children between 12 and 15 years of age. That is the reason why in the case of Kosovo, the respondents were younger than in the other country samples (covering a range until 15 years of age). In addition, Bosnia and Herzegovina used the national sample. In other Balkan countries (Croatia, Kosovo, and Serbia), the data was collected in one large and one medium-sized city,[272] while in North Macedonia, the study was conducted in two cities, including suburbs. The aim was to collect 900 cases (300 among 7th-graders, 300 among 8th-graders, and 300 among 9th-graders) in each city, with a minimum number of 1,800 cases per country. These variations within the sampling design reflect different local budgets, needs, and other practical factors. The schools were randomly selected, with an equal probability of selection between all school types.[273]

---

272 The sizes of the cities are based on the respective national classifications.

273 In order to facilitate drawing comparable random samples, research partners had access to a pre-programmed software package ("Survey Manager"). This is an Excel programme especially written for the ISRD3 study to manage the list of schools and classes in order to draw random samples of classes and to manage survey administration.

In Croatia, the official list of schools[274] in Zagreb and Varaždin (issued by the Ministry of Education in Croatia) was used as the sampling frame. Only in Zagreb, schools which had participated in the BECAN[275] survey were excluded so as to avoid overlapping. The total sample size of the students was 3,635, but only 1,741 of them (48 %) participated in the survey. One of the explanations for such a low percentage is the use of an opt-in consent policy, meaning that parents needed to approve in written form that they allowed their children to participate in this research. This is evident from the fact that 40.63 % of students were excluded from the survey because of missing parental consent (i.e., parents excluded their children from the survey or did not respond at all). Beside parental consent, the study was conducted with the approval of the Ministry of Science, of school principals, teachers, and participants. All of the students who got their parents consent participated in the study.

Bosnia and Herzegovina[276] used the national sample; here, the survey was conducted in schools covering all districts of the country except for the Brčko District.[277] The schools were contacted after the approval by the Pedagogical Institute of Srpska Republic, the Federal Ministry of Education, the science of Federation of Bosnia and Herzegovina and all cantonal ministries of education. Only two schools refused to participate in the study. In the end, 96 % of school principals gave their approval for conducting the study in their schools. In Bosnia and Herzegovina (like in Croatia), the opt-in policy was used upon request from the Ministry of Education at all cantonal levels. In total, 63 students refused to participate in the study, and another 648 did not have a parental consent. Thus, the overall sample of students participating in the study in Bosnia and Herzegovina was 3,066.

In Serbia,[278] researchers faced the same problem as in Croatia, since the Ministry of Education did not have a clear protocol to give approval for such a study. As mentioned before, there is a lack of empirical studies in the region, and therefore, institutions are not prepared or do not know how to respond. They did not have clear guidelines for conducting surveys in schools, so they gave a general approval and passed the responsibility to the local governments and school principals. In total, 20

---

274 According to the official school system in Croatia, schools are divided into two categories: primary and high schools. There are two types of high schools: gymnasiums and vocational schools. The duration of vocational school can be three or four years. The school system also knows primary and secondary art schools, with a specific school curriculum, which is different from non-art schools. Curriculums of vocational schools and gymnasiums also differ but have several same school subjects.

275 BECAN is an epidemiological study aiming at mapping child abuse and neglect (CAN) in the general population of 11- to 16-year-old children that attend as well as those that have dropped out of school. It also strives to identify the number of reported/detected cases of CAN being recorded in at least eight Balkan countries.

276 Some of the stated data were collected through the author's contact with the team that was conducting the research in Bosnia and Herzegovina.

277 *Maljević et al.* 2017.

278 This section is based on information available from *Stevković & Nikolić-Ristanović* 2015.

schools from Belgrade and Novi Sad participated in the survey. The principals of some schools refused to give consent for their schools because of different reasons, such as lack of time.[279] As a result, not even one private school participated in the ISRD3 study in Serbia. However, only three out of 1,336 students refused to participate in the survey.

North Macedonia used city-based samples in Skopje and Kumanovo (including the suburbs of these cities). Here, the school access rate amounted to 96 %, being the highest in the region. Together with Venezuela, North Macedonia is the only country in the whole ISRD3 sample that used a respondent consent policy. However, 22 % of students refused to participate in the study, even though they were informed that the questionnaire was anonymous. In total, 1,239 students participated in the study.

In Kosovo, the study was conducted in 18 schools and with a very high school access rate (92 %). They used an opt-out consent policy, and as a result, the student response rate was high at 84 %. That means that only 16 % of students refused to participate in the study. The overall sample of participants amounted to 1,078 students in Kosovo.

A school-based delinquency survey has its advantages and disadvantages. It has the advantage of including socially disadvantaged youth groups that would be more difficult to reach with home-based interviews.[280] However, a disadvantage of conducting the survey in schools is the problem with ensuring the access to schools and consent procedures.[281] There are also differences in school access rates among the Balkan countries. In Serbia, the school access rate is 75 %, while it reaches 96 % in North Macedonia and Bosnia and Herzegovina. Such variations are usual in cross-national surveys. In ISRD2, the overall school participation rate in Bosnia and Herzegovina was 100 % and in Slovenia 97 %, while in France, it was only 16 %. In the 2015 European School Survey Project on Alcohol and Other Drugs (ESPAD), the school participation rate was 98 % in the Croatian and North Macedonian sample[282] and only 43 % in the Netherlands.[283]

In contrast to the international sample of ISRD3, where student response rates were much lower than the willingness of the schools to participate, they are much more diverse in the Balkan region. Students' response rates mostly depended on the respective consent policy, which varied regarding how eager parents were to include their children. There are three possibilities: opt-in, opt-out, and respondent-informed consent. The opt-in policy requires that parents give explicit permission for their

---

279 For details, see *Nikolić-Ristanović* 2016.

280 See *Naplava & Oberwittler* 2002.

281 *Enzmann et al.* 2018, 13.

282 Croatia and North Macedonia are the only countries which participated in ESPAD survey in 2015.

283 For details, see http://www.espad.org/report/methodology/espad-2015 [29/10/2018].

children to participate in the study. In contrast, the opt-out policy means that parental permission is assumed in the absence of an explicit exclusion; thus, all students whose parents do not forbid participation can participate. In the respondent-informed consent policy, the personal decision of the respondent is sufficient: the child decides for himself or herself. The ISRD protocol requires informed consent from all respondents, which means that responding is voluntary. There is a large body of scholarly work on the response-rate effects of asking for parental consent.[284] However, if the parental consent procedure is used, the ISRD project recommends an opt-out policy where parents explicitly state their exclusionary intent if they want to exclude their child from the study. In the Balkan countries where the opt-in policy was used, the response rate of students was very low, such as in the case of Croatia (59 %). In contrast, where the opt-out or respondent-informed consent policy was used, the rates were much higher. In the case of Serbia where opt-out consent was used, the students' response rate was 92 %. When conducting research on juvenile delinquency, these challenges reflect cultural notions about the relative importance of protecting children *with* or *from* research.[285]

One of the issues of school-based data collection is the supervision condition. The main question is: who should supervise the classes where students are anonymously responding to a self-report survey? Previous research has shown that in comparison to an external supervisor, teacher's supervision does not produce statistically significant differences in self-reports about drug use and delinquency.[286] However, some researchers found that external supervision might solicit higher prevalence levels in some offences, most notably in drug use.[287]

ISRD data guidelines recommend that the survey should be administered by external assistants rather than teachers. Therefore, most of the Balkan countries had low rates of teacher's presence in the classrooms during the survey. All Balkan countries involved outside research assistance as data collectors in all classes; however, teachers stayed in some classes throughout the duration of data collection. In the case of Serbia, only 4 % of teachers were present, followed by Croatia with 13 %. In Bosnia and Herzegovina, 18 % of teachers were present during data collection. The highest rate was in Kosovo where 20 % of teachers were present during data collection.

---

284 See *Esbensen et al.* 1999; *Esbensen et al.* 2008; *Pokorny et al.* 2001; *White, Hill & Effendi* 2004.
285 *Enzmann et al.* 2018, 13.
286 See *Bjarnason* 1995; *Walser & Killias* 2012; *Kivivuori, Salmi & Walser* 2013.
287 *Kivivuori & Bernburg* 2011.

Table 1 Data collection in the Balkan countries: basic sample features[288]

	Data collection					Sample			
	Time	Method	Consent	External survey admin. (%)	Teacher presence (%)[a]	No. of students	No. of cities	School access rate (%)[b]	Student resp. rate (%)[c]
Bosnia and Herzegovina	2014–2015	Online	Opt-in	100	18	3066	9[d]	96	73
Croatia	2013–2014	p & p	Opt-in	100	13	1741	2	80	59
Kosovo	2013–2014	Online	Opt-out	100	20	1078	2	92	84
North Macedonia	2014	Online	RC	100	-	1239	2	96	78
Serbia	2013–2014	Online	Opt-out	100	4	1336	2	75	92

p & p: paper and pencil,

RC: respondent consent only,

a: % of data collection situations where the teacher was present,

b: % of initially sampled schools granting research access,

c: % of students responding, from the student body of the classes participating in the study,

d: national sample, a figure indicating locations/cantons.

---

288 *Table 1* is based on table 2.1, Data collection in the participating countries: Basic sample features from *Enzmann et al.* 2018, 8–9, Technical reports and by contacting local research teams.

4.3   The ISRD3 Measurement Instrument

Aside from the sampling procedure, the quality of cross-national research is given by the quality of the *instruments* used to measure variables.[289] The ISRD3 project used two measurement instruments: a *student questionnaire* and an *administration form*. The student questionnaire was the main instrument on which the major part of the analysis is based. Through the administration forms, interviewers in each country were obliged to keep track of the response rates and other issues related to the process of data collection. Some of the data that was used as a base for the technical reports can be seen in *Table 1*.

There were two versions of the questionnaire: paper-and-pencil and electronic. Apart from Croatia, all countries used the electronic version of the questionnaire. It made use of the offline software FluidSurveys.[290]

4.3.1   The ISRD3 questionnaire

The ISRD project used standardized questionnaires in order to ensure cross-national comparability. It was a very challenging process even in studies with fewer participants.[291] The first challenge was to ensure linguistic equivalence in the translations. However, this was not a problem for those Balkan countries which were already part of the ISRD project. For instance, the questionnaire of Bosnia and Herzegovina, which had already been tested in the ISRD2 study, was translated into three languages (Bosnian, Croatian, and Serbian) and written in two alphabets (Latin and Cyrillic).[292] That allowed other countries in the region to double-check their translations. The second challenge was cultural factors, such as interpretation and meaning of questions and terms. In differing cultural contexts, some questions might be harder to access and terms can differ.[293] Again, this was not a problem, as all examined countries in the region share a similar culture and a similar cultural sensitivity.

The ISRD3 questionnaire has a modular structure with a core set of fixed questions and a flexible part, which will vary from sweep to sweep. This allows for adapting the questionnaire to each sweep while still maintaining its compatibility with the previous sweep. It also allows for the addition of country-level optional models located

---

289 *Marshall Hean & Enzmann* 2012, 46.

290 FluidSurveys: http://fluidsurveys.com/.

291 *Marshall Hean & Enzmann* 2012.

292 All three languages are official languages in Bosnia and Herzegovina, as well as the two alphabets. The use of language and alphabet depends on the respective canton. The Croatian research team double-checked the translation with the Croatian version of the questionnaire in Bosnia and Herzegovina. In Serbia, *Liljana Steković* translated it into the Serbian language and then retranslated it from Serbian to English. After that, the questionnaire was tested with 45 respondents from one primary and one secondary school.

293 *Lynch & Addington* 2015; *Rodriguez, Pérez-Santiago & Birkbeck* 2015.

at the end of each questionnaire. The main aims of the ISRD3 project are theory-testing and development. This has given the researchers the possibility to test different theories, such as the social bonding and social control theories, the self-control theory, the routine activity/opportunity theory, and the social disorganization/collective efficacy – as well as the Procedural Justice Theory, the Institutional Anomie Theory, and the Situational Action Theory. In this research, the focus is mostly on the social control theory by *Hirschi* (1969).

The ISRD3 questionnaire consists of ten modules: demographic background (Module 1), family (Module 2), school (Module 3), victimization (Module 4), leisure and peers (Module 5), values and attitudes (Module 6), offending/delinquency (Module 7), substance-use questions (Module 8), norm-transmission strength questions to test the Institutional Anomie theory (Module 9), and procedural justice questions (Module 10). In addition to these ten modules, there is also an optional part, with a suggestion to add modules regarding gangs, cruelty to animals, and the response integrity question. Each module will be presented in the following sections.

4.3.1.1 Delinquency module

This module contained questions regarding self-reported illegal and risk behavior. These questions were based on the original National Youth Survey.[294] The core questionnaire had been designed for the ISRD1 project, with a focus on instruments to measure delinquency cross-nationally. A modified version was also used in ISRD2. In ISRD3, some changes were made regarding the self-reported delinquency questions ("Have you ever…?"). Questions about hacking and downloading music and films were replaced by a general question on illegal downloading. Some questions were reworded, such as the one on stealing from cars and snatching. Others were added, such as the question regarding graffiti. Overall, self-reported delinquency was measured by the following 14 items: illegal downloading, graffiti, vandalism, shoplifting, burglary, bike theft, vehicle theft, stealing from a car, stealing from a person, carrying a weapon, robbery/extortion, group fight, assault, and drug dealing.[295]

All items were asked on two time frames: *lifetime* prevalence ("Did you ever…?") and *last-year* prevalence ("Did you do this during the last twelve months?"), including the number of incidences ("Yes, _____ times"). Both time frames are used in this research. In contrast to ISRD2, there were no follow-up questions in ISRD3.[296]

---

294 *Elliott, Huizinga & Ageton* 1985.

295 For the exact questions, see the *Appendix*.

296 The ISRD2 questionnaire consists of follow-up questions, such as age of onset and detection (i.e., "How old were you when doing it for the first time?", "Were you detected and by whom?", etc.).

However, questions were added regarding contact with police because of illegal behaviour and the consequences thereof.

Numerous discussions and studies exist on the proper use of items that measure delinquency. There are many approaches to the use of these 14 delinquency items, and in this research, they are used in many ways.

First, the analyses are done by using each item *separately* (i.e., graffiti, theft, assault, etc.). As stated before, there are no big differences between Balkan countries in the interpretation of the specific questions. In addition, there are no big differences in the criminal codes regarding these 14 delinquent acts. Therefore, these items are quite easily comparable among these five Balkan countries.

Second, *composite* measures were employed in many analyses presented in the descriptive part and in the one that explains juvenile delinquency in the Balkans. The main aim was to use smaller and theoretically meaningful subscales. In this research, two very common distinctions were used based on different types of delinquency and the seriousness of delinquent acts.[297] The distinction of the seriousness of delinquent acts was based on the *frequency* of each act, although national criminal codes may treat some of these offences differently. Thus, minor offences are graffiti, group fighting, shoplifting, vandalism, and carrying a weapon.[298] Serious offences are less frequent or rare ones: theft, theft from a car, bicycle theft, car theft, assault, extortion, burglary, and drug dealing. The second distinction was made based on different types of offences: violent, property, and vandalism ones. Violent offences encompassed: extortion, carrying a weapon, group fighting, and assault. Property offences were shoplifting, burglary, theft, bicycle theft, car theft, and theft from a car – while the vandalism composite measure consisted of only two offences: vandalism and graffiti.[299] Similar to the single-measure items, all subcategories came in two versions: lifetime and last-year prevalence.

A third approach focused on overall delinquency. In this research, the overall delinquency scale was composed of all 14 offences: illegal downloading, graffiti, vandalism, shoplifting, burglary, bike theft, vehicle theft, stealing from a car, stealing from a person, carrying a weapon, robbery/extortion, group fighting, assault, and drug dealing. It is used as a rough measure of delinquency involvement (overall delinquency) and for a broad comparison. Much preferred is the use of a scale which produces simultaneously the information on seriousness and frequency. Therefore, in this research, variety scales were used. Variety scales are well-accepted criminal offending scales as they are relatively easy to construct, have a high reliability and validity, and, most importantly, are not compromised by the high frequency of minor

---

297 These two distinctions were also suggested by the ISRD3 technical reports.
298 Illegal downloading was not used as a minor offence as this would have disturbed the scale.
299 It should be noted that drug dealing and illegal downloading were not part of any mentioned type of offences.

offences.[300] There is a long discussion on how to create a meaningful and empirically useful scale of offences. *Hindelang et al.* (1981) recognize numerous measurement issues in criminological research, such as regarding the validity and reliability of self-report data and the unidimensionality of offending.[301] One of their results was that in self-report research, reliable scales are obtainable with relatively few self-report items of delinquency and that self-report measures are valid measures. Like many other researchers, in order to avoid the problem of a disproportionate weight on minor offences – such as in the case of the Guttman scaling –, they suggest to use the variety scale of offending.[302] It reports the total number of types of delinquent behaviour an individual has ever participated in.[303] In this study, the *raw variety* scale was used, which contains the sum of 14 offences (for both lifetime and last year) and *categorized variety* scores[304] (for both lifetime and last year). It should be noted that various of these scales, as all other scales, have several problems. They treat all forms of offending identically, do not differentiate between minor and serious offences, and they ignore the frequency of offending despite presenting these data simultaneously. However, in comparison with the problems of other scales, the ones encountered here are not that serious.[305]

4.3.1.2 Drug use

The module on substance use (drug and alcohol use) in the questionnaire is placed as the first segment of the flexible part. Here, many changes were made in comparison to the ISRD2 questionnaire. The concept is the same, but it is presented in a much more efficient way. The format of the questions regarding drug use was improved similar to the ones referring to different delinquency acts. Drugs are divided into three categories: cannabis; XTC, LSD, speed, amphetamines, or similar drugs; and heroin, cocaine, or crack. Both time frames are included: lifetime and last-year prevalence. However, in the case of cannabis use, the time frame is last month, in contrast to other drug-related questions, which are using last-year prevalence. The categorization of drugs in this research is based on the well-established ESPAD survey which provides a number of validated questions that have been used on international samples of youth. Interestingly, the ISRD3 questionnaire includes a question regarding the lifetime use of a fake drug (relevin) in order to assess over-reporting. In addition, this part contains a question that asks about the propensity

---

300 *Sweeten* 2012.

301 *Hindelang, Hirschi & Weis* 1981.

302 *Farrington* 1973; *Hirschi & Selvin* 1967; *Moffitt et al.* 2001; *Porterfield* 1943.

303 *Sweeten* 2012.

304 Variety score categories are: 0 = "no offences", 1 = "one offence", 2 = "two offences", 3 = "three offences and more offences".

305 *Elliott & Ageton* 1980.

to report.[306] This question has been successfully used in previous studies to examine the possibility of under- or over-reporting.

Consumption of drugs is not included in the delinquency measure, but drug dealing is. However, it should be noted that drug dealing is not included in any type of delinquency. As it can neither be categorized as a violent nor as a property or vandalism offence, it is presented as a separate item.

4.3.1.3 Alcohol use

Alcohol use, as well as drug abuse, was not a part of the delinquency measurement because the idea was only to include those behaviours that are illegal in all participating Balkan countries. Therefore, alcohol use – together with drug use and truancy – was classified as a risk behaviour. It is considered as a problematic behaviour that leads to more serious illegal behaviour.[307] The questionnaire focuses on the prevalence of the use of alcohol ("Have you ever drunk alcohol?"). This is followed by a question regarding the type of alcohol (beer, wine or strong spirits [e.g., whisky, vodka, schnapps,[308] etc.]) and frequency in terms of the type of alcohol in last month (30 days). It should be noted that the time lavel in questions related to the abuse of alcohol was different than in the questions related to delinquency. In the case of alcohol use, the time frame is last month, and in the module related to delinquency, it is last year (12 months). In the ISRD3 questionnaire, a question on binge drinking was added. This refers to the consumption of an excessive amount of alcohol within a short period of time and was measured as five or more drinks on one occasion. The longitudinal study showed that youths who binge drink when they are around 16 years old are more likely to develop an alcohol dependency at the age of 30.[309] Therefore, analyses in this research include the lifetime prevalence of the consumption of alcohol, last-month prevalence of the consumption of different types of alcohol and binge drinking by country.

4.3.1.4 Social-economic status

In ISRD3, questions related to the social-economic status are part of the demographics model. They are divided into two groups: the occupational status of parents and family affluence. In the occupational status of the family, two questions refer to the *unemployment* of the father and/or the mother. This is a more traditional

---

306 This is question 8.6: "Imagine you had used cannabis (cannabis / marijuana / hash), do you think that you would have said so in this questionnaire? I have already said that I have used it / Definitely yes / Probably yes / Probably not / Definitely not".

307 *Steketee et al.* 2013.

308 In the question related to strong spirits, researchers in the Balkans added schnapps (rakija) as a very common drink in the region.

309 *Viner & Taylor* 2007.

measure of the socio-economic status. The questions allowed three possible responses: "yes, he/she is unemployed; no, he/she is working; other[310] (he/she is retired, has a long-term illness, looks after the home, is a student, ...)". In the ISRD2 questionnaire, these questions had allowed many more possible answers, and the logic of the question was opposite (it had asked about the *employment* of the father and/or mother). Analyses of ISRD2 show that the best way of using these variables is to use them as a dichotomous variable. The same approach was used in the multivariate regression model of this research. The variable of 'mother unemployment' was divided into three dichotomous variables: mother's unemployment (yes/no), mother's employment (yes/no), and other (yes/no), referring to her retirement, long-term illness, etc.

Family affluence is divided into three questions: a source of family income; relative family affluence; and relative personal affluence. It is important to note that questions on relative family and personal affluence were based on the self-perception of the respondents in comparison with others. The questions provided a relatively large number of possible responses (seven in total), from "much worse off" to "much better off". The same logic was applied to the question concerning respondents' affluence, where they could choose on a scale from "much less" to "much more". The logic of comparison between the respondents and others he/she knows is a plausible indicator of family/personal affluence in the given society and is therefore comparable on the cross-national level. The question regarding family income was divided into two variables. The first one was constructed from the answer "My family receives unemployment or social welfare benefits",[311] which was presented as the variable *family funds, unemployment*. The second variable was based on the answer "My family gets income from the earnings, wages, or property" and was presented as *family funds, employment*, while the third option was an open question, *other*. In this third category, respondents could write their own answers. The first two variables were dichotomous, with the two categories *yes* and *no*.

In the ISRD2 questionnaire, family affluence was measured with questions which had initially been developed for studying health-wealth relationships in cross-national health behaviour research.[312] Among the family affluence indicators were some of the questions regarding having a room of one's own, having access to a computer at home, owning a mobile phone, and whether one's family owned a car. Analyses showed that it is doubtful if these questions actually measured affluence, as the answers showed little variation between the youths. Therefore, in ISRD3,

---

310 In the case of mothers, under the answer, the option "other housewife (kućanica, domaćica)" was added. Being patriarchal societies, it is a common situation in the Balkans that mothers stay at home and take care of the children and house, while fathers are seen as the main breadwinners of the family.

311 In the case of social welfare, each participating country was supposed to translate "social welfare" into an equivalent, appropriate category, so that it would be comparable.

312 *Currie et al.* 1997; *Boyce et al.* 2006.

questions measuring family affluence were changed to become simpler and to feature a higher validity.

4.3.1.5 Migrant status

In the ISRD3 questionnaire, the general concept of minority status was employed. It consisted of three simple questions about where the respondent was born and where his or her mother and father were born. The question format was open-ended, which allowed for any possible answers regarding the country of origin. Each country drafted a list of the most frequent countries of origin, with the possibility to add other countries. For the purpose of this research, the variable of *migrant* was created on the basis of the response to a question regarding the country of birth of the respondent as well as of the mother and father. However, in the analysis, the variable of *migrant* was also used as a simple dichotomy variable (native-born vs. first- or second-generation migrant) or even a trichotomy variable (native-born vs. first-generation migrant vs. second-generation migrant). In this regard, the questionnaire also had additional questions that were not part of the core definition used in this analysis, such as language spoken at home and type of minority group. Problems arose with regard to the question concerning the latter, as this was not used in the same way in all Balkan countries, and in the case of North Macedonia, it was not used at all. This question was also challenging for the analysis in a complex setting such as Bosnia and Herzegovina. Therefore, this question was excluded from the analysis.

It should be clarified that because of their difficult past and challenging economic situation, countries from the Balkans are emigration' countries of origin, unlike in Western and Central Europe, which are countries of immigration.[313] Large groups of residents from different ethnic backgrounds inhabit most of the Western and Central European countries, which is not the case in the Balkans. This is another reason why the *migration* variable was not considered as a core part of analysis in this thesis.

4.3.1.6 Religion

Methodologically, the available literature lacks a conceptualization of religion, which is seen as a key predictor variable. There is no common agreement on how to measure religion. According to *Clear* and *Sumter* (2002), various theories have failed to successfully conceptualize religion regarding its core meaning. As a multidimensional construct, it was based on various dimensions, such as belief (i.e., membership in a religious organization), effective (i.e., effect of religious systems on belief systems), and behavioural (i.e., frequency at which individuals are involved in religious practices or activities, also seen as involvement).[314] There is also a lack of agreement

---

313 OECD 2018.
314 *Fernander et al.* 2005

on the dimension of religiosity. It has been defined in terms of organizational religiosity (i.e., attendance of religious services) or subjective religiosity (i.e., the importance of religion and self-rated religiosity). Such ambiguous conceptualizations of religion have produced different indicators or measures that are not consistent and vary depending on which dimension of religion is utilized.[315] Another concept of measurement is based on the social control theory by *Hirschi* (1969). This theory proposes to measure religion through four elements: involvement, belief, commitment, and attachment.[316]

The ISRD3 questionnaire contains two questions about religion. The first one concerned the religious affiliation of the respondent: "What is your religion, or to which religious community do you belong?" This question is representative of one dimension of religion, which is belief. Each national researcher was able to add the most frequent religion in his/her country.[317] After collecting the data, religions were recorded so that a number was assigned to each religion. This provided the possibility to measure differences among juveniles belonging to any religion and those who do not. The second question was related to religiosity and measured how important religion is in a respondent's everyday life. This variable, called *religiosity*, was recorded on a scale ranging from "very important", "quite important", "a bit important", "a bit unimportant", "quite unimportant", to "very unimportant".[318] Not many variables dealt with religion, however, they covered the two main dimensions *religion affiliation* and *religiosity*, which gave the researchers the possibility to test some of the theories. This was a big breakthrough for the ISRD study, as ISRD2 did not have any questions regarding religion. Hopefully, more questions on this topic and its multidimensionality will be added in the ISRD4 questionnaire.

4.3.1.7 Family

With regard to delinquency, the family is one of the most important domains of this study.[319] Questions related to family were of central importance in this research, as the family plays a central role in Balkan societies. Therefore, in the analyses, the focus was on the variables and scales concerning the family. The ISRD3 questionnaire has many questions about a juvenile's family and a whole module dedicated to this aspect. There are different ways of using it. However, this thesis emphasizes the social control theory by *Hirschi* (1969). Therefore, variables and scales are used to test the theory, which is also one of the main goals of the ISRD projects. The analyses are based on the two main scales: *family control* and *family attachment*.

---

315 *Sumter et al.* 2018, 10.
316 For details, see *Chapter 4.3.1.6.*
317 Otherwise, if the same options would be used for all countries the questionnaire would be too long, or there would be too many variables to be recoded from the answer "other".
318 For details, see *Appendix 1.*
319 *Shoemaker* 2018, 93.

The parental attachment scale is composed of four questions: "How well do you get along with your father (or stepfather) and mother (or stepmother)", "How easily do you get emotional support and care from your parents?", and "Would you feel bad about disappointing your parents?". This scale is based on five answer levels, ranging from "totally agree" to "totally disagree" (Cronbach's Alpha = 0.76). The question regarding spending time with one's parent(s) was not included in the attachment scale because it did not work very well (Cronbach's Alpha = 0.56). In comparison with the ISRD2 questionnaire, the parental attachment scale was expended. Psychological questions on emotional support and disappointing parents were added.

The parental control scale was based on three dimensions. The first one concerned parent's knowledge about where their children are, what they are doing, and which friends they are staying with. The second one concerned parental supervision over their children, and the third dealt with child disclosure to parents. Based on these three elements, the scale worked very well (Cronbach's Alpha = 0.87). This three-dimensional parental control scale is a new scale based on the work of *Kerr* and *Stattin*,[320] which has recently been corroborated by *Eaton et al.*.[321] Parental control has been linked to various forms of delinquency in the empirical literature,[322] but the exact nature and meaning of the parental control construct and related measures have been analyzed in more depth in recent years. Over the years, many researchers have focused on activities parents actively engage in, such as tracking the child.[323] However, *Stattin* and *Kerr* (2000) noted that previous measures of parental control have typically assessed the amount of knowledge parents have about their children but not the process through which they discovered this information. As *Stattin* and *Kerr* (2000) as well as *Eaton et al.* (2009) noted, parental knowledge is strongly related to child disclosure. If a child's disclosure is not controlled, detected links between parental supervision and crime can be spurious and dependent on an unmeasured variation in the child's own behaviour. Therefore, the ISRD3 questionnaire included four options related to child disclosure: "I tell my parents who I spend time with", "… how I spend my money", "… where I am most afternoons after school", and "… what I do with my free time".

4.3.1.8 School

In the ISRD3 questionnaire, a number of questions were related to the school experiences of juveniles. For the purpose of this research, three scales were produced. The first one is an attachment to school; it is based on Lickert-type opinion statements about school ("If I had to move, I would miss my school"; "Most mornings I like going to school"; "I like my school"; "Our classes are interesting"). Cronbach's

---

320 See *Kerr & Stattin* 2000.

321 See *Eaton et al.* 2009.

322 See, e.g., *Biglan et al.* 1995; *Dishion et al.* 1995; *Metzler et al.* 1993.

323 *Dishion & McMahon* 1998.

Alpha worked very well here (0.81). In the ISRD2 project, school bonding or school climate scale had been used, but as this did not work very well (Cronbach's Alpha = 0.61), it was restructured into the school attachment scale. The second scale was school disorganization, which was part of the same module as school attachment, therefore using the same type of methodology. This question consisted of four sub-options: "There is a lot of stealing in my school"; "There is a lot of fighting in my school"; "Many things are broken or vandalized in my school"; "There is a lot of drug use in my school". Cronbach's Alpha also worked very well here (0.74). This measurement had also proven to work very well in the ISRD2 study, so it was maintained in the same way. The possible answers were structured on a four-level scale: "I fully agree"; "I somewhat agree"; "I somewhat disagree"; "I fully disagree".[324] The *Bonding to teachers* scale is a new scale comprised of two questions: "If you had to move to another city, how much would you miss your favourite teacher?" and "How important is it to you how your favourite teacher thinks about you?" (Cronbach's Alpha = 0.71). In this question, the emphasis is on the relationship between the respondent and his/her favourite teacher – and not only to the more abstract "school". Both questions used six-level scales as possible answers, ranging from "not at all/totally unimportant" to "very much/very important".

The ISRD 3 questionnaire includes a question regarding school performance. As there are many differences between the participating countries regarding the practice of repeating classes as well as grading systems, a subjective measure of school performance was used. The question was "How well do you do at school?", with seven possible answers ("excellent, I'm probably one of the best in my class(es)"; "well above average"; "above average"; "average"; "below average"; "well below average"; "poor, I'm probably one of the worst in my class(es)"). The second question about school performance was an objective one and asked whether the children had ever been held back, meaning if they had had to repeat a year (grade). Truancy was measured by asking if students had ever stayed away from school for at least a whole day without a proper reason in the last twelve months. This question also captured frequency by asking how often this happened.

4.3.2   Validity of self-report surveys in the Balkans

Self-report surveys were developed in the 1930s and 1940s in the USA and spread to Scandinavian and other European countries in the 1960s.[325] When looking at the history of self-report surveys,[326] it becomes clear that this method was invented and evolved in a specific cultural and societal context. Indeed, developing countries, such

---

324 It should be noted that this scale is coded in the opposite way in the dataset: 1 = fully disagree; 2 = somewhat disagree; 3 = somewhat agree; 4 = fully agree.

325 *Kivivuori* 2011.

326 For more details, see *Chapter 2.1.*

as those from the Balkan region, did not take part in most of the cross-national self-report studies and were not part of methodological studies on their reliability and validity.[327] Therefore, a question which arises is whether this method can be applied in countries with different cultural heritages and socio-political contexts? The main challenge is: would respondents tell the truth in the questionnaire?

The self-report method has nevertheless become the major instrument of data collection in the field of delinquency.[328] Previous studies have shown that it has a high degree of reliability and validly for most analytic purposes.[329] Many agree that self-report surveys are an appropriate method for testing theoretical correlates, but researchers are much more critical with respect to their validity as the basis for estimates regarding the level and nature of offending.[330] This is even more problematic when cross-national analyses are applied. Therefore, in this research, only the basics of the prevalence of juvenile delinquency will be presented as the context in which further analyses will be made. The next step in the analyses – and the most important one – is to test theoretical correlations and to see if the same factors have as much an impact on juvenile delinquency as they have in (more highly developed) Western nations.

The ISRD2 estimates of delinquency, drug and alcohol use were compared with the results of other, similar surveys, such as the Peterborough Study,[331] the Dutch self-report study,[332] and ESPAD.[333] They were all compatible and provided additional support for the validity of the ISRD2 study.[334] All of them were compared with domestic surveys in highly developed countries. However, the results in post-socialist countries were contradictory when compared to trends in self-reported offending and victimization.[335] One of the explanations was that the willingness to report committing an offence should be taken into consideration in these societies.[336] Therefore, *Enzmann et al.* (2018) incorporated questionnaire a few questions to test this in the ISRD3 study. It has recently used a further developed variant of the crosswise model[337] as a way of statistically correcting variants of a systematic response bias.

---

327 *Enzmann et al.* 2018, 19.

328 *Stone et al.* 2000.

329 *Thornberry & Krohn* 2000; *Thornberry & Krohn* 2003.

330 *Kivivuori* 2007; *Thornberry & Krohn* 2003.

331 *Wikström & Butterworth* 2006.

332 *Van der Laan & Blom* 2006.

333 *Hibell et al.* 2004.

334 *Enzmann et al.* 2018.

335 The countries in the post-socialist cluster with higher rates of self-reported victimization had lower rates of self-reported offending.

336 *Enzmann et al.* 2010, 178; *Pauwels & Svensson* 2008.

337 *Yu, Tian & Tang* 2008.

The respondent was asked two questions with yes/no responses: a sensitive and a non-sensitive question.[338] Respondents were then asked to uncover whether their answers to the two questions were the same ("yes" to both or "no" to both) or different ("yes" to one and "no" to the other). The probability distribution is known for the non-sensitive question. This allows the researcher to estimate the proportion of the sample answering "yes" to the sensitive question, which avoids the problem of asking the sensitive question directly.[339] *Enzmann et al.* (2018) presented the cultural variability of self-reported delinquency questions. They showed the last-year prevalence rates of self-reported delinquency (combined with shoplifting, burglary, assault, and extortion) based on the crosswise model and a direct question (see *Figure 1*). They reported a clear variability in the results of the direct and the indirect question for the different countries, which suggests that there is a differential validity of the self-reported responses for the ISRD3 countries. They also interpreted results in the way this differs between direct and indirect estimates as a measure of unwillingness or the inability to provide a truthful answer. If the analysis is made in this way, with a focus on the Balkan countries, Kosovo showed the highest and Croatia showed the lowest difference. This means that juveniles in the Kosovo sample had the highest unwillingness or inability to provide a truthful answer, and in the Croatian sample, they had the lowest.

In the next step, *Enzmann et al.* (2018) presented the impact of social desirability[340] on self-report estimates of offending, which was measured by the indirect question and operationalized as the difference in prevalence between the crosswise and the direct questions related to shoplifting, burglary, assault, and robbery. Based on this analysis, they reported that countries with a higher Human Development Index (HDMI) score tend to score lower regarding the social desirability effect, concluding that these countries are more familiar with social surveys – or less reluctant about expressing socially undesirable behaviour. Therefore, this should be taken into consideration when analysing data from the Balkan region, as most of these countries have low HDMI scores. Some of the suggested explanations were lack of general social trust, lack of trust towards research, and/or cognitive unfamiliarity with surveys. All of these suggested reasons could apply to the countries from the Balkan region, as they have relatively low levels of general social trust[341] and are relatively unfamiliar with surveys, which are rarely conducted in the region.[342]

---

338 For details, see the last question in the questionnaire, *Appendix 1*.
339 For details, see *Enzmann et al.* 2018.
340 See *Figure 1*.
341 *Mishler & Rose* 2001; *Rimac & Štulhofer* 2004; *Trzun* 2012.
342 *Getoš Kalac* 2014.

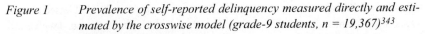

Figure 1   Prevalence of self-reported delinquency measured directly and estimated by the crosswise model (grade-9 students, n = 19,367)[343]

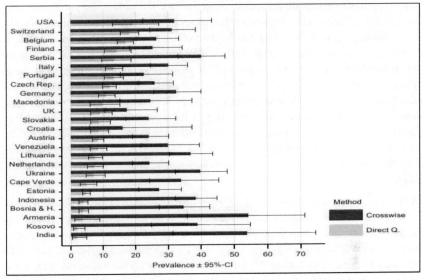

However, *Enzmann et al.* (2018) did not completely criticize self-report surveys on offending but warned that the validity of these surveys should be compared cross-nationally between culturally and economically similar countries. This is another reason why this research focuses only on countries that have more cultural and historical similarities than differences.

4.4   Statistics

The first part of the analyses aims at presenting prevalence rates of juvenile delinquency in the Balkans. It starts with an overview of the background information for each Balkan country, such as age, gender, nationality, etc. The differences in the samples are stressed out for better conceptualizing the data. The juvenile delinquency scale contains 14 different offences.[344] It is presented for the Balkan cluster as a whole as well as by country within it. It is divided into two parts based on the different time frames. The first time frame to be used is lifetime, based on the question "Have you ever…?", while the second one is last year. In order to provide a better

---

343 *Enzmann et al.* 2018, 24; countries are ranked based on the level of self-reported delinquency through the direct questions.

344 For more details, see *Chapter 4.3.1.1.*

overview of juvenile delinquency in the Balkans, the scale is divided based on two criteria: different types of offences and different levels of the offence. Twelve different types of offences are presented in three scales: the violent, the vandalism, and the property offence scale. Property offences are shoplifting, burglary, theft, bicycle theft, car theft, and theft from a car. Violent offences include extortion, carrying a weapon, group fight, and assault. It should be noted that as there is no consensus about vandalism, it should be placed under property or violent offences. In these analyses, they will be seen as a separate group, together with graffiti. The second division is based on the level of the offence; therefore, the analyses are run between minor and serious offences. The next step is lifetime versatility of juvenile delinquency, presenting the frequency of reported offences in the juvenile's lifetime. The aim of this analysis is to see how many different offences juveniles have reported. Lifetime delinquency will also be presented by gender and age based on the country level.

After presenting the phenomenology of juvenile delinquency in the Balkans, the next step is aetiology. Therefore, the following analyses focus on presenting different indicators which – based on the social control theory by *Hirschi* (1969) – have an impact on juvenile delinquency. The analyses start with an overview of the indicators by country and correlations between different variables measuring the same indicator. By providing a correlation matrix, the aim is to see which of the variables have the strongest correlation with lifetime juvenile crime and how strong the relationship is between the variables within the indicator. Based on these results, variables are added as independent variables in the multivariate analyses, while the dependent variable is the lifetime self-reported delinquency scale. Country-dichotomised variables are added in each model in order to test if there are differences among the countries. Serbia is used as a reference country for this purpose. There are also age differences between the country samples. Therefore, the variable *Age14* is added in the model. *Age14* is a computed variable that is centred near the mean age (14 years) of all respondents. An *Age14* variable is added to the model so as to constrain effects of age, not least since the mean ages differ clearly between the countries. Adding variable *Age14* controls for individual age effects on crime, and so the country dummies (as well as other variables) get rid of the age differences. The last variable to be added to the model is gender, coded 0 as a male and 1 as a female. These statistical models should give a better overview of the effect by different factors on juvenile crime in the Balkans.

Chapter 5

Findings

5.1 Descriptive Statistics

As a comparative study of juvenile crime and victimization, the ISRD has a large number of participating countries, which results in a large cultural diversity of participating countries and an explicitly standardized design.[345] Therefore, this research project includes only countries from the Balkan region[346] so as to minimize cultural diversity. It also uses the advantage of a standardized design for cross-national comparison. The first part of this chapter presents a brief overview of the sample characteristics. The second part describes the nature and distribution of overall delinquency in a combined sample called "Balkan cluster" as well as by country. This is followed by a section that presents the prevalence of different types of juvenile delinquency among the observed countries. The fourth part analyses the correlations between self-reported delinquency with gender and age. The following part investigates substance use, especially alcohol consumption and drug use. The last part refers to juvenile victimization.

With regard to the ongoing state-building process in the Balkan region, there is still a lack of criminological research on juvenile delinquency;[347] therefore, the aim of this chapter is to present and describe the spread of juvenile crime in the Balkans.

5.1.1 Sample characteristics

Table 2 shows how the sample has been obtained in the Balkan cluster and in the five countries which are forming this cluster, how it differs with regard to gender, age, migration status, and religion. "Migration status" distinguishes three groups: first-generation migrants (born abroad), second-generation migrants (born in the

---

345 *Enzmann et al.* 2018, 7.

346 This research contains data from Bosnia and Herzegovina, Croatia, Kosovo, North Macedonia, and Serbia. Even other countries from the Balkan region, such as Turkey and Greece, participated in the survey, but they did not finish data collection within the time of writing this thesis. Therefore, these countries were not included in the presentation of this research project. For more information on the participating countries in this project, see https://web.northeastern.edu/isrd/isrd3/ [16/06/2018].

347 For details, see *Chapter 2.2.*

country but with at least one parent born abroad), and natives (including third-generation migrants).

Table 2   Sample characteristics in the Balkan cluster and by country (%)

	Balkan cluster (n = 8460)	Bosnia and Herzegov. (n = 3066)	Croatia (n = 1741)	Kosovo (n = 1078)	N. Macedonia (n = 1239)	Serbia (n = 1336)
Age						
< 12	10.5	13.30	1.5	31.5	5.4	3.2
13	28.9	32.8	28.4	34.7	29.4	15.6
14	30.1	36.4	29.9	28.3	34.0	13.5
15	19.9	16.4	34.2	5.5	26.6	15.2
16+	10.6	1.1	6.1	0.0	4.6	50.5
Gender						
Female	50.6	51.4	53.2	49.0	49.2	47.8
Migration						
First generation	3.2	4.2	2.4	3.2	1.9	3.1
Second generation	15.0	10.6	19.6	6.4	9.8	31.0
Natives	81.8	85.2	78.1	90.4	88.3	65.9
Religion						
Catholic	22.0	8.6	88.6	2.6	0.6	2.5
Islam	40.9	61.0	1.1	94.5	42.9	1.3
Orthodox	31.3	24.9	0.5	0.1	52.5	91.5
Atheist & Agnostic	3.8	2.9	8.2	0.6	2.7	3.4
Other	2.0	2.6	1.6	2.2	1.3	1.3

In the Balkan cluster, the distribution of *gender* is well-balanced, although in some countries, there are slightly fewer males or females.[348] There are some age differences between the countries (mean age: 14 years). In most countries, the youngest

---

348 The national bureaus of statistics in the observed countries are making analyses based on age groups 0–14 or 10–14 and 15–19, which is not in line with the age group in this study. Therefore,

age cohort represents less than 14 % of the sample, while in Kosovo, it constitutes about one-third. On the other hand, the oldest age cohort is overrepresented in the Serbian sample with 50.5 %, while in Kosovo, this age group is not represented at all. Consequently, Kosovo has a younger sample on average than the rest of the countries (mean age: 13.06 years), while Serbia has definitely the oldest sample (mean age: 15.46 years). In the other three countries, including the Balkan cluster as a whole, the age distribution is more balanced. It will be part of the analyses in correlation with the prevalence of different types of juvenile delinquency by countries, as the age-crime curve increases to a peak in the teenage years and then decreases.[349]

Migration status is an important variable in the ISRD3 study, similar to the ISRD2 study.[350] However, this is not the case in the Balkan cluster due to the political and historical background of these countries. According to the ISRD3 research sample, Serbia has by far the highest percentage of migrants (34.1 %), followed by Croatia (22.0 %), while in Kosovo, the proportion of migrants is lowest (9.6 %). The proportion of the first generation of migrants is almost the same in all countries, with the highest in Bosnia and Herzegovina (4.2 %) and the lowest in North Macedonia (1.9 %). This difference comes from the proportion of the second generation of migrants, with the highest in Serbia (31 %) and the lowest in Kosovo (6.4 %). The problem of the migration variable in these countries is that they were all part of one country (Yugoslavia) before the 1990s. Therefore, migration cannot be seen in the same light as in the rest of Europe. Most of the first- and second-generation migrants' origin is in the Balkan countries.

Religion plays an important role in the Balkan region, as most of its inhabitants embrace religion as an element of national belonging.[351] Croatia has a Catholic majority, Serbia an Orthodox majority; in Kosovo, the majority of people identify as Muslims, while in North Macedonia, the majority of people identify themselves as Muslims or Orthodox; the same goes for Bosnia and Herzegovina, including a smaller proportion of people that identify as Catholics.[352] The distribution of religion in the sample is similar to the one at the national level in the observed countries. Therefore, in the Croatian sample, 88.6 % of respondents consider themselves as Catholics, in the Serbian sample, 91.5 % reported that they belong to an Orthodox religion, and in the case of Kosovo, 94.5 % identified as Muslims. When looking at

---

it is doubtful to do a comparison based on age between the research sample and national samples. See https://www.dzs.hr/default_e.htm, http://www.stat.gov.rs/en-us/oblasti/stanovnistvo/statistika-polova/, http://publikacije.stat.gov.rs/G2017/PdfE/G20176008.pdf, http://www.stat.gov.mk/Publikacii/2.4.16.10.pdf [04.08.2018].

349 *Farrington* 1986, 189.
350 *Marshall Hean & Enzmann* 2012, 34.
351 Pew Research Center 2017; for more, see *Chapter 4.3.1.6.*
352 For details, see Pew Research Center 2017; Pew Research Center 2015.

Bosnia and Herzegovina and North Macedonia, the sample was mostly evenly spread between Muslims and Orthodox Christians. In Bosnia and Herzegovina, 61 % of respondents identified as Muslims, 24.9 % as Orthodox, and 8.6 % as Catholics. The Orthodox religion was represented in 52.5 % of the North Macedonian sample, and Muslims constituted 42.9 % here.

5.1.2 Prevalence of juvenile delinquency in the Balkans

This chapter describes the basic findings concerning the prevalence of juvenile delinquency in the Balkan cluster as well as between the individual countries. They are still in a process of state-building, although in different stages of it, and they are facing economic and societal challenges which demand better and more innovative policy-making. Hence, these countries need reliable and accessible data so that policy-makers have a realistic understanding of the problems to be dealt with and to ensure that the policies they create are well-targeted and effective. Therefore, the first part of this chapter focuses on the distribution of juvenile delinquency in the Balkans, with an aim to see which differences exist between the observed countries.

Tables 3 and *4* demonstrate lifetime and last-year prevalence of 14 delinquent acts that were reported by the juveniles in the sample. These acts are comprised of responses to the questions "Did you 'ever' commit such acts?" and "Have you done so during the 'last year' prior to the administration of the survey?". These percentages should not be seen as an exact illustration of the volume of juvenile delinquency in the Balkans, but give a rough overview of the prevalence of different delinquent acts in the region. Self-report rates have many weaknesses, as much as official data and victimization surveys. Actually, there is no ideal measurement of delinquency, and each source has its positive and negative aspects that should be taken into consideration when analysing and presenting the data. Furthermore, lifetime prevalences are rather rough indicators of delinquency that do not reflect the current situation (mostly because of the age differences among the respondents).[353] Therefore, in the next step of analyses, last-year prevalence rate will be included, as well as an age-crime curve.

Missing answers are presented because a high number of missing values may be an indication of a possible underreporting of certain acts. However, this is not the case in this dataset. The percentage of missing data is relatively low in the lifetime and last-year prevalence tables.

---

353 *Enzmann* 2010, 57.

Table 3 Lifetime prevalence of 14 delinquent acts

	Balkan cluster		Bosnia and Herzegovina		Croatia		Kosovo		North Macedonia		Serbia	
	%	% missing	%	% missing	%	% missing	%	% missing	%	% missing	%	% missing
Illegal downloading	32.1	2.5	19.2	5.9	59.6	0.7	8	1.2	18.7	0.3	57.6	0.1
Graffiti	18.6	23	16.5	5.4	16.7	0.7	7.7	1.2	17.8	0.3	35.5	0
Shoplifting	9	2.3	4.3	5.4	10.9	0.7	1.3	1.2	7.7	0.3	25	0
Vandalism	6.4	2.4	4.5	5.5	7.8	0.7	2.1	1.2	6.7	0.3	12.4	0
Group fight	8.1	2.5	6.3	5.8	6	0.9	4.9	1.2	12.9	0.3	13.4	0
Theft	4.4	2.5	2.3	5.8	5.7	0.9	1	1.2	4.2	0.3	10.3	0.1
Carrying a weapon	5.4	2.5	3.6	5.8	4.1	1	3.7	1.2	6.5	0.3	11.4	0.1
Drug dealing	2.3	2.7	1.3	6	3.4	1.5	0.7	1.2	2.2	0.3	4.6	0
Car break	2.4	2.4	1.1	5.7	0.8	0.9	0.6	1.2	1.9	0.3	3.2	0
Bicycle theft	2.1	2.4	1.1	5.6	1.7	0.9	0.5	1.2	1.7	0.3	6.8	0.1
Assault	2.3	2.5	1.8	5.9	1.5	0.9	1.4	1.2	2.9	0.3	4.6	0
Car/motor theft	1.4	2.4	1.1	5.7	0.8	0.9	0.6	1.2	1.9	0.3	3.2	0
Extortion	1.3	2.4	1.5	5.7	0.7	0.9	0.8	1.2	1.9	0.3	1.5	0
Burglary	1	2.4	1.1	5.6	0.6	0.9	0.7	1.2	1.4	0.3	1.2	0.1

Thus, in the case of Kosovo and North Macedonia, missing data are the same for all delinquent acts (1.2 % and 0.3 %). In other countries – as well as in the Balkan cluster as a whole –, missing data vary ± 0.3 %, with an exception in the case of drug dealing in Croatia (1.5 %, 1.8 %) and in the Serbian sample for last-year prevalence (0.4–10.2 %). The highest rate of missing data for most of the countries is found for non-serious offences (e.g., illegal downloading last year), because there is a possibility that juveniles do not remember it. However, in the case of serious offences, there is also the problem of non-reporting (e.g., drug dealing). Some offenders may not want to disclose committing serious offences because they fear the consequences, embarrassment, shame, or any other reason. This explanation can be applied especially in the case of ex-communist countries.

In the Balkan cluster, 45.6 % of respondents reported having "ever" commit one or more of the 14 offences. Looking at the country level, the results vary from 17.5 % for Kosovo to 76.5 % in the case of Serbia, followed by Croatia (65.6 %), North Macedonia (35.2 %), and Bosnia and Herzegovina (34.2 %). Therefore, significant differences can be seen among the Balkan countries in overall lifetime delinquency.

When looking at individual delinquent acts in the Balkan cluster, it is apparent from *Table 3* that most of the young offenders reported acts of a non-serious nature, such as illegal downloading and graffiti. Illegal downloading has extremely high rates in some countries (see Croatia and Serbia). Therefore, the rates of overall lifetime delinquency are different when excluding illegal downloading. Serbia still has the highest rate at 61.9 %, followed by Croatia with twice the number of respondents having "ever" committed one or more of the 13 remaining offences (29.5 %). Bosnia and Herzegovina and North Macedonia have slightly lower rates than Croatia (25.0 % and 27.9 %). Kosovo has the lowest rate at 13.1 %. When excluding illegal downloading from the delinquency scale, the highest difference is found in the Croatian rate, going down from 65.6 % to 29.5 %, since Croatia has the highest percentage of illegal downloading among all observed countries. In order to explore the aetiology of such a high rate of illegal downloading, it would be useful in the future to include information about internet access levels and of daily online usage. With this information, it would be possible to test if the rate of illegal downloading simply reflects exposure to opportunities. Some of these questions were part of the ISRD2 questionnaire, but they were excluded from the ISRD3 questionnaire. However, World Bank data from 2016 on individuals using the internet show that in Croatia, 73 % of the population use the internet, and almost the same proportion can be seen in North Macedonia (72 %), followed by Serbia where 67 % use the internet, and the lowest percentage is found in Bosnia and Herzegovina (55 %).[354] These

---

354   The World Bank 2016. For Kosovo, no data was available.

data of the World Bank, however, do not vary as much as reported illegal downloading in the ISRD3 sample. However, almost the same pattern can be seen when compared to the latter's country rates, except in the case of North Macedonia where fewer students reported illegal downloading in comparison to all individuals using the internet. Another cause could be that juveniles at this age are not familiar with what is legal – especially what is illegal in terms of downloading, which could be seen in the ISRD2 study for the case of Bosnia and Herzegovina.[355] However, there insufficient data for testing this issue in the ISRD3 study. Thus, informatics as well as knowledge about the unauthorized use of protected content is something that should be taken into consideration for implementing the new curriculum of primary and secondary schools. The development and implementation of the new curriculum is still an ongoing process in Croatia.

When comparing rates of other delinquent acts (i.e. apart from the above-mentioned ones), Serbia has the highest rates in all delinquent offences except for extortion where North Macedonia has a higher rate (1.9 % vs. 1.5 %). At the other end, the lowest rates are found in the Kosovo sample, with two exceptions: in the case of carrying a weapon, the slightly lower rate is found in Bosnia and Herzegovina (3.6 %), and in the case of extortion, it is found in Croatia (0.7 %). Overall, these results indicate that the country with the highest rate of delinquency in the Balkan region is Serbia, followed by Croatia.

Table 4 shows last-year prevalence of juvenile delinquency per country and in the complete Balkan cluster. If comparing this with lifetime prevalence (*Table 3*), the ranking order of the most frequently committed delinquent acts is almost the same, no matter whether one considers acts committed "ever" or "last year". The two most frequently reported delinquent acts are still non-serious offences: illegal downloading and graffiti. Group fighting is the third-most reported delinquent act in the case of Bosnia and Herzegovina,[356] Kosovo, and North Macedonia. However, in the case of Serbia, the third-most reported delinquent act is shoplifting. In the Croatian sampling, it is not shoplifting (as in lifetime prevalence) but vandalism. Group fighting is the only delinquent act in which North Macedonia has the highest rate among the whole cluster. In contrast, the results of the Health Behaviour in School-aged Children (HBSC) study – an international report of 2001/02 – show that North Macedonia has among the lowest rates of psychical fighting in the observed countries, even lower than Croatia.[357]

---

355 *Budimlić, Maljević & Muratbegović* 2010.

356 In the case of Bosnia and Herzegovina, prevalence rates are much lower than in the ISRD2 study. For details, see *Budimlić, Maljević & Muratbegović* 2010.

357 *Currie et al.* 2004.

Table 4   Last-year prevalence of 14 delinquent acts

	Balkan cluster		Bosnia and Herzegovina		Croatia		Kosovo		North Macedonia		Serbia	
	%	% missing	%	% missing	%	% missing	%	% missing	%	% missing	%	% missing
Illegal downloading	27.2	5.9	17.4	6.8	50.6	7.9	7.6	1.2	17	0.3	45.7	10.2
Graffiti	13.6	3.3	13.7	6	12.6	1.4	7.4	1.2	14	0.3	19.4	3.7
Shoplifting	5.1	2.8	2.4	5.6	6.3	1.3	0.9	1.2	5.5	0.3	12.9	1.9
Vandalism	4.8	2.8	3.2	5.8	6.5	1.2	1.8	1.2	5.5	0.3	8.3	1.4
Group fight	6.7	3	5.2	6	5.1	1.4	4.6	1.2	11.4	0.3	9.4	1.9
Theft	2.5	2.8	1	5.9	4	1.2	0.8	1.2	2.5	0.3	5	1.4
Carrying a weapon	4	3	2.5	6.1	3.5	1.5	3.5	1.2	5.4	0.3	7.2	1.9
Drug dealing	1.5	3	0.6	6.1	3	1.8	0.5	1.2	1.5	0.3	2.8	1.3
Car break	1.1	2.6	0.8	5.8	1.3	1.1	0.5	1.2	1.3	0.3	1.7	0.6
Bicycle theft	0.8	2.6	0.4	5.7	1.1	1.1	0.2	1.2	1	0.3	1.6	0.7
Assault	1.4	2.8	0.8	6.1	0.9	1.1	1	1.2	1.9	0.3	3	1
Car/motor theft	0.7	2.6	0.4	5.7	0.6	1	0.4	1.2	1.1	0.3	1.6	0.4
Extortion	0.7	2.6	0.5	5.9	0.5	1	0.6	1.2	1	0.3	0.9	0.4
Burglary	0.5	2.6	0.4	5.7	0.3	1	0.5	1.2	0.8	0.3	0.5	0.7

Overall, in the Balkan cluster, group fighting is the third-most reported act, after illegal downloading and graffiti. Based on data regarding the lifetime and last-year prevalence of group fights, it could be concluded that they are a part of the primary and secondary school children's culture in the Balkans, as well as graffiti. Possibly, group fights are a result of competition between juveniles in school.[358] The rates of other delinquent acts are very low, especially in the case of serious offences. Therefore, it is aimless to talk about least reported offences.

In total, the rate of last-year overall delinquency in the Balkan cluster is low (22.9 %). Illegal downloading was not included in the last-year overall delinquency scale, while its rates are so high in some countries that it has a strong impact on the scale. The highest rate of last-year overall delinquency was found in Serbia (39.2 %), followed by North Macedonia (23.7 %) and Croatia (22.1 %). The lowest rate is found in Kosovo (12.6 %), which was expected because of the different age distribution in the Kosovo sample and the low score in the social desirability test (see *Figure 1*).

5.1.3   Different types of juvenile delinquency in the Balkans

In this section, the analyses will employ composite measures by making use of the number (but not all) of the items. The use of smaller and theoretically meaningful subscales is a common practice, although there is no general agreement on the best way to create such a composite measure.[359] Based on the analyses of the previous ISRD study waves, there will be two common distinctions: minor and serious offences as well as property, violent, and vandalism offences. Property offences are shoplifting, burglary, theft, bicycle theft, car theft, and theft from a car. Violent offences are extortion, carrying a weapon, group fighting, and assault. It should be noted that because there is no consensus about the vandalism offence, i.e. whether it should be placed under property or violent offences, in these analyses, it will be seen as a separate group, together with graffiti. Likewise, drug dealing and illegal downloading are not part of any of the above-mentioned types of subscales. Although national criminal codes may classify some of these offences differently, the classification was based on ISRD study here. Generally speaking, minor offences are the most frequent ones: graffiti, group fighting, shoplifting, vandalism, and carrying a weapon. Serious offences are the less frequent or rare ones: theft, theft from a car, bicycle theft, car theft, assault, extortion, and burglary.

---

358 *Budimlić, Maljević & Muratbegović* 2010.

359 *Marshall Hean & Enzmann* 2012, 49.

Figure 2   *Lifetime prevalence of different types of juvenile delinquency by country (%)*

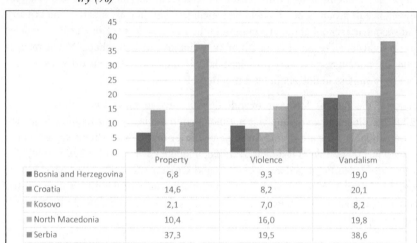

	Property	Violence	Vandalism
■ Bosnia and Herzegovina	6,8	9,3	19,0
■ Croatia	14,6	8,2	20,1
■ Kosovo	2,1	7,0	8,2
■ North Macedonia	10,4	16,0	19,8
■ Serbia	37,3	19,5	38,6

When comparing the prevalence rates of lifetime property and violent offences, *Figure 2* shows a significant difference between the participating Balkan countries. Serbia features much more prominent in both rates than the other countries. At the other end, Kosovo has the lowest rates. Notwithstanding, Kosovo has a high rate of violent offences in relation to property crime. Croatia and Serbia are the only countries that have a lower rate of violent than of property offences. Comparing all three groups of delinquent acts, the highest rates in all countries can be found in vandalism offences, mostly because of graffiti, which also becomes evident when visiting these countries.

In terms of the prevalence rate of different types of juvenile delinquency in the last twelve months, *Figure 3* shows that the distribution of different types of delinquency is almost the same as in lifetime delinquency rates.[360] Again, Bosnia and Herzegovina, Kosovo, and North Macedonia have a higher rate of violent than of property offences, contrary to the results in Croatia and Serbia, with North Macedonia featuring the highest rate of violent offences among all examined countries. One of the possible explanations why Serbia does not have a high rate of violent crimes – compared to other types of crime in which it has very high rates – can be the implementation of various anti-violence programmes in schools, such as "School without Violence – Towards a Safe and Enabling Environment for Children"[361] that was conducted in 2005. UNICEF originally initiated the programme, which is one of the broadest and most ambitious programmes for preventing youth violence in Serbia.

---

360 Please note that *Figure 2* uses a different scale than *Figure 3*.

361 *Simeunović-Patić, Meško & Ignjatović* 2016, 408.

In general, the distribution of property and violent offences differs among these countries. Croatia and Serbia have more problems with property offences, while Bosnia and Herzegovina, Kosovo, and North Macedonia have higher rates of violent offences.

Figure 3   *Last-year prevalence of different types of juvenile delinquency by country (%)*

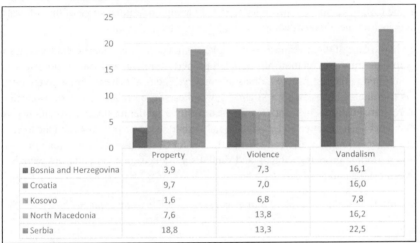

	Property	Violence	Vandalism
■ Bosnia and Herzegovina	3,9	7,3	16,1
■ Croatia	9,7	7,0	16,0
■ Kosovo	1,6	6,8	7,8
■ North Macedonia	7,6	13,8	16,2
■ Serbia	18,8	13,3	22,5

A Pearson's correlation coefficient was run in order to determine the relationship between lifetime between property, violent, and vandalism offences by country. All these relationships were statistically significant in all observed countries. The highest positive moderate linear correlation was found between violence and vandalism in North Macedonia ($r = 0.46$). This suggests that juveniles in North Macedonia who commit violent offences also commit vandalism. Results suggested that the lowest correlation is between property and vandalism offences in Serbia ($r = 0.12$). Correlations between lifetime property, violent, and vandalism offences in the other countries were between $r = 0.2$ and $r = 0.3$.

The results suggest that there are statically significant differences in prevalence rates among countries, and further analyses will focus on the risk factors which have an impact on decreasing or increasing delinquency rates.

In order to further illustrate differences between the countries, *Figure 4* shows that with respect to minor and serious offences. Interestingly, only in the case of last-year minor offences, North Macedonia has a higher rate than Croatia. This signifies that almost every fourth respondent in North Macedonia reported committing at least one minor offence in the previous twelve months, and every third one in the case of Serbia. Furthermore, in Serbia, every second respondent reported having committed at least one minor offence in his or her life. It should be emphasized that the minor-offence scale did not include illegal downloading, since the rate would then be even much higher and would have a strong impact on the distribution, resulting in a contamination of the results. Compared to other countries, Serbia shows a big difference between last-year and lifetime offences, contrary to Kosovo which features almost no difference. This might be influenced by the age of respondents in the sample: Kosovar participants had a mean age of 13.06 years, while Serbians had 15.46 years. In the case of Kosovo, if juveniles reported having committed some of the offences in their lifetime, this was congruent with the last twelve months.

As in the case of the lifetime analyses, a Pearson's correlation coefficient was run so as to determine the relationship between property, violent, and vandalism offences committed in the last twelve months by country. The results were similar to the ones for lifetime offences, with a slightly lower Pearson correlation. All relationships were statistically significant. The highest positive moderate linear correlation was found between violence and vandalism in North Macedonia ($r = 0.44$) and the lowest one between property and vandalism offences for Serbia ($r = 0.13$). Correlations between lifetime property, violent, and vandalism offences in other countries were between $r = 0.2$ and $r = 0.3$.

Figure 4   Distribution of minor and serious offences by country (%)

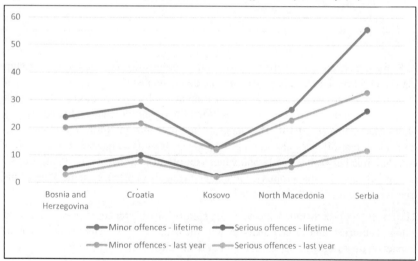

These findings have important implications for developing further national programmes of education and training institutions to adopt intervention measures in response to violence, as well as measures in the field of prevention, especially in Bosnia and Herzegovina, North Macedonia, and Kosovo. Croatia and Serbia should focus more on prevention programmes regarding property crime. Further analyses of this survey will focus on indicators that have an impact on different types of delinquency.

5.1.4 Versatility

Figure 5 presents lifetime versatility, which shows whether juveniles in the Balkan countries had committed one or more different offences during their lifetime. A variety scale was used for self-reported delinquent behaviour variables in order to create a theoretically meaningful and empirically useful scale of delinquency acts containing all 14 offences. Variety scales are easy to construct, possess high reliability and validity, and are not compromised by the frequency of non-serious crime types, which is very important in this case.[362] The scale was compared by summing up all lifetime prevalences of the 14 different offences.

Figure 5   Lifetime offending versatility by country (%)

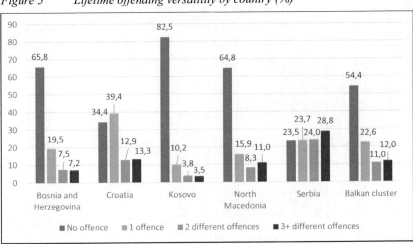

In the Balkan cluster, 45.6 % of juveniles reported having committed one or more delinquent acts in their lifetime. The results vary at the country level. Only in the cases of Croatia (mean of 1.20) and Serbia (1.94), the number of juveniles who reported one or more delinquent acts is higher in comparison to the ones who reported none (65.6 % for Croatia, 76.5 % for Serbia). In contrast, in Bosnia and Herzegovina (mean of 0.70), Kosovo (0.35) and North Macedonia (0.89), a high number of juveniles reported that they did not commit any of the 14 offences in their lifetime. A

---

362 *Sweeten* 2012.

Table 5 Gender differences between different types of lifetime juvenile delinquency by country (%)

	Bosnia and Herzegovina		Croatia		Kosovo		North Macedonia		Serbia		Balkan cluster	
	Female %	Male %	Female %	Male %	Female %	Male %	Female %	Male %	Female %	Male %	Female %	Male %
All offences	44.3	55.7	49.6	50.4	31.7	68.3	36.8	63.2	42.4	57.6	43.9	56.1
Vandalism	53.7	46.3	50.6	49.4	36.8	63.2	37.6	62.4	37.0	63.0	45.0	55.0
Property	41.6	58.4	43.3	56.7	31.8	68.2	36.7	63.3	41.8	58.2	41.3	57.7
Violence	25.0	75.0	21.3	78.7	25.3	74.7	22.3	77.7	15.7	84.3	21.3	78.7
Soft drug	25.0	75.0	36.0	64.0	20.0	80.0	21.1	78.9	31.0	69.0	28.7	71.3
Hard drug	36.0	64.0	40.0	60.0	15.4	84.6	10.5	89.5	10.5	89.5	23.1	76.9
Serious offences	38.8	61.2	41.1	58.9	22.2	77.8	34.3	65.7	39.5	60.5	38.5	61.5

second finding is that many of the juveniles who reported having committed one or more offences did restrict their involvement in offending behaviour to only one offence. This is especially the case in the Croatian sample where most juveniles reported only one offence in their lifetime, and from *Table 3*, it can be seen that most reported offences are minor ones. A third finding is that three or more offences were "ever" committed by 12 % of the respondents. However, higher rates are found for Serbia where 28.8 % of juveniles reported three or more offences in their lifetime.

5.1.5 Gender

According to media in the Balkans, female juvenile delinquency is increasing and females are more and more involved in serious offences. Historically, feminist theories have explained women's participation in crime as the result of emancipation.[363] However, some theorists have strongly denied that, focusing on biological differences as one possible explanation.[364] Other theorists correlated this with female victimization experiences, attributing female delinquency as a response to the fact that females are often victims of sexual abuse.[365] Most of the previous research found that females consistently show considerably lower delinquency rates than males.[366] Despite political and social eruption, which brought a better economic position of women and girls in most European countries over the second half of the 20th century, a comparison of male and female delinquency continues to show lower rates among females.[367] The same result can be seen in this self-report research for the Balkan countries, with some exceptions.

Gender differences in delinquency involvement found in the ISRD3 study in Balkan countries are in accordance with official data: females clearly commit a lower number of delinquent acts than males do. *Table 5* presents the lifetime prevalence rates for different offence types by country and gender. The results show considerable variations according to the type of delinquent behaviour. However, these variations are not as high as in the ISRD2 post-socialist cluster, according to which boys committed three times as many offences as girls.[368] Looking at the overall prevalence of delinquency in Balkan countries, males committed little more offences than females (43.9 % for females; 56.1 % for males). In Croatia, there is almost no difference between males and females (49.6 % for females, 50.4 % for males).

---

363 See *Adler* 1975; *Simon* 1975; *Austin* 1993.
364 *Maccoby & Jacklin* 1980.
365 *Chesney-Lind* 1989; *Cain* 1990.
366 *Junger-Tas, Ribeaud & Cruyff* 2004, 333.
367 *Junger-Tas, Ribeaud & Cruyff* 2004, 334.
368 For details, see *Junger-Tas* 2012a.

In order to see whether there are differences in the offence types reported by females and males, *Table 5* also presents gender differences based on lifetime vandalism, property, and violent crime. In terms of property offences, in all investigated Balkan countries, males reported higher prevalence rates than females, as expected. However, the smallest difference can be found in the case of Croatia (43.3 % for females, 56.7 % for males), mostly because of female involvement in minor property offences such as shoplifting (42.9 %; see *Table 5*). Females in Bosnia and Herzegovina and Serbia are also involved in shoplifting, in contrast to other Balkan countries where their percentage is twice as low as the one of males.

Table 6 shows that males are twice or even more times as likely as females to have been involved in serious property offences such as burglary and bicycle or car theft, except for Bosnia and Herzegovina where 42.9 % females reported having committed burglary in their lifetime. With regard to violent offences, in the Balkan cluster, males reported three times cases than females (21.3 % for females, 78.7 % for males). Therefore, violence among females is a relatively rare event in all countries, mostly because females tend to not participate in group fights – as mentioned before, group fights are a common way of male competition in primary schools in the Balkans. It is worth remarking that when comparing the prevalence rates of property offences to the ones of violent offences, the overall gender gap is considerably more pronounced with respect to the former than to the latter behaviour. However, this is not so obvious when looking at vandalism. The most striking result to emerge from the data is that in Bosnia and Herzegovina and Croatia, more females reported having committed vandalism offences in their life. This is mostly due to females reporting higher prevalence rates for graffiti than males.[369]

---

369 One of the possible obstacles is that the meaning of the graffiti question used in the ISRD3 questionnaire was not very clear. The problem is that in some places (such as both cities in Croatia), graffiti can be recognized as a legitimate art form if it is produced in spaces designated for it – as long as the content is acceptable. The question "Have you ever in your life painted on a wall, train, subway or bus (graffiti)?" should more clearly refer to graffiti as an illegal act, such in the case of illegal downloading.

The governments of Zagreb and Varaždin, the Croatian cities where the ISRD3 study was conducted, have implemented programmes for the prevention of grafitti vandalism in which they educate young people in schools about the amount of damage graffiti causes to the city. In collaboration with the School of Applied Arts and Design, the city of Zagreb, however, does promote graffiti as a form of art by providing spaces such as walls and parks, where the graffiti is allowed. For more information, see https://www.zagreb.hr/en/edukacija-i-informiranje-mladih-kao-prevencija-van/108271, http://varazdin.hr/ [05/06/2018].

Talking to my colleagues from Bosnia and Herzegovina while visiting its capital Sarajevo, it became obvious to me that it is a city with a large graffiti subculture. The problem is that some of the graffiti is not regarded as a form of street art but as vandalism. Therefore, the Police Department of the Sarajevo Canton Ministry, in cooperation with ICITAP (International Criminalization Assistance Programme in BiH) and the Municipal Administration of the City of Sarajevo, carried out the "Graffiti Removal" campaign – an area without grafitti – in 2018. For more information, see http://mup.ks.gov.ba/aktuelno/obavjestenja/poziv-gradanima-i-predstav nicima-medija-kampanja-uklanjanje-grafita [05/06/2018].

Table 6   *Gender differences between lifetime offences by country (%)*

	Bosnia and Herzegovina		Croatia		Kosovo		North Macedonia		Serbia	
	Female %	Male %	Female %	Male %	Female %	Male %	Female %	Male %	Female %	Male %
Illegal downloading	34.7	65.3	48.8	51.2	18.6	81.4	33.6	66.4	40.3	59.7
Graffiti	55.8	44.2	55.2	44.8	37.3	62.7	37.7	62.3	37.1	62.9
Shoplifting	45	55	42.9	57.1	35.7	64.3	35.4	64.6	41.3	58.7
Vandalism	33.6	66.5	31.6	68.4	17.4	82.6	33.7	66.3	21.8	78.2
Group fight	21.4	78.6	21	79	20.8	79.2	20.6	79.4	14	86
Theft	42.3	57.7	42.4	57.6	18.2	81.8	38.5	61.5	47.4	52.6
Carry weapon	25.5	74.5	13.9	86.1	35	65	16	84	15.1	84.9
Drug dealing	36.6	63.4	45.8	54.2	0	100	29.6	70.4	29.5	70.5
Car break	40	60	24.1	75.9	12.5	87.5	28.6	71.4	31.1	68.9
Bicycle theft	45.7	54.3	20.7	79.3	0	100	33.3	66.7	37.4	62.6
Assault	41.1	58.9	15.4	84.6	6.7	93.3	25	75	12.9	87.1
Car theft	39.4	60.6	35.7	64.3	14.3	85.7	30.4	69.6	20.9	79.1
Robbery/ extortion	36.2	63.8	15.4	84.6	0	100	26.1	73.9	20	80
Burglary	42.9	57.1	18.2	81.8	37.5	62.5	17.6	82.4	18.8	81.3

It should be noted that Kosovo has the biggest discrepance between genders for all delinquent acts. In most delinquent acts, female participation is lower than 20 %, and in some, they do not participate at all (such as drug dealing and extortion). Even the number of males reporting to have committed these offences is low, yet this can also be seen from the perspective of female rights in the society and way it is functioning regarding gender equality in Kosovo. The analyses of the gender structure of the groups of friends respondents spend time with showed statistically significant differences between Kosovo and other Balkan countries. In Kosovo, only 44.4 % of juveniles reported that their group of friends consists of both genders – in contrast to Croatia where 68 % of juveniles reported spending time with friends of both sexes. An equal position for females and males in the society is still a challenge in Kosovo.[370]

---

370 OSCE Mission in Kosovo 2015.

While the legal framework [371] ensures equal opportunities, the challenge is the implementation of these laws and social norms in practice. In Kosovo, the majority of males still totally or partially agree that the most important role of females is to take care of home, cooking, and childcare for the family.[372]

In general, females in the Balkans – with statistically significant differences between the countries – have lower levels of delinquency than males, in particular with respect to violent offences, soft and hard drug abuse, and serious delinquent acts. Both lower delinquency levels and lower drug use may point to a greater reluctance among females to take risks.

5.1.6   Age

Numerous studies have shown that age is strongly related to offending.[373] As early as *Quetelet* in the 1800s, social statisticians presented a strong relationship between age and crime that is now known as the age-crime curve.[374] As can be seen in official crime statistics and self-report studies, the crime rate increases during adolescence to a peak in the late teenage years and then declines rapidly through adulthood.[375] However, debates surround the question how much variation occurs in the age-crime curve by crime type and in different social contexts. Therefore, *Figure 6* presents the age-crime curve for lifetime prevalence of property, violent, and vandalism offences in the Balkan cluster. For property and violent offences, they follow the same age distribution until the age of 16; however, while vandalism follows the same trend, its rate is higher. It is clear that in case of property and vandalism, the age-crime curve rapidly increases from 12 to 17 years of age, while in the case of violence, it only increases until the age of 16 and then stagnates. However, when analysing the data for last-year prevalence of property, violent, and vandalism offences for the same age group, the results are not as clear as for lifetime offences (see *Figure 6*). The age-crime curve for last-year vandalism also increases, with a stagnation at the age of 15 to 16. In the case of violence, it even decreases after 16 years of age. Therefore, for violent offences in the Balkan cluster, the age-crime curve reaches its peek at the age of 16, which is not the case for property and vandalism offences. It should be noticed that in the Balkan countries, 15 to 16 years is an age in which juveniles transfer from primary to secondary school. As mentioned before, violence is a common part of primary school children's culture and the result of rivalries.

---

371   Law on Gender Equality (05/L-020); https://gzk.rks-gov.net/ActDetail.aspx?ActID = 10923 [05/06/2018]; Regulation on Rules of Procedure of the Ombudsperson Institution (02/2016); https://gzk.rks-gov.net/ActDetail.aspx?ActID = 12504 [05/06/2018].

372   OSCE Mission in Kosovo 2018.

373   *Huizinga et al.* 2003, 52; *Farrington* 1986; *Marvell & Moody* 1991.

374   See *Steffensmeier et al.* 1989; *Bouffard* 2009, 28.

375   *Farrington* 1986.

While violence is fading, property crime is rising, and the transition from primary to secondary school is an element influencing juvenile behaviour.

Figure 6   Age-crime curve for lifetime prevalence of different types of offending in the Balkan cluster

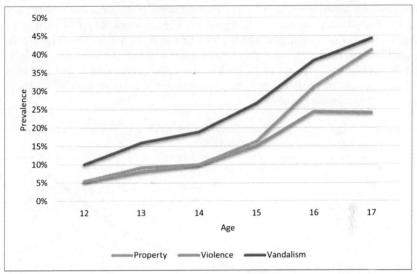

Figure 7   Age-crime curve for last-year prevalence of different types of offending in the Balkan cluster

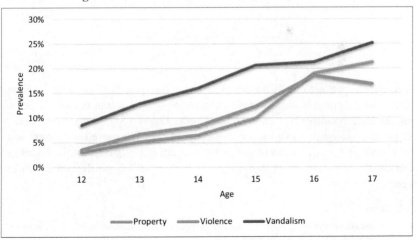

In order to see if this also stands on the country level, data in *Figure 8* shows differences in the age-crime curve for violence between Kosovo and the Balkan cluster. Kosovo stands out here because of the difference in average age compared to the other countries in the sample. Most of the 9th grade juveniles in Kosovo were 14 to 15 years of age, while they were 15 to 16 years old in the other countries. The results show that the Kosovar age-crime curve for violence is in the same line with the one for the whole Balkan cluster until the age of 14. Then, towards the age of 15, it drops sharply in the Kosovo sample, which is in a line with the previous finding that the transition from primary to secondary school is one of the elements influencing juvenile behaviour.[376] At the age of 15, the Kosovar crime curve drops to the same level it had at the age of 12. In contrast, the age-crime curve for violent offences rapidly increases towards the age of 14.

Figure 8   *Age-crime curve for last-year prevalence of violent offences in the Balkan cluster and Kosovo[377]*

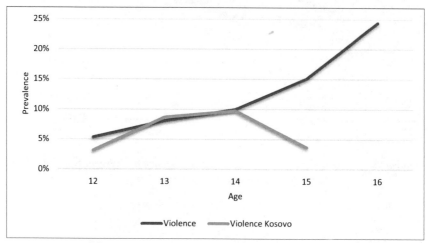

Property offences are mostly contained in the Croatian and Serbian samples. Therefore, *Figure 9* presents the age-crime curve for property offences in Croatia, Serbia, and the Balkan cluster as a whole. Interestingly, *Figure 9* shows that in the case of Serbia, the age-crime curve has a nearly constant rate. The curve is constantly very high, with a peak at 13 years of age and then again at 17. In contrast, in the case of Croatia, the age-crime curve shows a clear increase and follows the general Balkan trend.

---

376 Results are only presented until 15 years of age because in the Kosovo sample, there are no 16-year-old juveniles. For details, see *Table 1*.

377 *Figure 9* presents the property age-crime curve for Croatia only until the age of 16 because the remaining age groups would only encompass data for Serbia.

Figure 9   Age-crime curve for last-year prevalence of property offences in the Balkan cluster, Serbia, and Croatia

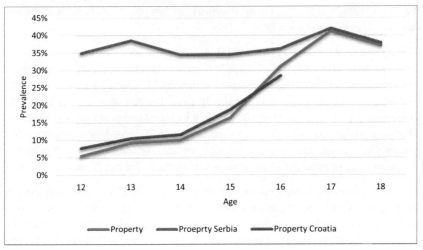

5.1.7   Substance use

There is a long history of alcohol and drug use in relation to criminal activities. The existence of a correlation between the consumption of alcohol and/or the use of drugs and juvenile crime has long been acknowledged.[378] Therefore, this section presents and discusses the results of prevalences for the use of alcohol, soft drugs, hard drugs, and extreme drugs per country. In Europe, there is growing concern about the increasing number of juveniles who drink alcohol and use drugs.[379] Several studies indicate that one quarter to one third of all adolescents drink alcohol.[380] According to the results of the European School Survey on Alcohol and Other Drugs 2011 (ESPAD),[381] more than half of the students had been drinking alcohol during the past 30 days prior to the survey. Particularly low prevalence rates were reported for Albania, Bosnia and Herzegovina, and Montenegro. On average, more boys than girls had been drinking alcohol in the month prior to the survey. Countries with large such differences between genders included the Balkan countries of Albania, Bosnia and Herzegovina (Republic of Srpska), Montenegro, and Serbia. Particularly low levels (5–9 %) of illicit drug use can be noticed in Bosnia and Herzegovina

378   *Gottfredson & Hirschi* 1990;
379   *Steketee* 2012, 118.
380   *Hibell et al.* 2012, *Steketee* 2012, 118.
381   For more information about the ESPAD project and some findings, see *Chapter 2.3.*

(Republic of Srpska), Montenegro, Albania, and Serbia. There is a lack of self-re-port studies among Balkan countries with a focus on alcohol and drug use, but from the ESPAD study, it becomes clear that there are significant differences in the use of alcohol between these countries.

There are several questions in the ISRD3 questionnaire about the use of alcohol and three questions about the use of drugs in terms of prevalence, incidence, and other characteristics. The students were asked if they had consumed alcohol, and if so, how frequent the had done so in the last 30 days. The last question was related to binge drinking. They were also asked if they had used soft drugs such as cannabis (marijuana or hashish) or hard drugs such as XTC, LSD, speed, or amphetamines – and finally, extreme drugs including heroin, cocaine, or crack. The recall period in the survey was lifetime use or the previous month (i.e., the last 30 days).[382]

Figure 10 shows that the overall prevalence rate for alcohol use is relatively high in the Balkans: 45.8 % of all students had drunk alcohol in their lifetime and 33.6 % in the last month. However, there are big differences in alcohol use between the countries. The highest rates of lifetime use of alcohol were in Serbia (79.6 %) and Croatia (75.3 %), opposite to low rates in Bosnia and Herzegovina (29 %) and North Macedonia (36.6 %), with an extremely low rate in Kosovo (11.6 %). The results are similar in the case of last-month use of alcohol. Serbia and Croatia have the highest rates (around 60 %), while the other countries have lower rates. The juve-niles in this study often consumed low-alcoholic drinks (24.7 % beer and alcopops and 18.2 % wine). Beer and alcopops are thus the most popular drinks among young people in the Balkan region. The majority does not consume strong alcohol fre-quently (see *Figure 11*). However, one out of every three students had drunk strong alcohol at least once over the previous month. Only in Serbia, the consumption of strong spirits was higher than that of wine and even higher than the use of beer and wine in other countries. It should be noted that the question regarding strong spirits included schnapps (*rakija*[383]) which is a very popular drink in the region.

---

382 For more information about the alcohol and drug use questions, see *Chapter 4.*

383 By the Regulation (EC) No. 110/2008 of the European Parliament and of the Council of 15 January 2008, Rakija or Rakia is defined as follows: "Spirit (preceded by the name of the fruit) obtained by maceration and distillation is a spirit drink: (i) produced by maceration of fruit or berries listed under point (ii), whether partially fermented or unfermented, with the possible addition of a maximum of 20 litres of ethyl alcohol of agricultural origin or spirit and/or distillate deriving from the same fruit per 100 kg of fermented fruit or berries, followed by distillation at less than 86 % vol […]", adding that "(b) [t]he minimum alcoholic strength by volume of a Spirit (preceded by the name of the fruit) obtained by maceration and distil-lation shall be 37.5 %".

Figure 10   *Prevalences of lifetime and last-month alcohol use for the Balkan cluster and per country*

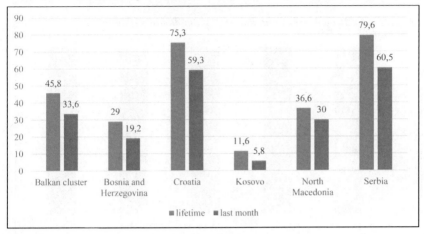

Figure 11   *Prevalences of last-month use of beer or alcopops, wine, and strong spirits for the Balkan cluster and per country*

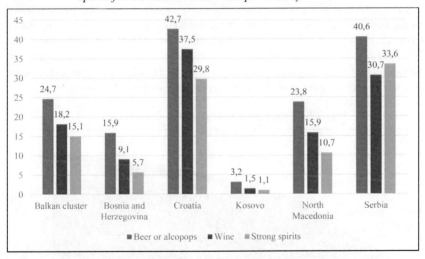

In Balkan countries with low levels of reported lifetime alcohol use have a high number of juveniles who declared themselves as Muslims. Alcohol is forbidden in Islam. *Figure 12* presents lifetime use of alcohol by religion. Among juveniles who declared themselves as Muslims, only 20 % reported consuming alcohol. Contrarily,

more than half of Christian juveniles reported use of alcohol in their lifetime (70 %
and 60 %). Atheists also reported a high level of alcohol consumption (68 %).

Figure 12   *Prevalences of lifetime use of alcohol by religion*

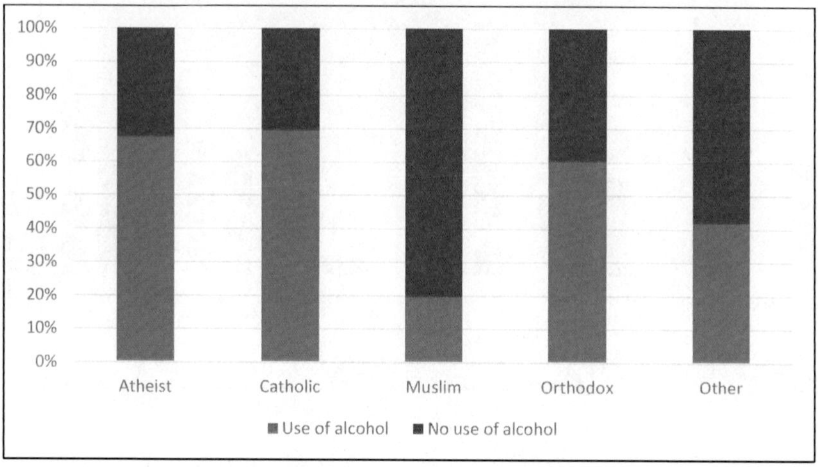

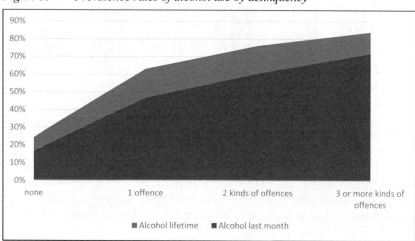

Figure 13 shows the prevalence rates of the two indicators of alcohol use in relation
to the variable versatility, which combines the frequency and seriousness by measuring the number of different types of offences committed. The results show that
when the number of different types of committed offences increases, the percentage
of subjects who have used alcohol does so, too. In this case, the greatest difference
can be seen with regard to the abuse of alcohol in a student's lifetime.

Figure 13   *Prevalence rates of alcohol use by delinquency*

The use of soft drugs is less popular among juveniles than that of alcohol, as can be seen in *Figure 14*.[384] On average, 7.4 % have used cannabis, marijuana, and/or hash, while and only 4.5 % of all students have used any of these substances in the 30 days prior to the study. There are, however, some significant differences between the countries. Their order regarding the use of cannabis is similar to the results for self-report delinquency. More than 20 % of juveniles in Serbia reported a lifetime use of cannabis. In Croatia, 9 % of juveniles reported the use of cannabis in their life. In the other countries, this figure was below 5 %. The use of XTC, LSD, speed, ampheta-mines, or similar drugs is much lower; yet considering the age range (12–16 years), it is alarming nevertheless (1.7 % had tried it). Serbia has the highest rate, with 4.3 % having used XTC, LSD, speed, amphetamines, or similar drugs. Other countries are under 1.5 % in the use of hard drugs. The results regarding the use of heroin, cocaine, or crack show that the average consumption in the region is 1.1 %, with the highest rate in North Macedonia (1.5 %), followed by Serbia (1.4 %) and Kosovo (1.2 %). As expected, the prevalence rate of drug use is much lower than the one for alcohol consumption in the Balkan region.

Figure 14   *Lifetime prevalence of drug use by country*

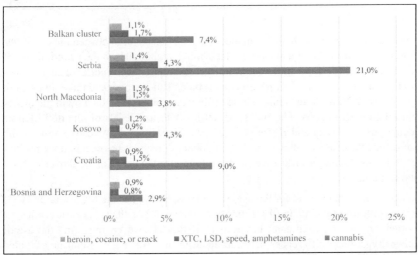

Figure 15 shows the prevalence rates for the use of the three different drug categories in relation to the variable versatility, which combines frequency and seriousness by measuring the number of different types of offences committed. The results show that as the number of types of committed offences rises, the percentage of subjects

---

384 *Steketee* 2012, 120.

who have used different type of drugs increases. In this case, the greatest difference can be seen with regard to the use of cannabis in a student's lifetime.

Figure 15   Prevalence rates of drug use by delinquency

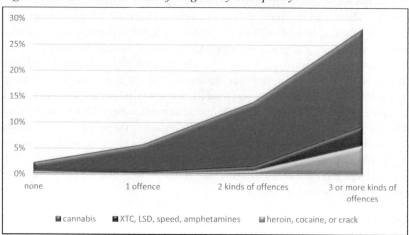

There are significant differences in alcohol and cannabis use between the countries. The students from Croatia and Serbia have much higher rates in their lifetime use of alcohol than those from other countries. For example, they reported a seven times higher use of alcohol in their lifetime than students in Kosovo, and three times more than those in North Macedonia. These differences can be explained by in the different religion affiliations. The Balkan countries with low levels of reported lifetime alcohol use – Bosnia and Herzegovina, North Macedonia, and Kosovo – are at the same time the countries in which a high number of juveniles has declared themselves as Muslims. A similar difference has been found for the use of alcohol over the previous month.

When looking at the data for the use of cannabis, Serbia has the highest rate (21 %) again, followed by Croatia (9 %). In other countries, less than 5 % of juveniles reported ever having used cannabis in their lifetime. However, regarding the use of other drugs, there differences between countries are rather low. In all investigated countries, less than 5 % juveniles reported the use of XTC, LSD, speed, amphetamines, heroin, cocaine, or crack.

5.1.8   Juvenile victimization

In general, a strong correlation is assumed between victimization and delinquency among juveniles.[385] This does not mean that all victims are offenders or, vice versa,

---

385 *Gruszczynska, Lucia & Killias* 2012, 95.

that all offenders become victims of crimes. However, juveniles are victimized disproportionately often compared to other age groups, and crime is an essential aspect of the quality of life at this age. As the delinquency rates in the Balkan region are low, it would be interesting to see if the victimization rates go in the same direction.

Figure 16   Prevalence rates of victimization by country (%)

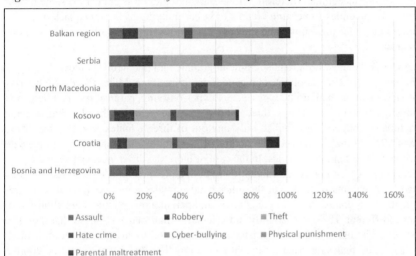

The questionnaire included items on robbery, assault, theft, hate crime, cyber-bullying, physical punishment, and parental maltreatment in a student's lifetime. *Figure 16* presents different types of victimization by country and in the Balkan region as a whole. The distribution of victimization among the countries is a bit different than the distribution of delinquency. Serbia has the highest rate of victimization, followed by North Macedonia and Bosnia and Herzegovina. In the case of Serbia, almost half of students were victims of physical punishment in their lifetime, and one out of three students became a victim of theft. Physical punishment is most common in Bosnia and Herzegovina (30.5 %), Croatia (34 %), and Serbia (45.7 %), while theft is most common in Kosovo (20.3 %) and North Macedonia (29.9 %). The highest rates of hate crime can be observed in North Macedonia (9 %). This is not surprising as previous studies showed that there is a big problem regarding hate speech in North Macedonia. The Helsinki Committee for Human Rights of the Republic of Macedonia (2015) stated that a partcular problem and thus a reason for inciting hate speech and hate crimes is the political ideology of ethno-nationalism which dominates North Macedonian policies. It openly and indirectly promotes the glorification of one's own nation and spreading prejudice to the extent of a demonization of other cultures and ethnicities, which constitutes grounds for the dissemination of hate speech. The Helsinki Committee for Human Rights of the Republic of Macedonia concluded that the situation in North Macedonia recently gained such proportions in politics that it was followed by an intensive increase in hate speech and hate crimes.

In other countries, the rates of hate crime are under 5 %. The highest rates of parental maltreatment and assault were observed in Serbia and Croatia. The distribution of cyber-bullying is almost the same and varies from 16 % in Croatia to 19 % in Serbia and North Macedonia. Therefore, in the Balkan region, it is almost the same probability for juveniles to become victims of cyber-bullying as there is a lack of policy programmes for prevention and the education of juveniles as well as parents in this matter.

Gender is the most important socio-demographic variable in this context. *Figure 17* presents the victimization rates by gender and crime type. Males faced a higher risk of victimization in all crime types except cyber-bullying, parental maltreatment, and physical punishment. Almost three out of four males reported that they had become victims of robbery. In contrast, only one out of three females reported this. More than 50 % of males had become victims of assault. Again, males have to face hate crime more often than females. In the case of theft, the differences between the genders are less pronounced. Around 50 % of both males and females reported that they had been victims of theft. On the other hand, females are cyber-bullied more frequently than males. Physical punishment and parental maltreatment are almost gender-indifferent. However, slightly more females than males reported that they had become victims of physical punishment and parental maltreatment. Overall, in all crime types, males reported victimization in more than 40 %, while females reported victimization in more than 30 %.

Figure 17   Victimization rate by gender (%)

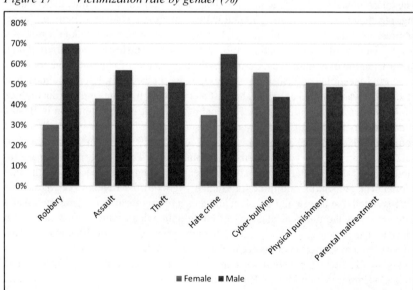

A survey carried out by *Villmow* and *Stephan* in the 1970s included a combination of self-reported crime and victimization items. One interesting finding from this study was that those juveniles who reported heavy participation in crime were also among those who reported a lot of victimization. In this analysis, the focus was on overlapping delinquency and victimization. *Figure 18* presents juveniles who in this study reported committing at least on offence,[386] as well as those who reported victimization in different crime types. The results show that 40 % of juveniles who reported committing crimes also reported that they had become victims of physical punishment. It should be noticed that victimization by physical punishment was asked in a way that it referred only to the physical punishment by one's mother and/or father.[387]

Every third juvenile who reported committing delinquency acts also reported that he/she had been a victim of theft. Less than 13 % of these juveniles also reported that they had become victims of robbery, assault, hate crime, and physical punishment.

Overall, victimization from physical punishment by parents had the highest overlap with delinquency.

Figure 18   Overlap of victimization and delinquency

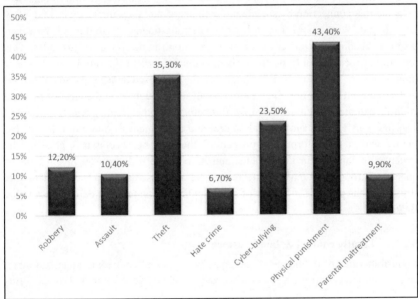

---

386   A dummy variable for delinquency was used in the analysis.
387   See *question 4.1 f)* in the *Appendix*.

5.2   Indicators of Juvenile Delinquency in the Balkan Region

5.2.1   Impact of the family on juvenile delinquency

Throughout history, theories concerning the aetiology of juvenile delinquency have taken into account different factors as the main causes which affect juvenile behaviour, but the family has undoubtedly always played a central role.[388] The family serves as an important moderator of delinquency, with the potential to increase or decrease criminogenic factors such as spending time with delinquent peers and engaging in a risky lifestyle.[389]

In this chapter, the analysis is based on the most influential theory on the role of the family in juvenile delinquency, *Hirschi's* social control theory (1969). *Hirschi* stated that juveniles who have strong bonds with their parents would embrace their parents' values and attitudes. The idea is that these juveniles do not want to disappoint their parents, and as a result, they behave in a norm-confirming way. They try to fulfil their parents' expectations in order to strengthen their bonds with the family. One of the hypotheses of *Hirschi's* theory was that juveniles with strong family bonds will replicate this connection by socializing with peers, and they might try to find a few good friends with whom they will develop strong bonds.[390] He did not, however, take into account the power of the peer group on the behaviour of juveniles. This research is focusing only on the Balkan countries, where the family plays a very important role. Therefore, in this part, the analysis is based on informal social control with a focus on the family. The family is analysed through several concepts: parental control, parental attachment, family structure, and other family-related variables. The first part focuses on parental control and attachment as the two pillars of the family within the informal social control theory. The second part presents the structure of families in the Balkans and its possible influence on juvenile delinquency. Through the multivariate regression analysis, the third part explains the strength of the possible influence of family indicators on juvenile delinquency in the Balkans.

5.2.1.1 Family control & family attachment

Control theories of delinquency recognize two types of control: indirect and direct control. Indirect control is present when an individual has incorporated social norms

---

388   *Hirschi* 1969; *Nye* 1958; *Sampson & Laub* 1993.
389   *Higgins & Albrecht* 1977; *Dong & Krohn* 2016.
390   *Junger-Tas* 2012b, 185.

of significant others into his social interaction.[391] Direct control exists when an individual's activities are supervised and/or monitored by significant others.[392] Therefore, when indirect control is explained through the informal control theory, the family is seen as the most conventional institution in which juveniles build their social norms and values as a result of their attachment to the family.[393] In his early work, *Hirschi* argued that parents have an influence on juvenile delinquency mostly through attachment – as a condition for internalizing societal values, giving a preference to indirect control and disregarding direct control. The same path was followed by *Nye* (1958)[394] who focused more on indirect control and introduced the importance of a present family for juvenile socialization. Less parental attachment produces a lack of emotional support in juveniles, which they compensate by engaging in deviant behaviour.[395]

On the other hand, some theories emphasize more direct rather than indirect control. The coercion theory[396] by *Larzelere* and *Patterson* (1990)[397] recognizes the importance of direct control as well as the interaction between direct and indirect control. *Wells* and *Rankin* (1988) concluded that direct control is statistically significant in conjunction with juvenile delinquency. They saw the weakness of previous research on direct control in the scale, which presented family control. By focusing only on broken homes and family sizes and disregarding other factors such as monitoring, it did not target the right indicators. After producing the modest scale control – contained from normative regulation, monitoring, and punishment –, they concluded that indirect and direct control are statistically significant and also work independently of each other. Later studies used this logic in conducting measures of direct control and also presented a statistically significant relation between direct parental control and delinquency.[398]

The relationship between both types of control (indirect and direct) and juvenile delinquency was mostly tested in Western countries. However, little attention has been paid to how the effects of parent control play out in different cultures. Previous cross-national studies have suggested that the family can play a different role in different cultures in relation to juvenile delinquency.[399] However, in almost all cultures, it is seen as an important factor in juvenile delinquency. This chapter tests the situation in the Balkan region.

---

391 *Broidy* 1995.
392 *Broidy* 1995.
393 For details, see *Hirschi* 1969; *Nye* 1958.
394 *Nye* 1958.
395 *Hoeve et al.* 2012.
396 *Patterson* 1995.
397 *Larzelere & Patterson* 1990.
398 *Hagan* 1989; *Sampson & Laub* 1993.
399 *Junger-Tas* 2012; *Minkov & Hofstede* 2012.

In this part, the results drawn from the analyses of ISRD3 data will be presented. The focus is only on the Balkan countries which participated in the survey: Bosnia and Herzegovina, Croatia, Kosovo, North Macedonia, and Serbia. The aim is to test the impact of the family on juvenile delinquency in the Balkan region. Could we apply the same theories here which were based on empirical research in more highly developed countries, such as Western Europe and the USA? Are there any cultural differences in family structure and functioning, and if so, does this have an impact on juvenile delinquency? The Balkan region is unquestionably an integral part of Europe but also presents historically and criminologically a region *sui generis*.[400] Therefore, it is a suitable region for testing theories drawn from developed countries.

5.2.1.2 Parental control impact on juvenile delinquency

The parental control scale is based on three dimensions. The first dimension is parental knowledge about where their children are, what they are doing, and which friends they are staying with. The second dimension is parental supervision over the children, asking if they go out, whether their parents ask them what they are doing, where are they going, and whom they are spending time with, whether parents tell them what time they need to be back home, and if they are obliged to call their parents; do their parents check their homework, and do they make sure that their children only watch films/DVDs rated appropriate for their age group. The third dimension is child disclosure to parents based on these questions: do the respondents tell their parents whom they spend time with, how they spend their money, where they are during most afternoons after school, and what they do in their free time. Based on these dimensions, the parental control scale worked very well (Cronbach's Alpha = 0.87).[401] The aim of this scale is to avoid the weaknesses of *Hirschi's* early work. It was constructed with variables focusing on monitoring, supervision, as well as disclosing and discarding variables such as broken home and family size, which was supported by a high Cronbach's Alpha. The juvenile delinquency scale is a dichotomised variable containing 14 delinquent acts.[402] Therefore, it has two categories, one containing respondents who did not report committing any of these acts in their lifetime, while the second category refers to juveniles who reported at least one delinquent act.

Table 7 presents the correlation between the parental control scale and the juvenile delinquency scale, explaining the influence of parental control on juvenile delinquency. Where juveniles reported the weakest parental control (presented here with the value 1), 81 % also reported that they committed at least one delinquent act in their lifetime. *Table 7* shows that with increasing parental control, fewer juveniles reported having committed at least one delinquent act in their lifetime. Only 11 % of

---

400 *Sundhaussen* 2014; *Getoš Kalac* 2014.

401 For more details, see *Chapter 4*.

402 The methodology of constructing the variables is presented in *Chapter 4*.

the ones who reported strong parental control also reported one of the delinquent acts from the ISRD3 questionnaire. *Table 7* suggests that the stronger parental control becomes, the less juvenile delinquency is reported in the Balkans. Therefore, parental knowledge, supervision, and children's disclosure to parents all play a role in juvenile delinquency in the Balkans. Parental control has an impact on decreasing juvenile delinquency through monitoring of children and prevents them from getting into potentially dangerous situations such as spending time with delinquent peers and engaging in a risky lifestyle;[403] but *Table 7* does not give any information about how strong the influence is and whether differences exist between the countries.

Table 7   *Correlation of the parental control scale and the juvenile delinquency scale in the Balkans*

	Parental control				
	weak			strong	
	1	2	3	4	5
Balkan	(N = 105)	(N = 594)	(N = 2353)	(N = 4433)	(N = 705)
% of juveniles with reported offences	81%	80%	65%	35%	11%

Therefore, *Table 8* presents the correlation between the parental control and the juvenile delinquency scales in the five participating countries. The same methodology as presented above was used to construct the scales. In all five countries, there is a difference between the impact of strong and weak family control on the percentage of juveniles who reported having committed at least one delinquent act in their lifetime. Only Bosnia and Herzegovina and Croatia do not have a clear drop of reported delinquency when parental control is weak.[404] In the weakest part of the parental control scale (value 1), Kosovo is the only country where all juveniles reported at least one delinquent act in their lifetime. However, it should be emphasized that in this case, the number of respondents is very low (N = 2). In Serbia, 95 % of juveniles with very weak parental control reported juvenile delinquency. Contrary to that, among all other countries in the Balkans, Serbia has the highest percentage (52 %) of juveniles who reported having committed at least one delinquent act and very strong parental control. Only 8 % of juveniles in Bosnia and Herzegovina, 6 % in Kosovo, and 13 % in North Macedonia reported delinquency despite very strong parental control. It could be concluded that the pattern between Balkan countries is similar but with some differences in the level of reported delinquency.

---

403 *Higgins & Albrecht* 1977; *Jessor et al.* 1995.

404 It is presented only between the weakest and weak part of family control scale (family control presented under Nos 1 and 2).

Table 8   *Correlation of the parental control scale and the juvenile delinquency scale by country*

	Family control				
	weak			strong	
	1	2	3	4	5
Bosnia and Herzegovina	(N = 21)	(N = 121)	(N = 683)	(N = 1803)	(N = 233)
% of juveniles with reported offences	57%	68%	50%	29%	8%
Croatia	(N = 37)	(N = 187)	(N = 656)	(N = 778)	(N = 41)
% of juveniles with reported offences	78%	83%	75%	55%	24%
Kosovo	(N = 2)[405]	(N = 9)	(N = 113)	(N = 697)	(N = 244)
% of juveniles with reported offences	100%	67%	41%	17%	6%
North Macedonia	(N = 4)	(N = 76)	(N = 294)	(N = 699)	(N = 162)
% of juveniles with reported offences	75%	74%	54%	28%	13%
Serbia	(N = 41)	(N = 201)	(N = 607)	(N = 456)	(N = 25)
% of juveniles with reported offences	95%	88%	81%	65%	52%

The correlation between age and crime is one of the most well-known relationships in criminology.[406] Both *Hirschi* (1969) and *Nye* (1958) connected parental control with the age of juveniles. They argued that with age, youths spend less time with their parents, that parents' control is fading and becomes less relevant as a protective factor. *Table 9* shows the correlation between parental control and age in the Balkan cluster. It is statistically significant with a correlation coefficient of r = -0.33. The

---

405 The number of students who answered this question in Kosovo was very low.
406 *Rocque, Posick & Hoyle* 2016.

results in *Table 9* suggest that parental control decreases when the juveniles get older. In cases where control is strong (values 4 and 5), it clearly decreases with increasing age. Contrarily, low parental control (values 1 and 2) increases unexceptionally with age. Therefore, the age scale will also be added as a protective factor to the multivariate analyses.

Table 9   Dependency of parental control scale by age in the Balkan cluster

Age	Parental Control Scale				
	1 weakest	2	3	4	5 strongest
12	N(4)	N(12)	N(121)	N(556)	N(164)
	0.5%	1.4%	14.1%	64.9%	19.1%
13	N(17)	N(108)	N(520)	N(1513)	N(270)
	0.7%	4.4%	21.4%	62.3%	11.1%
14	N(20)	N(159)	N(728)	N(1426)	N(198)
	0.8%	6.3%	28.8%	56.3%	7.8%
15	N(28)	N(163)	N(608)	N(801)	N(81)
	1.7%	9.7%	36.2%	47.7%	4.8%
16	N(11)	N(74)	N(198)	N(140)	N(10)
	2.5%	17.1%	45.7%	32.3%	2.3%
17	N(20)	N(54)	N(152)	N(63)	N(2)
	6.9%	18.6%	52.2%	21.6%	0.7%

5.2.1.3 Parental attachment impact on juvenile delinquency

A number of studies have shown that not only parental control but also parental attachment is independently related to decreasing juvenile delinquency.[407] *Wells* and *Ranking* (1988) concluded that it has the same impact on juvenile delinquency as family control.[408] Many studies found evidence to suggest that poor attachment relationships with parents increase the risk of delinquent behaviour.[409]

Therefore, there is a general agreement that delinquents are less attached to their parents than non-delinquents.[410] The hypothesis is that if there is a strong attachment between parents and juveniles, there will be the stronger resistance by juveniles

---

407 See, e.g., *Esbensen & Deschenes* 1998; *Hawkins, Catalano & Miller* 1992; *Masten* 1994; *Matsueda & Heimer* 1987; *Stice & Barrera* 1995.

408 *Wells & Rankin* 1988.

409 *Hoeve et al.* 2012.

410 *Williams* 2012, 387.

against getting involved in delinquent behaviour, because they do not want to disappoint their parents. In order to test this hypothesis, an attachment scale was used, based on five level questions ranging from "totally agree" to "totally disagree", asking about how well juveniles get along with their mothers and fathers, how easily they can get emotional support or care from their parents, and whether they would feel very bad about disappointing them (Cronbach's Alpha = 0.76). The question regarding spending time with the parent(s) was not included in the attachment scale because it did not work very well (Cronbach's Alpha = 0.56). The correlation of the family attachment scale and the juvenile delinquency scale in the Balkan region, as presented in *Table 10*, is not as clear as the correlation between family control and juvenile delinquency, as presented in *Table 7*. The lowest impact in terms of reducing juvenile delinquency is on the juveniles who reported average family attachment (values 2 and 3). About 73 % of them reported that they had committed at least one delinquent act in their lifetime. Among the juveniles who reported the weakest family attachment (value 1), 55 % reported that they had not committed any delinquent act in their lifetime. On the other hand, where family attachment was strongest (as reported by more than one-half of respondents), only 32 % reported ever having committed a delinquent act. It could be concluded that family control has a much stronger influence on juvenile delinquency in the Balkans than family attachment. Family control can thus be associated with low levels of juvenile delinquency, which is only partly the case with family attachment.

Table 10   Correlation between the family attachment scale and the juvenile delinquency scale in the Balkans

	Parental attachment				
	weak				strong
	1	2	3	4	5
Balkan	(N = 51)	(N = 127)	(N = 612)	(N = 2992)	(N = 4082)
% of juveniles with reported offences	45 ± 7	69 ± 4	74 ± 2	59 ± 1	32

Table 11 presents the same correlations as *Table 10*, but by country. The scale attachment has a clear negative correlation only in the cases of Croatia and Serbia, however only with a slight slope. In Croatia, if attachment is very strong (presented as value 5 in the table), only 55 % of juveniles did not report having committed a delinquent act, while the number is even higher for Serbia, at 66 %. Weaker trends to lower delinquency in correlation with stronger family attachment could as well be seen in the cases of North Macedonia and Kosovo, while Bosnia and Herzegovina shows a reverse U-shape with low delinquency for both weakest and strongest family attachment.

Table 11   *Correlation of the family attachment scale and the juvenile delinquency scale by country*

	Family attachment				
	weak			strong	
	1	2	3	4	5
Bosnia and Herzegovina	(N = 29)	(N = 28)	(N = 91)	(N = 893)	(N = 1794)
% of juveniles with reported offences	21%	54%	64%	46%	27%
Croatia	(N = 6)	(N = 46)	(N = 215)	(N = 904)	(N = 499)
% of juveniles with reported offences	100%	78%	77%	69%	55%
Kosovo	(N = 3)	(N = 11)	(N = 23)	(N = 184)	(N = 649)
% of juveniles with reported offences	33%	27%	17%	25%	16%
North Macedonia	(N = 7)	(N = 16)	(N = 60)	(N = 350)	(N = 737)
% of juveniles with reported offences	57%	63%	47%	49%	28%
Serbia	(N = 6)	(N = 26)	(N = 223)	(N = 661)	(N = 403)
% of juveniles with reported offences	100%	89%	89%	78%	66%

Some age differences occur in the country samples;[411] therefore, the parental attachment scale is correlated with age. *Table 12* presents the dependency on the parental attachment scale by age in the Balkan cluster. In the literature, it is unclear to what extent the link between attachment and delinquency changes over the lifecourse. There are at least two rival hypotheses. According to *Hirschi* and *Gottfredson* (2001),[412] the link between attachment to parents and delinquency should remain

---

411 For more details, see *Chapter 5.1.*
412 *Hirschi & Gottfredson* 2001.

similar across childhood, adolescence, and emerging adulthood. Contrary, dynamic developmental theories assume that change is possible. According to *Sampson* and *Laub* (2005), strong bonds to one's family and school impede delinquent behaviour during childhood and adolescence, while in adulthood, social ties are being passed on from family and school to labour or marriage. Therefore, the influence of family ties should wane in late adolescence and young adulthood when the individual establishes other important social ties. Thus, the theory of *Hirschi* assumes that the attachment-delinquency link is independent of age, while *Sampson* and *Laub* state that it is strongest during childhood and gradually decreases during adolescence and early adulthood.

Table 12   *Dependency of the parental attachment scale by age in the Balkan cluster*

Age	Parental attachment scale				
	1 weakest	2	3	4	5 strongest
12	*N(4)*	*N(8)*	*N(20)*	*N(198)*	*N(570)*
	7.7%	5.9%	3.2%	6.4%	13.5%
13	*N(13)*	*N(20)*	*N(120)*	*N(798)*	*N(1384)*
	25.0%	14.8%	19.3%	26.0%	32.9%
14	*N(16)*	*N(45)*	*N(174)*	*N(906)*	*N(1278)*
	30.8%	33.3%	28.0%	29.5%	30.4%
15	*N(14)*	*N(37)*	*N(153)*	*N(703)*	*N(723)*
	26.9%	27.4%	24.6%	22.9%	17.2%
16	*N(2)*	*N(13)*	*N(73)*	*N(222)*	*N(118)*
	3.8%	9.6%	11.7%	7.2%	2.8%
17	*N(2)*	*N(7)*	*N(50)*	*N(150)*	*N(79)*
	3.8%	5.2%	8.0%	4.9%	1.9%

Table 12 suggests that when looking at the highest value of parental attachment (value 5), the age drop becomes very clear. However, when analysing value 4 – which suggests some less attachment than value 5 does –, the results are opposite and show that attachment is increasing with age. In the case of very weak parental attachment, there is no clear scale or pattern of decreasing or increasing the level of family attachment with age.

The correlation of parental attachment and age is statistically significant with a correlation coefficient of r = -0.22. When comparing this correlation with the one between parental control and age, the results suggest that age has a stronger impact on parental control than on parental attachment.

5.2.1.4 Family structure

Family structure is an important background factor bearing a wealth of information about the respective country and cultural differences.[413] In ISRD2, the highest percentage of families who consisted of two biological parents (83.5 %) and the lowest number of single parents were found in Southern Europe, while the lowest percentage of intact families was found in Latin America and the Northern European cluster.[414]

In ISRD3, 90.5 % of juveniles from the Balkan region reported living with both parents; compared to the clusters from ISRD2, this is the highest percentage. Only 6.9 % of juveniles were living with one parent and 2.5 % with other people than their biological parents (such as grandparents, other family members, and foster families). The very high number of juveniles living with both parents can be ascribed to the cultural and economic situation in the region. In most parts of the Balkans, divorce is still perceived as a shame for a family.[415] For some couples, a separation is impossible for economic reasons because they are financially not able to move live in separate units.

Croatia has the highest number of children living with their parents in the EU. The average age at which young people leave their parents' home is 32 years.[416] Traditionally, family structures in the Balkan region can be seen as a two-parent nuclear family and collectivist culture with traditional values.[417] Parents promote values such as conformity and demand respect for adults and strict rearing.[418] In this context, it is not surprising that family control is more protective against juvenile delinquency than family attachment.

---

413 *Junger-Tas* 2012.

414 *Junger-Tas* 2012, 189.

415 A very common saying in the Balkans is that it is better to be in a bad marriage than alone.

416 EUROSTAT 2018.

417 *Ispa et al.* 2004.

418 *Ispa et al.* 2004.

Table 13　Pearson correlation between family variables and juvenile delinquency

		Juvenile delin- quency scale	Parental control scale	Parental attach- ment scale	Dinner with parents	Death of father/ mother	Serious illness of a parent	Parents consume alcohol/ drugs	Violence between parents	Serious conflicts between parents	Separa- tion/di- vorce of parents	Family struc- ture
Juvenile delin- quency scale	Pearson correlation	1										
	Sig. (2-tailed)											
	N	8202										
Parental control scale	Pearson correlation	-.382**	1									
	Sig. (2-tailed)	.000										
	N	8190	8435									
Parental attachment scale	Pearson correlation	-.226**	.400**	1								
	Sig. (2-tailed)	.000	.000									
	N	7864	8088	8105								

		Juvenile delinquency scale	Parental control scale	Parental attachment scale	Dinner with parents	Death of father/mother	Serious illness of a parent	Parents consume alcohol/drugs	Violence between parents	Serious conflicts between parents	Separation/divorce of parents	Family structure
Dinner with parents	Pearson correlation	-.181**	.322**	.274**	1							
	Sig. (2-tailed)	.000	.000	.000								
	N	8187	8421	8095	8442							
Death of father/mother	Pearson correlation	.030**	-.017	-.047**	-.004	1						
	Sig. (2-tailed)	.007	.126	.000	.716							
	N	8177	8406	8069	8404	8419						
Serious illness of a parent	Pearson correlation	.109**	-.089**	-.073**	-.084**	.124**	1					
	Sig. (2-tailed)	.000	.000	.000	.000	.000						
	N	8170	8396	8060	8392	8399	8406					

		Juvenile delinquency scale	Parental control scale	Parental attachment scale	Dinner with parents	Death of father/ mother	Serious illness of a parent	Parents consume alcohol/ drugs	Violence between parents	Serious conflicts between parents	Separation/di- vorce of parents	Family struc- ture
Parents consume alcohol/ drugs	Pearson correlation	.096**	-.120**	-.159**	-.097**	.061**	.073**	1				
	Sig. (2-tailed)	.000	.000	.000	.000	.000	.000					
	N	8171	8399	8064	8394	8406	8396	8408				
Violence between parents	Pearson correlation	.119**	-.131**	-.197**	-.113**	.062**	.092**	.312**	1			
	Sig. (2-tailed)	.000	.000	.000	.000	.000	.000	.000				
	N	8169	8395	8059	8391	8399	8390	8398	8405			
Serious conflicts between parents	Pearson correlation	.196**	-.239**	-.290**	-.221**	.016	.112**	.253**	.438**	1		
	Sig. (2-tailed)	.000	.000	.000	.000	.131	.000	.000	.000			
	N	8166	8392	8056	8390	8399	8388	8397	8392	8403		
	Pearson correlation	.113**	-.115**	-.179**	-.110**	.040**	.063**	.186**	.247**	.231**	1	

		Juvenile delin-quency scale	Parental control scale	Parental attach-ment scale	Dinner with parents	Death of father/ mother	Serious illness of a parent	Parents consume alcohol/ drugs	Violence between parents	Serious conflicts between parents	Separa-tion/di-vorce of parents	Family struc-ture
Separation/ divorce of parents	Sig. (2-tailed)	.000	.000	.000	.000	.000	.000	.000	.000	.000		
	N	8170	8356	8061	8393	8398	8388	8397	8392	8393	8406	
Family structure	Pearson correlation	.086**	-.040**	-.122**	-.073**	.224**	.052**	.088**	.095**	.065**	.292**	1
	Sig. (2-tailed)	.000	.000	.000	.000	.000	.000	.000	.000	.000	.000	
	N	8196	8428	8099	8437	8411	8399	8401	8398	8395	8399	8451

**) Correlation is significant at the 0.01 level (2-tailed).

5.2.1.5 Multivariate regression of family-related variables

When applying a multivariate linear regression, the focus should be on selecting the best possible independent variables that contribute to the dependent variable. Therefore, the correlation matrix is presented for all independent variables with a focus on family variables and the dependent one, which is lifetime juvenile delinquency. The correlation value gives an idea of which variable is significant, and by which factor. Based on the correlation matrix, the focus is on estimating the coefficients by minimizing the error function. The purpose of this section is to show the probability of offence perpetration under the influence of independent family variables.

Table 13 presents the strength of family variable relationships, i.e. how dependent family variables are on each other. Both scales (family attachment and family control) are negatively correlated with the juvenile delinquency scale and statistically significant. This means that self-reported delinquency decreases in conjunction with stronger family control and higher family attachment. Accordingly, the stronger family control and the higher family attachment, the lower is juveniles' involvement in delinquency. However, there are some differences when comparing the correlation coefficient between those two scales and juvenile delinquency. Family control has a stronger correlation with juvenile delinquency than family attachment ($r = -0.38$ and $r = -0.23$).

Table 13 also presents the correlation between family control and family attachment, showing a strong relationship ($r = 0.4$) between juveniles' attachment to their parents and the latter control practices. Therefore, parents who have a warm and supportive relationship with their children also have effective parental control over them. This is also in line with previous research findings.[419] Juveniles with a lack of parental control and supervision might think that their parents do not care about them.[420] Concerning other family variables, e.g. regularly having dinner with one's parents also has a strong positive correlation with family control ($r = 0.32$) as well as family attachment ($r = 0.27$), meaning that parents who have dinner together with their children are practicing stronger control and attachment – and even stronger control than attachment. Serious conflicts between one's parents have a high negative correlation with family control ($r = -0.24$) as well as family attachment ($r = -0.29$), which also goes for another variable which contains the issue of violence between parents. Among the above-presented variables, low negative correlations can be found in the cases of a serious illness or

---

419 *Cernkovich & Giordano* 1987; *Loeber & Stouthamer-Loeber* 1986.
420 *Riley & Shaw* 1987.

the death of a parent. This means that this type of a bad family event does not have a strong effect on juvenile delinquency.

Table 14 presents a multivariate regression of juvenile delinquency depending on family control, family attachment, other family variables, age, and gender, as well as country-specific effects. Age14 is a computed variable that is cantered near the mean age of all respondents (14 years). An age14 variable is added to the model so as to constrain effects of age, not least since the mean ages differ clearly between the countries. Adding variable age14 controls for individual age effects on delinquency,[421] so that the country dummies (as well as other variables) get rid of the age differences.[422]

In this model, the self-reported lifetime delinquency scale was used as a dependent variable. When focusing on family factors, it shows that parental control and attachment, family structure, serious illness of parents, and serious conflicts between parents are statistically significant at the level of $p < 0.05$ to juvenile delinquency. The parental control scale has a great influence on delinquency, as shown by the biggest standardized beta coefficient of -0.25. Family attachment is also statistically significant but with a standardizing beta coefficient of -0.05. This result is contrary to the ones from developed countries, where parental control is seen as being less relevant as a predictor of delinquency compared to parental attachment. In the Balkans, family control has a stronger influence on juvenile delinquency than family attachment, although the effect of parental attachment may be reduced through its high correlation with family control ($r = 0.4$). Both scales have a negative effect on juvenile delinquency. Therefore, with stronger parental control and attachment, juvenile delinquency might decrease. Other family variables which are statistically significant but have a positive beta coefficient (opposite to two parental scales) are family status, serious illness of parents, and serious conflict or violence between parents. Family status has a positive impact, meaning that juveniles living with both parents might decree delinquency. Furthermore, serious illness of parents and serious conflict or violence between parents raise the probability of a delinquent child. Gender is also statistically significant, with a beta coefficient of 0.14. There is no big difference

---

421 See, e.g., *Hirschi & Gotfredson* 2001 (theory of crime postulate), that age in itself has an effect on crime.

422 That is important since the age structure of the respondents differs between the countries (see *Chapter 5.1*). What is left may be a more culture-specific effect of the different countries. Nevertheless, except for the individual effect, one could think about so-called context effects, e.g., effects of being in contact with a certain age group and its rules. In this example, not only the individual age will be important, but also the mean age of the group the respondents are mostly in contact with. Such an effect could not be captured with the individual age. For further research, it should be considered to calculate such two-level effects, but this would exceed the scope of this analysis.

between the countries in this model, except in the case of Serbia. The parameters of the four other countries could be seen as being equal within the calculated errors. Therefore, only in Serbia, the delinquency scale is about 0.4 higher than in the other countries. In total, this model explains 21 % of the variance concerning delinquency, including the effects of the different countries. The variance concerning delinquency seems to be mainly driven by the age differences of the respondents in the different countries, as coud be seen in *Figure19*, where the parameters of the family and employment models (see below) are plotted against the mean age of the respondents in the different countries.

Table 14   *Multivariate regression of juvenile delinquency depending on family control, family attachment, other family variables, age, and gender, as well as country-specific effects ($R^2 = 0.21$)*

Model	B	Std. Error	Beta	t	Sig.
Constant	3.61	0.17		21.2	0.000
Control: Serbia	0.00				
Kosovo	-0.56	0.08	-0.11	-7.4	0.000
Croatia	-0.28	0.06	-0.07	-4.8	0.000
North Macedonia	-0.32	0.06	-0.07	-4.9	0.000
Bosnia and Herzegovina	-0.46	0.06	-0.14	-8.0	0.000
Scale control	-0.54	0.03	-0.25	-20.1	0.000
Scale attachment	-0.13	0.03	-0.05	-4.2	0.000
Family structure	0.22	0.05	0.05	4.8	0.000
Death of father/mother	0.01	0.09	0.00	0.1	0.914
Serious illness of parents	0.24	0.04	0.07	6.4	0.000
Parents consume alcohol/drugs	0.10	0.09	0.01	1.1	0.289
Violence between parents	0.17	0.09	0.02	1.9	0.052
Serious conflicts between parents	0.20	0.06	0.04	3.3	0.001
Separation/divorce of parents	0.10	0.06	0.02	1.6	0.100
Dinner together with parents	-0.01	0.01	-0.02	-1.8	0.065
Age14	0.11	0.01	0.09	7.4	0.000
Gender (female)	0.47	0.03	0.14	14.2	0.000

Figure 19   *Country parameters of the family and the employment model plotted against the mean age of respondents in the different Balkan countries*

5.2.2   Impact of the economy on juvenile delinquency

The socio-economic disadvantage has long been viewed as a risk factor which has an influence on elevated rates of crime.[423] In the literature, its influence on crime has been subject to considerable discussions, and perhaps it is the most controversial correlate of crime. Over time, many researchers have examined the direct influence of socio-economic disadvantages on juvenile delinquency – and with different findings. In fact, criminological theories from the early and middle decades of the 20th century that have dominated the field for many years took as their starting point the hypothesis that most delinquents come from a socially disadvantaged background. Some of the studies which reported the influence of the socio-economic status on juvenile delinquency were later rejected. In his work, *Cohen* (1956) differentiated working- and middle-class boys, arguing that there is a lack of opportunities in social status and prestige for working-class boys, which draws them to the bottom of the status hierarchy and thus to crime.[424] Criticism of his work addresses the lack of validated data and contradictory concepts.[425] *Mannheim et al.* (1957) conducted a survey in all London courts and thus with several magistrates, with a sample of 400 boys.[426] They concluded that there are certainly significant differences in the distribution of the social classes over some court areas. However, this hypothesis also no

---

423 *Rutter, Giller & Hagell* 1998.
424 *Cohen* 1955.
425 *Rabow* 1966.
426 *Mannheim, Spencer & Lynch* 1957.

longer has acceptance because it failed to stand up to further empirical testing – the correlation was not as strong or as consistent as assumed.[427]

Other empirical studies have shown that there are no significant correlations between juvenile delinquency and socio-economic status – the first finding coming from an early self-report research. *Nye, Short,* and *Olson* (1958) conducted a study among high-school groups in western and midwestern communities in Washington, based on self-reported behaviour rather than on official data.[428] Their conclusion was that there is no significant difference in the delinquent behaviour of boys and girls of a different socio-economic status. Their study did not focus on explaining the aetiology of juvenile delinquency, but falsified theories which were based on the theoretical assumption of a correlation between class differences and juvenile delinquency. *Akers* (1961) conducted a study in high schools in northeastern Ohio, with the primary purpose to retest the hypothesis of the above study by using (insofar as possible) the same approach, but at a different locality.[429] Their study showed the same results, i.e. no significant differences in the delinquent behaviour of juveniles of a different socio-economic status. Later studies have examined the possible severity of offences in socio-economic differentials. A study conducted by *Elliot* and *Ageton* using self-report data found no significant correlation between social class and status offence, hard drug use, or public disorder. However, they found a correlation between social class and predatory crime, property crime, and crime against the person.[430] Other studies used different criminological techniques and measures with the conclusion that there is no statistically significant relationship between delinquency and the socio-economic status (*Arnold* 1966[431], *Hirschi* 1969). At the end of the 20th century, critics began to challenge the validity of the self-report method and the findings of this method.[432] Researchers now shift towards finding other specific conditions under which socio-economic status and delinquency are related, or other factors on which the socio-economic status may have an influence in terms of decreasing or increasing delinquency.

Testing the influence of socio-economic disadvantages on crime rates – across various societies and by using a wide range of factors, including income,[433] poverty,[434] and socio-economic status[435] – produced new insights. A number of researchers have reported that inequality, extreme poverty, and social exclusion matter

---

427   *Rutter, Giller & Hagell* 1998, 199.
428   *Nye, Short & Olson* 1958.
429   *Akers* 1964.
430   *Elliott & Ageton* 1980.
431   *Arnold* 1966.
432   *Hindelang, Hirschi & Weis* 1981.
433   *Farrington* 1990; *Patterson et al.* 1992.
434   *Currie* 1998.
435   *Farrington* 1990.

in shaping a society's experience of violent crime.[436] Some of the factors will be addressed in more detail below. A much-debated question is whether socio-economic disadvantages, in general, have a direct influence on engaging in crime or whether this is mediated by a series of adverse family, school, and neighbourhood factors. Up to now, a number of studies have highlighted the influence of these factors. *Nye*, *Short*, and *Olson* did not find any statistically significant differences between the socio-economic status and juvenile delinquency, but what they pointed out is that juveniles from a middle-class status reported less delinquent acts than those from a lower or higher socio-economic status. Family factors suggested that slightly more effective social control and socialization by middle-class parents help reduce delinquent behaviour.[437] In their discussion, *Rutter* and *Giller* also found a connection (though not a strong one) between social status and delinquency, which they mainly attributed to the extremes of the social scale.[438] Their connection is strongly evident, with measures of parental unemployment and reliance on welfare rather than with indices of parental education.[439] In their longitudinal study of 378 families from rural Iowa – which at that time was suffering an economic crisis in agriculture –, *Conger et al.* studied the impact of economic pressure on parents and their early-adolescent children.[440]

Taken together, all these results suggest that economic pressure does have an effect on crime rates, but the impact is rather indirect and takes effect through family factors such as parental depression, marital conflict, and parental hostility. *Farnworth et al.* (1994) analysed the results of the first four waves of the Rochester Youth Development Study, in which each subject and his/her parent or gradient were interviewed at six-month intervals.[441] The aim of the study was to determine which aspect of social disadvantages was most closely related to which types of delinquency. Longitudinal analyses showed that the main effect came from long-term unemployment and a continuous dependence on welfare. The strongest correlation was found with street crimes such as assault, car theft, bike theft, and purse-snatching. It was concluded that an underclass status was a key risk factor, having the strongest impact on street crime.

5.2.2.1 Economy in the Balkan region

This research has focused only on Southeastern European countries from the ISRD3 cluster. The Regular Economic Report (RER) covers economic developments, prospects, and policies in six Southeastern European countries (SEE6): Albania, Bosnia

---

436 *Currie* 1998, 114.

437 *Nye, Short & Olson* 1958, 389.

438 *Rutter & Giller* 1983, 136.

439 *Rutter & Giller* 1983, 137.

440 *Conger et al.* 1994.

441 *Farnworth et al.* 1994.

and Herzegovina, Kosovo, North Macedonia, Montenegro, and Serbia. The economy of these six Southaastern European countries (SEE6) recovered from the 2012 recession, growing by 2.2 % on average in 2013 (the year of the ISRD3 survey). Each of the SEE6 countries marked positive growth rates in 2013, with growth at or exceeding 3 % in Kosovo, North Macedonia, and Montenegro. External demand for SEE6 exports, especially by the European Union (EU), was the key driver of the recovery.

Overall, the SEE6 countries have limited success in translating their economic recovery into job creation. Unemployment has remained high at an average rate of 24.2 % in 2013. High unemployment rates and the large numbers of chronic unemployment are prevalent among vulnerable groups such as youth and the low-skilled.

Although the association between socio-economic disadvantages and crime can be explained by a theoretical framework, there is lack of empirical research to test the influence of different factors on young people's exposure to socio-economic disadvantages and the development of crime.[442] This study sought to examine this association by taking a foothold in the informal control theory, which relies on the social control theory proposed by *Hirschi*.[443] This theory claims that the motivation towards behavioural deviance is constant among individuals and that it is social bonds that constrain these impulses – but focusing on the informal mechanism of social control as well as operating within families, schools, and social networks. The idea is to test this theory in the countries which are undergoing political, economic, and social transitions on different levels. From an economic point of view, when comparing the Balkan countries with Western European countries or the USA, the former are facing strong economic crises with high rates of unemployment, mostly among young people.

5.2.2.2 Unemployment rates among young people/families in the Balkan region

The South East Europe Regular Economic Report (SEE RER)[444] reported that labour is still the largest source of income in the SEE6 countries. It is followed by pensions and social assistance the share of which varies among countries, but together, they help explain the relatively low reliance on labour market income. As we will see in the following RER data, the labour market in the SEE6 countries is very weak and features the highest levels of youth unemployment in Europe. Its fast increase has strongly been affected by the global financial crisis, and 27.1 %, it is nearly twice as high as in the EU11 countries. Engagement in decreasing youth unemployment should be the focus of policy-makers in the region. The SEE RER

---

442 *Fergusson, Swain-Campbell & Horwood* 2004.

443 *Hirschi* 1969.

444 World Bank Group 2015; The World Bank 2014.

highlighted that the tenacity of the rise of regional youth unemployment bears the risk of creating a "lost generation" of workers with weak job prospects and economic potential. The authors emphasize that this is the first young generation to have been fully educated post-transition, so they bring to the labour market a different mindset and skills than their parents. We have to conclude that this will might lead to countries losing their most productive generation, which might furthermore pose risks for long-term economic growth and threatens to exacerbate inequality and social tensions.

In Kosovo, the labour market situation is alarming and calls for urgent reaction for improving the current economic situation. In 2014, the unemployment rate was at 35 %, while the employment rate was at 26.9 %. The alarming situation is that among all unemployed, 69 % are unemployed long-term, and 61 % among the youth. A similar economic situation is found in Bosnia and Herzegovina with an unemployment rate of 27.5 % in Q1 (1st quarter in the financial calendar) in 2014. Youth unemployment is one of the biggest problems of the labour market in Bosnia and Herzegovina. The rate is extremely high, and in 2015, it was the highest in the region at 62 %. Among the unemployed, 82 % have been seeking employment for over one year. The labour market situation is a little better in North Macedonia, but still, the unemployment rate was at 28 % here in 2014, while the employment rate was at 41.2 %. At 53.1 % in 2014, the youth unemployment rate was the third-highest in the region. The Serbian labour market was also strongly affected by the global financial crises. Here, the unemployment rate increased from 13.6 % in 2008 to 20.3 % in 2014. As in all SEE6 countries, the unemployment rate among young people is also high, at 43.1 %. Croatia[445] is the country with the lowest rates in the region, but if we compare it with the rates of other EU countries, the Croatian unemployment rate (17.3%) is among the highest, only lower than Greece and Spain. In 2014, the unemployment rate of young people was at 45.5 %, down from 50 % in 2013. It is important to emphasize that the unemployment rate in Croatia fluctuates with the tourist season, whose direct contribution to the Croatian GDP was 12.5 % in 2014,[446] which is the highest contribution among all EU-28 countries. Its influence is reflected in the Croatian unemployment rate. According to the Croatian Bureau of Statistics,[447] in the 2014 Q3 – which is the high tourist season in Croatia –, the unemployment rate was at 15.7 %. As could thus be expected, it was higher at 18.3 % in the 2014 Q4. In the 2015 Q1, the rate was still high at 18.1 %, and in the Q2, it decreased to 15.5 % because the tourist season starts in spring.

---

445 EUROSTAT 2014.
446 World Travel & Tourism Council 2015, 8.
447 DZS 2014; http://www.dzs.hr/Hrv/system/first_results.htm [01/06/2018].

As World Bank statistics[448] show, the unemployment rate among females[449] in the region was very high in 2014. In this respect, the worst situation in the observed countries was found in Bosnia and Herzegovina with a rate of 29.8 %, followed by North Macedonia with 28.1 %. The figure was slightly better in Serbia at 25.9 %. Statistically, the best situation was found in Croatia at 16.6 %. The share of women actively looking for work in the aforementioned countries was significantly higher than in Western European countries, such as Germany with a rate of 4.8 %, Austria 5 %, and Switzerland 4.7 %.

Figure 20   Unemployment rate among respondents' parents by country

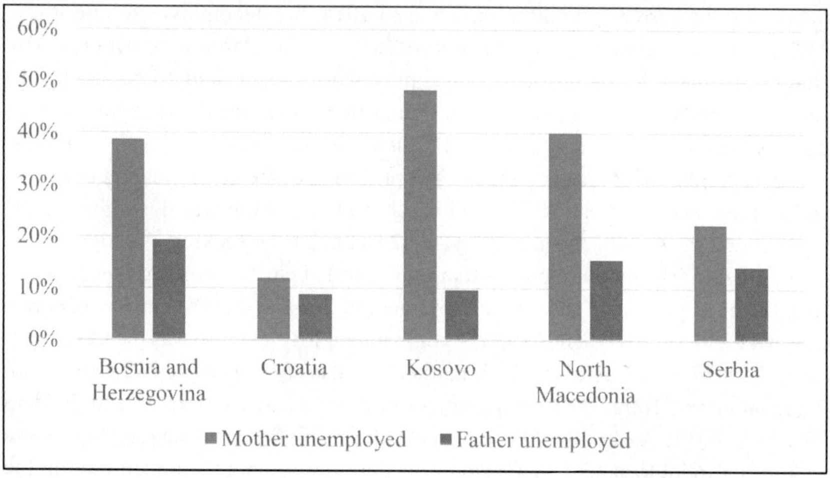

Figure 20 presents the unemployment rate of respondents' mothers and fathers by country. It is obvious that these are very high in all Balkan countries, which is consistent with the national and international data presented above. The fathers' unemployment rate is highest in Bosnia and Herzegovina (19 %), followed by 15 % in North Macedonia and 14 % in Serbia. Kosovo has a very low unemployment rate among fathers (10 %) in comparison to the one of mothers, which is the highest among all Balkan countries (48 %). This means that almost half of Kosovar respondents reported that their mother is unemployed. This is alarming and implies that Kosovo is a patriarchal society where the role of the mother is to take care of household and family, while the father is the one to provide the family income. North Macedonia also has a high rate of mother unemployment (40 %). Parents' unemployment rates are lowest in Croatia, the only EU country in the Balkan cluster.

---

448   Worldbank 2015, http://data.worldbank.org/indicator/SL.UEM.TOTL.FE.ZS [01/06/2018].

449   Unemployment here refers to the share of the labour force that is without work but available for and seeking employment.

5.2.2.3 Maternal employment and juvenile delinquency

The focus of researchers on the effects of maternal employment on child development started in the USA in the 1950s when a large number of women entered the paid workforce.[450] In the beginning, researchers were trying to find a correlation between maternal employment and child development, but not much research was conducted on the correlation between maternal employment and juvenile delinquency. Through the years, research showed different effects, suggesting various causes. An early researcher who was dealing with maternal employment and delinquency found a small positive effect and explained this with low maternal supervision.[451] This meant that working mothers are less able to control and discipline their children, the result being juvenile delinquency. Most contemporary researchers, however, found little or no effects between maternal employment and delinquency.[452] On the other hand, some research have found that children of regularly employed mothers are less likely to commit a delinquent act.[453] The reason could be seen in an economic dimension such as the associated improvement of family income.

Parental unemployment can be correlated with juvenile delinquency in that it can cause psychological and behavioural problems and bad school performances among children. Both of these effects occur in correlation with juvenile delinquency.[454] This could also be present in the Balkan region through maternal employment, since here the mother still has the main position in child rearing.

5.2.2.4 Multivariate regression of economy-related variables

The correlation matrix in *Table 15* shows that not all independent economy variables are statistically significant to the dependent variable (lifetime juvenile delinquency). This stands in contrast to the family variableswhich were all statistically significant with juvenile delinquency on a 0.01 level. However, father as well as mother unemployment and family funds from employment are statistically significant with lifetime juvenile delinquency. Among all statistically significant variables in *Table 15*, mother unemployment has the highest correlation ($r = -0.10$). Family funds due to unemployment (mostly from welfare systems) are in a statistically significant correlation with mother and father unemployment at a level of 0.001. The highest correlation can be found for unemployed fathers at $r = 0.23$. However, there is no correlation with juvenile delinquency. Contrary to this, family funds gained from employment (mostly wages) are in a statistically significant correlation with juvenile delinquency and expectedly with father and mother unemployment at a level of 0.05.

---

450   *Vander Ven et al.* 2001.

451   *Roy* 1963.

452   *Vander Ven et al.* 2001; *Harve* 1999.

453   *Vander Ven et al.* 2001, 238.

454   *Baker et al.* 2009; *Harland et al.* 2002; *Madge* 1983; *Mazerolle* 1998.

Table 15   Pearson correlation of economy-related variables and juvenile delinquency

		Juvenile delinquency scale	Father unemployment	Father employment	Mother unemployment	Mother employment	Family funds, unemployment	Family funds, employment
Juvenile delinquency scale	Pearson Correlation	1	-.002	.040**	-.102**	.018	-.006	-.081**
	Sig. (2-tailed)		.853	.000	.000	.106	.600	.000
	N	8202	8202	8202	8202	8202	8202	8202
Father unemployment	Pearson Correlation	-.002	1	-.096**	.171**	-.017	.229**	-.028*
	Sig. (2-tailed)	.853		.000	.000	.118	.000	.011
	N	8202	8460	8460	8460	8460	8460	8460
Father employment	Pearson Correlation	.040**	-.096**	1	-.034**	.129**	.015	.012
	Sig. (2-tailed)	.000	.000		.002	.000	.165	.251
	N	8202	8460	8460	8460	8460	8460	8460
Mother unemployment	Pearson Correlation	-.102**	.171**	-.034**	1	-.129**	.172**	.048**
	Sig. (2-tailed)	.000	.000	.002		.000	.000	.000

		Juvenile delinquency scale	Father unemployment	Father employment	Mother unemployment	Mother employment	Family funds, unemployment	Family funds, employment
Mother employment	N	8202	8460	8460	8460	8460	8460	8460
	Pearson Correlation	.018	-.017	.129**	-.129**	1	.032**	-.010
	Sig. (2-tailed)	.106	.118	.000	.000		.004	.353
	N	8202	8460	8460	8460	8460	8460	8460
Family funds, unemployment	Pearson Correlation	-.006	.229**	.015	.172**	.032**	1	-.128**
	Sig. (2-tailed)	.690	.000	.165	.000	.004		.000
	N	8202	8460	8460	8460	8460	8460	8460
Family funds, employment	Pearson Correlation	-.081**	-.028*	.012	.048**	-.010	-.128**	1
	Sig. (2-tailed)	.000	.011	.251	.000	.353	.000	
	N	8202	8460	8460	8460	8460	8460	8460

**) Correlation is significant at a 0.01 level (2-tailed).

*) Correlation is significant at a 0.05 level (2-tailed).

In this case, none of the correlations is high. Nevertheless, all variables will be included in the multivariate regression model.

The reference variables to be used in this model are Serbia, mother other, father other and family funds other; other refers to the status different from employment and unemployment. It is, for example, in case a person is getting funds as retirement money or in case of a serious illness, as well as receiving family funds from sources other than employment and welfare, such as if other family members working abroad transfer money to the family.

The results of the multivariate regression show that the employment status of the mother has an influence on the lifetime prevalence of juvenile delinquency in the Balkans. In the model presented here, the dependent variable is the juvenile delinquency scale, containing 14 lifetime delinquency acts from the ISRD3 questionnaire. More about the structure of the scales is presented in *Chapter 4*. The results in *Table 15* show that out of all economy-related variables, only mother unemployment is statistically significant for self-reported juvenile delinquency. Therefore, no other variables concerning the employment status of the family are statistically significant. This means that mother and father employment as well as unemployment and family income do not play a role in juvenile delinquency in the Balkans. As *Table 15* shows, the unemployment status of the mother will reduce delinquency at a rate of 0.17 on the delinquency scale.[455] This assumes that the other variables are held constant. As the results show, the father employment status does not have an influence on juvenile delinquency. Where the mother is seen as the main person in child-rearing and is the one who stays at home and takes care of the family, children will achieve a stronger attachment to their family and the family can practice stronger control, which will result in juveniles not getting involved in delinquent behaviour. Going a step further, it could be concluded that fathers do not play an important role in child-rearing in the Balkans, and whether or not they stay at home does not have an influence on juvenile delinquency. The family is patriarchal in the Balkans, where the father is mainly responsible for the family income and the mothers are responsible for taking care of the children. Testing the same model in the Western European countries Germany, Austria, and Switzerland, the results were diametrically opposed. Here, father unemployment was the only variable which was statistically significant for juvenile delinquency. A possible explanation is the very low level of unemployment in these countries, and father unemployment can also be seen as an indication of a dysfunctional family.

In the model presented in *Table 16*, country differences can be identified if compared with Serbia as a reference country. However, there are also differences between other countries in the Balkans, the highest being between Kosovo and Croatia (r = -0.98

---

455   For details about the structure of these variables, see *Chapter 4*. For details about the distribution of these variables by country, see *Chapter 5.2.2.2*.

and r = -0.40). It is important to emphasize that in this model, R^2 is not very high and 14 % of the variance are explained by the model. When analysing the data based on the multivariate regression model by adding only country dummy variables, R^2 is 9 %. This variance is mainly caused by the (age-driven) differences between the countries.

Table 16   Multivariate regression of self-reported juvenile delinquency depending on the employment status of the parents, age and gender ($R^2 = 0.14$)

Model	B	Std. Error	Beta	t	Sig.
Constant	1.33	0.07		19.4	0.000
Serbia (reference)	0				
Kosovo	-0.98	0.07	-0.21	-13.7	0.000
Croatia	-0.40	0.06	-0.10	-6.9	0.000
North Macedonia	-0.66	0.06	-0.15	-10.2	0.000
Bosnia and Herzegovina	-0.77	0.06	-0.23	-12.2	0.000
Mother other (reference)	0				
Mother unemployment	-0.17	0.04	-0.05	-4.3	0.000
Mother employment	-0.03	0.09	0.00	-0.4	0.716
Father other (reference)	0				
Father unemployment	0.04	0.05	0.01	0.8	0.402
Father employment	0.11	0.08	0.02	1.5	0.146
Family funds other (reference)	0				
Family funds, unemployment	0.00	0.09	0.00	0.0	0.972
Family funds, employment	0.00	0.05	0.00	0.0	0.983
Age 14	0.20	0.01	0.17	13.8	0.000
Gender (female)	0.50	0.03	0.16	15.2	0.000

The multivariate regression model presented in *Table 16* suggests that despite the country differences, mother unemployment has the strongest impact on juvenile delinquency in the Balkans. However, it would be wrong to conclude that juvenile delinquency automatically decreases if mothers stay at home and take care of their children. As seen in *Chapter 5.2.2*, the unemployment rate among young people/families in the Balkan region is very challenging due to the economic situation, especially in the case of youths and females who have very high unemployment rates.

Therefore, by considering the whole context of the region, the results should be interpreted in the light of country development. With respect to the societies and policy-makers in the region, the focus should be on the process of developing policies and programmes with the aim of encouraging fathers to participate in their children's rearing, as their participation is now established in developed countries. Additionally, young people and mothers should be better included in the labour markets of these countries.

Maternal unemployment is seen to have a control effect. Therefore, it was added to the parental control model,[456] but then it was not significant.[457] Therefore, in this model, the effect of employed mothers vanished by the other effects such as parental control, which is statistically significant with a beta coefficient of -0.25. Therefore, in order to reduce juvenile delinquency, the focus should not only be on maternal unemployment but more strongly on parental control in general.

5.2.3   Impact of the school on juvenile delinquency

Today, juveniles spend a large part of their lives in school which, as such, plays an important social role in juvenile delinquency.[458] It is a place where young people socialise and form their cultural norms and values. Throughout history, school has been widening its role from being a strictly educational place to become an educational as well as a social and cultural bonding institution. In his social control theory, *Hirschi* stated that the stronger the social bonds are within conventional societies – such as families, schools, and communities –, the lesser the likelihood that an individual will commit a criminal offence.[459] Some theories even claim that school has replaced the family in terms of socialising youth in modern society – such as the general theory of crime by *Gottfredson* and *Hirschi*.

In the first part of this section, the education system in the Balkans will be presented. Violence in school is also related to the school itself and to the educational system in general.[460] In the second part, the focus will be on the social control theory by testing the role of school on juvenile delinquency. The results will present how well the juveniles in this research perform in school and to what extent they are attached to their respective school. The last part will aim at defining – with the multivariate linear regression model – which school variables are related to juvenile delinquency and which ones are not.

---

456   It refers to *Table 14*.
457   For more details, see *Appendix 1*.
458   *Junger-Tas* 2012b, 211.
459   *Tibbets & Hemmens* 2015.
460   *Rutter et al.* 1979.

5.2.3.1 Education systems in the Balkan region

In the Balkan region, the educational system has gone (and is still going) through a process of reformation and modernisation. The transition from socialism to democracy and a market-oriented society has sparked a need for adjusting curricula and ways of teaching with the aim to modernise the educational systems of the countries in this region. According to the Social Research Centre in assistance with the UNICEF education system, in order to make them more efficient and up-to-date, the teaching quality needs to be improved, adequate public funds for the educational system have to be allocated, lifecourse education should be developed, and, most importantly, education needs to be linked to the needs of the job market.

There are different education systems in the region which can be divided into four levels: preschool rearing and education, elementary, secondary, and higher education. Elementary school is free of charge for all children. The differences are found in its duration. In Croatia and Serbia, children start elementary school at the age of six/seven; it ends with the 8th grade. In Bosnia and Herzegovina and North Macedonia, elementary school ends with the 9th grade. Kosovo has a different educational system from the above-mentioned countries. Here, it is divided into primary and secondary education, both being mandatory and free of charge in publicly funded educational institutions. Primary school starts when the child is six years of age and ends with the 5th grade. Lower secondary education includes classes from six to nine, i.e. students aged 12–15.

The differences in the educational systems have an impact on the sampling of this study. The target group was juveniles between 13 and 16 years of age, which in the cases of Croatia and Serbia included the 7th and 8th grades of primary school and the first grade of secondary school. In Bosnia and Herzegovina, North Macedonia, and Kosovo, the target group were juveniles from 7th to 9th grade of primary school (lower secondary education).

5.2.3.2 School functioning and bonding

Along with the family, school is one of the main environments in which young people develop their personality.[461] The focus of this chapter is on juveniles' attachment to school and deviant phenomena in school. The hypothesis is that the higher juveniles' attachment to school, the stronger is its influence on decreasing juvenile delinquency – following the logic from the social control theory by *Hirschi* (1969). Juveniles with strong bonds to school have a high risk of losing these bonds when participating in delinquent behaviour. Control theories assume that we all have an urge for committing delinquent acts, but we will refrain from doing so because someone/something prevents us.[462] The difference between committing and refraining

---

461 *Egli, Lucia & Berchtold* 2012.

462 *Agnew & Brezina* 2012.

from delinquency does not lie in motivation, but in the extent to which natural motives are controlled. All juveniles are exposed to roughly the same direct control in school, but some will engage in delinquent behaviour nevertheless. There are many explanations for that phenomenon, one of which being that juveniles who do not engage in delinquent behaviour have more to lose. This is called a *stake in conformity*, in which case juveniles do not want to lose the stake by getting involved in delinquent behaviour.[463] The ones who have much to lose will be more anxious about engaging in delinquency because the stakes are high. In the context of school, there are two dimensions of the *stake in conformity*: attachment to school and teachers as well as the actual investment in school through good grades and ambitious plans for the future.

The first dimension is an emotional attachment to school, which is in the same line as emotional attachment to parents as presented in *Chapter 5.2.1.1*. Juveniles with a strong emotional attachment to teachers have more to lose by committing a delinquent act.[464] In the traditional educational system, such as the one in the Balkan region, where juveniles have the same teacher for several years, the bonds and thus the *stake in conformity* are even higher. Families in the region are more static, they do not move around the country, which can also be explained through political regimes in history. Thus, most juveniles spent their whole education life in the same city. In this context, bonds with school become strong. Therefore, school bonding is seen as a positive indicator for decreasing juvenile delinquency.[465]

The second level of a *stake in conformity* is an actual or anticipated investment into conventional society. Many juveniles invest a lot of time and energy into getting good grades, participating in various school activities, and building up a good reputation in order to be rewarded in the future with a good faculty and/or good job opportunities.[466] Therefore, engaging in delinquency puts all of this at stake.

The ISRD3 questionnaire contains a number of questions regarding school functioning. So as to test the above-mentioned hypothesis, two scales were made. The first scale presents school attachment based on the statements "If I had to move, I would miss my school; most of the days, I like going to school; I like my school; classes are interesting". This scale worked very well, with a Cronbach's Alpha 0.81.[467] In this scale (presented in *Figure 21*), correlations are strong, the lowest being between "classes are interesting" and "If I had to move, I would miss my school" (0.39). The hypothesis is that children would miss their school not because of the curriculum and institutional factors but because of their attachment to the teachers and other children in school.

463 *Toby* 1957.
464 *Agnew & Brezina* 2012.
465 *Costello & Vowell* 1999; *Hirschi* 1969; *Loeber & Stouthamer-Loeber* 1986; *Mack et al.* 2007; *Wright et al.* 1999.
466 *Chapple, McQuillian & Berdahl* 2005; *Sampson & Laub* 1993.
467 For more details about the school attachment scale, see *Chapter 4*.

Figure 21   *Attachment to school variables by country*

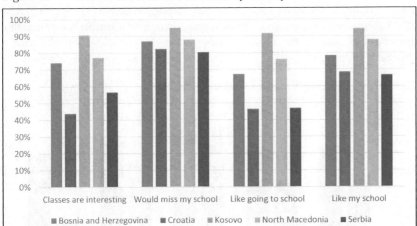

Figure 21 presents each variable from the school attachment scale by country. In all investigated countries, more than half of the students reported that their school classes are interesting, except in the case of Croatia, where only 44 % of students thought so. For the last seven years, Croatia has been struggling to implement a curriculum reform in the primary and secondary education systems. The New National Curriculum was accepted by the Croatian Parliament on 17th October 2014, but it had still not been put into practice at the time of writing. With the change of the government in 2016, some slight modifications were made in the national curriculum, all of which had the aim to create useful and meaningful education, in line with the developmental age and interests of juveniles and closer to their everyday lives. The Croatian Ministry of Science and Education has recognized that school education needs to be developed in line with modern society; therefore, one of the aims of the new National Curriculum is an education that will prepare children for life in the 21st century, for a world of work, continuing education, and lifelong learning.[468] Thus, the high percentage of juveniles who think that until now, their classes are not interesting could be expected. *Figure 21* shows the high percentage of juveniles in most countries who said they would miss their school if they had to move somewhere else, so they allegedly like their schools. However, in the cases of Croatia and Serbia, more than half of the students reported that they did not like going to school. Therefore, it can be argued that in Croatia and Serbia, students like their school and would miss it rather because of their friends and not because of the school as an institution.

---

468   For details, see The Ministry of Science and Education in Croatia, https://mzo.hr/hr/rubrike/ nacionalni-kurikulum [01/07/2018].

Likewise, in most Balkan countries, more than half of the students would miss their teachers if they had to move home, with the exception of Serbia (32 %) (see *Figure 22*). Together with the question about the importance of a teacher's opinion, this question was part of the bond-to-teacher scale. It worked very well, with a Cronbach's Alpha of 0.71.[469]

Figure 22   Teacher-bonding variables by country

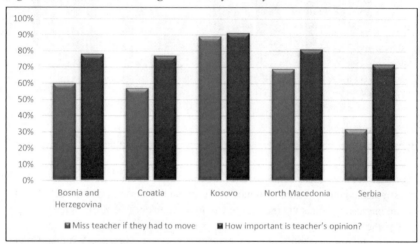

The third scale that was used regarding the school is school disorganization. It contains four questions about stealing, fighting, vandalism, and drug use in the respective school. The scale worked very well, with a Cronbach's Alpha of 0.74. The strongest correlations are between "fighting in school" and "stealing" (0.57) and between "fighting in school" and "vandalism" (0.51). *Figure 23* shows that delinquency is omnipresent within Balkan schools. Bosnia and Herzegovina has the highest rate of reported vandalism within schools (56 %), followed by Serbia (49 %) and Croatia (40 %), while the lowest rate is found in Kosovo (35 %). Bosnia and Herzegovina also has the highest rate of reported fighting in school among all studied countries (49 %), followed by Kosovo (47 %). *Figure 23* suggests that in Kosovo, fighting in school is the most frequent among the observed delinquent acts. Bosnia and Herzegovina also has the highest rate of stealing in schools (34 %). Furthermore, the results suggest that there is a big problem with drug use in Serbian schools, where every third student reported intensive drug use in their school. In other Balkan countries, around 9 % of students reported drug use in schools. Overall, in most countries, vandalism is the biggest problem in schools, except in the case of Kosovo, where fighting is more prevalent at 47 %. These results show in which direction school

---

469   For details about the teacher bonding scale, see *Chapter 4*.

programmes on delinquency prevention and education should go and which delinquency acts they should focus on.

If comparing these results with self-reported delinquency, there is a big discrepancy
between the rates.[470] In Bosnia and Herzegovina, only 4.5 % of respondents reported
that they had committed vandalism acts in their lifetime, while 56 % reported vandalism in schools. In Kosovo, 47 % of students reported much fighting in their
school, but only 4.9 % reported having participated in group fights. In Croatia, 40 %
reported vandalism in their school, with only 7.8 % having committed vandalism
acts in their lifetime. In the Serbian sample, there are less differences between self-
reported delinquency in general and in school – here, 32 % of students reported
fighting in their school and only 13 % in their lifetime.

Figure 23   *School disorganization variables by country*

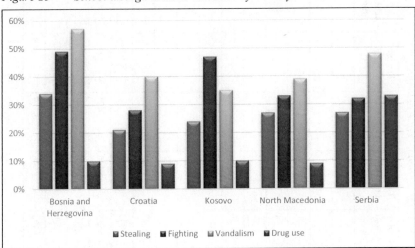

5.2.3.3   Multivariate regression of school-related variables

Here, the same methodology was used as in the correlation between family and economy. Therefore, the first part presents the Pearson correlation between all school-
related variables. The second part presents the results of the multivariate regression.
The purpose of these analyses is to present the model of delinquency as predicted by
school variables. The aim is to show the probability of delinquent acts under the
influence of independent variables and to compare the influence of predictors on
delinquency in the Balkan countries. In this case, independent variables are school-
related ones.

---

470   For data about self-reported delinquency in the Balkan countries, see *Chapter 5.1.*

Table 17 Pearson correlation of school-related variables and juvenile delinquency

		Juvenile delinquency scale	School attachment scale	Teacher bonding scale	School disorganization scale	Truancy	School achievement	Repeated grade	Age	Gender
Juvenile delinquency scale	Pearson Corr.	1								
	Sig. (2-tailed)									
	N	8202								
School attachment scale	Pearson Corr.	-.285**	1							
	Sig. (2-tailed)	.000								
	N	8192	8430							
Teacher bonding scale	Pearson Corr.	-.235**	.482**	1						
	Sig. (2-tailed)	.000	0.000							
	N	8196	8418	8427						
School disorganization scale	Pearson Corr.	.155**	-.085**	-.129**	1					
	Sig. (2-tailed)	.000	.000	.000						
	N	8189	8419	8415	8421					
Truancy	Pearson Corr.	.261**	-.195**	-.157**	.094**	1				
	Sig. (2-tailed)	.000	.000	.000	.000					
	N	8175	8390	8396	8387	8399				

		Juvenile delinquency scale	School attachment scale	Teacher bonding scale	School disorgani-zation scale	Truancy	School achieve-ment	Repeated grade	Age	Gender
School achievement	Pearson Corr.	-.105**	.148**	.211**	-.063**	-.160**	1			
	Sig. (2-tailed)	.030	.000	.000	.000	.000				
	N	8178	8388	8393	8385	8371	8399			
Repeated grade	Pearson Corr.	.105**	-.047**	-.068**	.094**	.125**	-.098**	1		
	Sig. (2-tailed)	.000	.000	.000	.000	.000	.000			
	N	8181	8387	8393	8384	8373	8378	8399		
Age14	Pearson Corr.	.280**	-.258**	-.261**	-.024*	.232**	-.161**	.112**	1	
	Sig. (2-tailed)	.000	.000	.000	.030	.000	.000	.000		
	N	8188	8413	8409	8405	8382	8383	8383	8442	
Gender (female)	Pearson Corr.	.154**	-.039**	-.115**	.093**	.057**	-.118**	.056**	.025*	1
	Sig. (2-tailed)	.000	.000	.000	.000	.000	.000	.000	.023	
	N	8195	8423	8419	8415	8392	8392	8391	8441	8452

**) Correlation is significant at a 0.01 level (2-tailed).

*) Correlation is significant at a 0.05 level (2-tailed).

All school-related variables, as well as age and gender, are statistically significant at a level of 0.01 with self-reported lifetime juvenile delinquency, as presented in *Table 17*. Among them, the highest correlation with juvenile delinquency is in the case of school attachment (r = -0.29). The correlation is negative, meaning that with a higher level of school attachment, juvenile delinquency rates decrease. The scale for school disorganization has not such a high correlation (r = 16). Contrary to school attachment, this is a positive correlation; therefore, a higher level of disorganization in school results in a higher level of self-reported delinquency. Furthermore, the school attachment and the school disorganization scales are both statistically significant with all variables in the presented matrix. In the case of school attachment, the strongest correlation is found with the teacher bonding scale (r = 0.48). As expected, there is a strong correlation between school and teacher attachment, and both variables have a strong influence one one another. Attachment to school is mainly achieved through the teachers who are the ones to transfer certain social values and norms to children. Therefore, when investing into a society in order to develop and transform it, we also need to invest into teachers as individuals and not only into schools as institutions. School attachment has a negative correlation not only with juvenile delinquency (r = -0.29) but also with truancy (r = -0.20), school disorganization (r = -0.09), and repeating grades (r = -0.05). Truancy, which is related to repeating classes, can be explained in two ways: with a lack of juvenile presence in school, it is harder to make a connection; and/or with a lack of attachment to school comes a lack of interest in school and a sense of failure. In the case of school disorganization, the strongest positive correlation was found with the juvenile delinquency scale (r = 0.16); in general, it is negatively correlated with all positive school variables and positively with all negative school variables (truancy and juvenile delinquency). The result regarding the impact of the school disorganization scale on reported juvenile delinquency was not expected. However, this suggests that in the schools were juveniles reported a high level of fighting, stealing, vandalism, and drug use, fewer students had to repeat grades. However, juveniles who had been involved in delinquent behaviour also reported that vandalism is present in their school, as well as the consumption of drugs, stealing, and/or fighting. All school variables are statistically significant with age and gender at a level of 0.01, except for the case of age and school disorganization which is statistically significant at a 0.05 level. As all variables are statistically significant with more or less strong correlations, they are all added to the multivariate regression model.

Table 18 shows the results of the multivariate regression of self-reported juvenile delinquency depending on the school factors, age, and gender. In the presented model, school factors, age, and gender are independent variables, while the self-reported scale of lifetime juvenile delinquency is the dependent variable.[471] Serbia is

---

471   More about the structure of the scales is presented in the *Chapter 4*.

used as a reference country. All variables related to school are statistically significant at a level of 0.01, except in the case of school achievement that is not statistically significant. Among these school-related variables, truancy and school attachment have the highest beta coefficient at 0.15. Truancy has a positive beta coefficient, meaning that along with more truancy, there is also more delinquency.

Table 18   *Multivariate regression of self-reported juvenile delinquency depending on the school factors, age, and gender ($R^2 = 0.21$)*

Model	B	Std. Error	Beta	t	Sig.
Constant	1.53	0.12		12.8	0.000
Serbia (reference)	0				
Kosovo	-0.66	0.07	-0.14	-9.2	0.000
Croatia	-0.27	0.06	-0.07	-4.8	0.000
North Macedonia	-0.37	0.06	-0.08	-5.9	0.000
Bosnia and Herzegovina	-0.58	0.06	-0.17	-10.5	0.000
Attachment to school	-0.30	0.02	-0.15	-12.0	0.000
Bonding to teacher	-0.05	0.01	-0.05	-3.9	0.000
School disorganization	0.24	0.02	0.11	11.2	0.000
Truancy	0.59	0.04	0.15	14.3	0.000
School achievement	0.02	0.01	0.02	1.9	0.056
Repeated grade	0.55	0.13	0.04	4.2	0.000
Age 14	0.14	0.01	0.12	9.9	0.000
Gender (female)	0.41	0.03	0.13	12.8	0.000

In addition to *Table 18*, data suggest that those who are often truant are not strongly attached to their school and even claim to hate it. Contrarily, attachment to school has a negative beta coefficient. Therefore, attachment to one's school has an influence on respondents' juvenile delinquency in a way that higher attachment to school correlates with less delinquency. As expected, school disorganization also has an influence on delinquency, with a beta coefficient of 0.11. School achievement does not have an influence on delinquency, which is remarkable. A possible explanation is that a low level of school achievement does not automatically spark an engagement in crime, while the cause(s) for this should be sought somewhere else. However, repeating a grade has a slight influence on juvenile delinquency (beta coefficient of 0.4).

In the model presented in *Table 18*, there are differences between the countries if compared with Serbia as a reference country. Nevertheless, more differences can be seen between other countries in the Balkans, mainly between Kosovo and Croatia ($r = -0.66$ and $r = -0.27$). The results suggest that there is no big difference between Croatia and North Macedonia ($r = 0.27$ and $r = 0.37$) or between Kosovo and Bosnia and Herzegovina ($r = 0.66$ and $r = 0.58$) It is important to emphasize that in the model presented in *Table 18*, R^2 is 21 %. Therefore, 21 % of the variance can be explained by the model. When analysing the data based on the multivariate regression model by adding only country dummy variables, R^2 is 9 %. This variance explanation is mainly caused by the age-related differences between the countries.

5.2.4   Impact of religion on juvenile delinquency

The relationship between religion and delinquency has been studied since the early 1900s.[472] Since *Hirschi's* and *Stark's* (1969) publication "Hellfire and Delinquency",[473] the role of religion in crime and delinquency has been extensively examined. They changed the path of criminological research on religion. The results of their study indicated that religiosity and delinquency had not much relationship. This was an astonishing result at that time because most researchers were convinced of the prosocial impact of religion on human behaviour.[474] Subsequent research repeated the study by *Hirschi* and *Stark* (1969), and these replications both supported[475] and refuted[476] the original findings. After so much contradiction, the debate heated up on whether or not religiosity helps reduce delinquency.[477] Many studies concluded that the relationship between religion and delinquency lacked explanatory consensus.[478] One of the explanations for such diverse results was made through the morality of a society. Referring to their religiosity, the idea was that in moral societies, a strong relationship would be found between religion and delinquency, but in secularized societies, there would be little or no relationship.[479] This was substantiated in that studies in religious communities reported a high relationship, while studies in secular communities failed to find any such relationship.[480] Other researchers try to explain differences through the validity of the measures. In the past, they used various ways to measure religiosity, trying to find out which of its

---

472   *Knudten & Knudten* 1971.
473   *Hirschi & Stark* 1969.
474   *Stark* 1984.
475   *Burkett & White* 1974.
476   *Albrecht, Chadwick & Alcorn* 1977; *Higgins & Albrecht* 1977; *Jensen & Erickson* 1979.
477   *Kelly et al.* 2015, 506.
478   *Evans et al.* 1995; *Tittle & Welch* 1982.
479   *Stark, Kent & Doyle* 1982.
480   *Kelly et al.* 2015, 506.

aspects are important for delinquency. Empirical studies examining adolescents' religiosity and delinquency mostly focused on two measurements: religious involvement (religious service attendance) and religious salience (perceived importance of religion in one's life). In most research which used these measurements of religiosity, a negative association with delinquency was found, and when adding social control and social learning variables, findings remained statistically significant.[481] Others focused on explaining the relationship between religiosity and crime through different types of crime. Specifically, researchers argued that religion may not be significantly correlated with serious crimes, but it may be negatively correlated with minor ones like drug use.[482] They considered that minor disobedience violates norms, which is not clearly seen as lawbreaking in the respective society but is in conflict with religious values.[483]

The focus of this research is on the social control theory, which takes a look at specific elements within a religion that theoretically have an influence on delinquency. As stated before, *Hirschi's* (1969) social control theory considers that a lack of conventional social bonds increases the likelihoods of individuals to commit delinquent acts. The strength of these bonds is measured through the four elements of involvement, belief, commitment, and attachment. The more and stronger these ties are due to these elements, the smaller is the likelihood that an individual will engage in criminal behaviour. Consequently, these four elements will be described in terms of their application to religion. Involvement in the social control theory is based on the premise that an individual who is highly involved in community activities will not commit any delinquency. From the religion perspective, involvement can be understood as time spent with the institution and can be measured through attending religious service. Individuals who do so relatively often have lower odds of committing delinquent acts. In "Hellfire and Delinquency", *Hirschi* and *Stark* (1969) tested this correlation and found no effect. Subsequent research tested the correlation between religious involvement and delinquency with different measures, different types of crime and different sample age groups. Thus, when focusing on different types of delinquency, research reported that religious service attendance is related to status offences among adolescents.[484] However, no correlation was found between serious offences. Furthermore, in the case of youths and young adults, some research showed that religious service attendance among persons with a religious affiliation decreases the possibility of young people beginning to engage in alcohol and drug consumption.[485] Some research showed that combining religious involvement with the family

---

481 *Cochran & Akers* 1989; *Johnson & Siegel* 2008; *Regnerus* 2003.

482 *Burkett & White* 1974; *Cochran* 1988.

483 *Miller & Vuolo* 2018.

484 *Burkett* 1993.

485 *Bachman et al.* 2002; *Ulmer et al.* 2010.

indicators parental control and parental attachment in conjunction with some family characteristics decreases juvenile delinquency.[486]

The element of commitment in connection with religion in the social control theory is seen in a way that if an individual has invested time into building a religious identity, that individual may not want to commit delinquent acts that could result in the loss of such an investment. This is seen as a ratio between an investment and its gain (or loss). In practice, involvement in religion is measured through private prayer and commitment to the religion, which represents deep personal religious values beyond group-level involvement.[487] Religiosity proved to have an influence on the use of hard drugs like cocaine and heroin,[488] but praying showed an influence on soft drugs use, too.[489]

The third element of the social control theory by *Hirschi* (1969) is attachment. It is examined through the consideration of an individual's stated closeness to religion and the importance of his/her religious identity. Religion movements have formal but also informal social sanctions for delinquency behaviour, and a most dominant factor for informal social sanctions is religiosity. In general, those individuals who hold their religion to be very important are less likely to commit a crime. Researchers found that religiosity of juveniles significantly correlates with delinquency.[490] *Bachman et al.* (2002)[491] found that religiosity – seen as religious importance to the individual – had a negative relationship with cigarette use, alcohol abuse, marijuana use, and cocaine use. Furthermore, some researchers have found that individuals who reported that religion is important to them showed a decrease in their seducibility to delinquent behaviour.[492]

The fourth element is belief, which can be considered as an individual's identification with a particular religion, and therefore, the assumption is that a strong belief influences delinquency.[493] If individuals have a strong religious belief, there is a high probability that they will employ it in their everyday life and that they would see a delinquent act as immoral behaviour. This element was mostly tested through the influence of delinquency on belief, showing that delinquent behaviour can affect one's belief in religious institutions.[494]

---

486 *Petts* 2009.
487 *Miller & Vuolo* 2018.
488 *Benda & Corwyn* 1997.
489 *Reisig, Wolfe & Pratt* 2012.
490 *Litchfield, Thomas & Li* 1997.
491 *Bachman et al.* 2002.
492 *Regnerus & Elder* 2003.
493 *Miller & Vuolo* 2018.
494 *Uecker, Regnerus & Vaaler* 2007; *Benda & Corwyn* 1997.

Most of the above-mentioned research was conducted in the USA and Western European countries. There is, however, a lack of criminological research on the impact of religion on juvenile delinquency in the Balkans. This research provides the first overview of the correlation between religion and juvenile delinquency in the Balkans.

5.2.4.1 Religion affiliation, religiosity, and juvenile delinquency

In this section, the focus is put on the relationship between different religious affiliations, religiosity, and juvenile delinquency. Religion plays an important role in the Balkan region, as most of its inhabitants embrace religion as an element of national belonging.[495] Croatia has a Catholic majority, Serbia has an Orthodox majority; in Kosovo, the majority of people identify as Muslims, while in North Macedonia and Bosnia and Herzegovina, a majority identifies as Muslims or Orthodox, including a smaller proportion of Catholics.[496] The research sample contains the same structure by country.[497] Three of the countries have a clear representation of mainly one religion (Croatia, Kosovo, and Serbia), and two countries have a mixture of two or more religions (North Macedonia and Bosnia and Herzegovina) (see *Table 2*). In the overall sample, the proportion of the different religious affiliations is presented in *Table 2*. Muslim is the strongest representative religion in the sample, followed by Orthodox and Catholics. It should be noted that only 3.8 % of respondents reported that they considered themselves as atheists, and only 1.9 % reported other religious affiliations. It is clear that other religious affiliations than Catholic, Muslim, or Orthodox are very rare in the Balkan cluster. This is in line with the results from the Pew Research Centre research conducted in Central and Eastern Europe. Research has shown that in most Balkan countries, people who say that religion is important to them are more likely than others to voice strong pride in their national citizenship. Therefore, one of the explanations used for such a low presence of other religious groups and the low level of atheists is that belonging to a certain religious affiliation is important for being a "true" citizen of that country. It should be noted that religious affiliation is strongly connected with national belonging, and ethnicity is strongly related to religious affiliation. Bosnia and Herzegovina is very diverse with respect to religions, since no single religious group forms a clear majority, which is due to the ethnic division within the country.

As seen in previous research, religiosity also plays a role in juvenile delinquency. The focus is on religiosity differences and different influences it appears to have

---

495 Pew Research Centre 2017; for more, see *Chapter 4.3.1.6*.
496 For details, see Pew Research Centre 2017; Pew Research Centre 2015.
497 For more, see *Chapter 5.1*.

on delinquency. Religiosity was brought up in the ISRD3 questionnaire in the following format: "How important is religion to you (personally) in your everyday life?", and the response options were as follows: 1 = very unimportant, 2 = quite unimportant, 3 = a bit unimportant, 4 = a bit important, 5 = quite important, 6 = very important. *Figure 8* presents religiosity by country. In Kosovo and North Macedonia, the highest rate of respondents reported that religion is very important in their everyday lives (64 % and 60 %). In Bosnia and Herzegovina, also more than half of respondents said that religion is very important for them. However, in Croatia and Serbia, the rate of those who reported the highest value for this question was "very unimportant" (18 % and 20 %). In comparison with other countries from the region, this is around three times lower. In Serbia, most juveniles reported that religion is a bit important in their everyday lives (42 %). In Croatia, the highest rate was recorded for the value "quite important" (33 %). If looking at religiosity as a dichotomised variable with two categories (important and unimportant), more than 78 % of juveniles reported that religion is important in their everyday lives. The highest rate would be found in Kosovo (94 %), followed by North Macedonia (92 %) and Bosnia and Herzegovina (92 %). Croatia would have the lowest rate at 78 %. Overall, it can be concluded that juveniles in the Balkans have a high level of religiosity, meaning that religion plays an important role in their everyday lives. Therefore, it is important not only to see their level of religiosity but also its impact on crime.

Figure 24   Religiosity by country

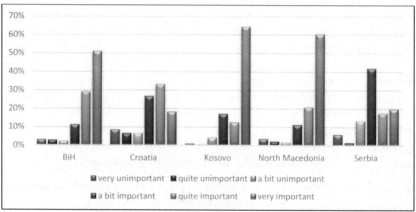

Table 19 Pearson correlation of religion-related variables and juvenile crime

		Juvenile delinquency scale	Religious affiliation	Religiosity	Gender	Age14
Juvenile delinquency scale	Pearson Corr.	1				
	Sig. (2-tailed)					
	N	8202				
Religious affiliation	Pearson Corr.	-.050**	1			
	Sig. (2-tailed)	.000				
	N	8184	8440			
Religiosity	Pearson Corr.	-.191**	.247**	1		
	Sig. (2-tailed)	.000	.000			
	N	8075	8295	8308		
Gender	Pearson Corr.	.164**	.023*	-.001	1	
	Sig. (2-tailed)	.000	.037	.964		
	N	8195	8438	8304	8452	
Age14	Pearson Corr.	.280**	-.010	-.219**	.025*	1
	Sig. (2-tailed)	.000	.350	.000	.023	
	N	8188	8427	8296	8441	8442

**) Correlation is significant at a 0.01 level (2-tailed).

*) Correlation is significant at a 0.05 level (2-tailed).

5.2.4.2   Multivariate regression of school-related variables

Table 19 is a correlation matrix for religion-related variables as well as gender, age, and self-reported juvenile crime. The results suggest that all religion-related variables are statistically significant in correlation with crime at a level of 0.01. Religion affiliation has a low beta coefficient of -0.05, while it is a bit stronger in the case of religiosity (-0.19). The correlation between religious affiliation and religiosity is also statistically significant, with a beta coefficient of 0.25. This result suggests that religious affiliation has an impact on religiosity. Age does not prove to have a correlation with religious affiliation but, as expected, with religiosity (beta coefficient of -0.22). At a level of 0.01, gender is not in a statistically significant correlation with both religion-related variables. In total, all religion-related variables will be included in multivariate analyses as they have a statistically significant correlation with the self-reported juvenile crime scale.

Table 20 shows the results of the multivariate regression of self-reported juvenile crime depending on the religion factors, age, and gender. In the presented model, these three variables are independent, while the self-reported scale of lifetime juvenile crime is a dependent variable.[498] In this model, the religion variables were used as dichotomised variables. Each religion is presented by one dichotomised variable, using atheist and other religion[499] as a reference point. Results suggest that there is almost no difference between religions, but there is a difference if compared with a reference point (atheist and others). All religion affiliations have a negative beta coefficient. Religiosity also has an influence on juvenile crime, but with a lower beta coefficient of -0.09. The effect is negative, meaning that with higher religiosity, there is a lower rate of juvenile crime.

In the model presented in *Table 20*, there are differences between the countries if compared with Serbia as a reference country. Between Serbia and Kosovo, the difference is at its maximum (r = -1.0). Croatia shows the lowest difference to Serbia, so it has the highest difference between Kosovo. The results suggest that there is no big difference between Bosnia and Herzegovina and North Macedonia (r = 0.63 and r = 0.76). It is important to emphasize that in the model presented in *Table 20*, R^2 is 15 %. Therefore, 15 % of the variance can be explained by the model. When analysing the data based on the multivariate regression model by adding only country dummy variables, R^2 is 9 %. Overall, it can be argued that there is a negative impact of religiosity on juvenile crime. With higher religiosity, there is a lower probability for juvenile crime. However, the impact is not as strong as in the case of parental control. There is also a difference between juveniles who reported that they belong

---

498   More about the structures of the scales is presented in *Chapter 4*.

499   Other religions such as Protestants and Evangelicals participated in the overall sample with 1.9 %.

to one of the three dominant religions in the Balkans and those who reported that they are atheist or belong to some other religion.

Table 20 Multivariate regression of self-reported juvenile crime depending on the religion factors, age, and gender ($R^2 = 0.15$)

Model	B	Std. Error	Beta	t	Sig.
Constant	2.08	0.10		20.2	0.000
Serbia (reference)	0				
Kosovo	-1.00	0.09	-0.21	-11.7	0.000
Croatia	-0.39	0.09	-0.10	-4.3	0.000
North Macedonia	-0.63	0.07	-0.14	-9.4	0.000
Bosnia and Herzegovina	-0.76	0.07	-0.22	-11.4	0.000
Other religion (reference)	0				
Catholics	-0.35	0.09	-0.09	-4.0	0.000
Muslims	-0.26	0.09	-0.08	-3.0	0.002
Orthodox	-0.32	0.09	-0.09	-3.7	0.000
Religious attachment	-0.10	0.01	-0.09	-7.4	0.000
Age14	0.19	0.01	0.16	12.9	0.000
Gender (female)	0.50	0.03	0.16	15.2	0.000

Chapter 6

Conclusion

6.1 Descriptive Statistics

The ISRD3 study is the first self-report study with a primary focus on crime conducted in the Balkan region.[500] Therefore, it is also the first study that can provide a review of juvenile crime in the region. Consequently, it faced some challenges, which is reflected in the sample characteristics. Bosnia and Herzegovina used a national sample because of its complex structure, while other countries conducted the survey only in the capital and one medium-sized city. The differences between the country samples are the most obvious with regard to the age of the respondents. The Kosovo sample has younger participants than the other countries (mean age: 13.06 years), while the Serbian sample has the oldest respondents (mean age: 15.46 years). This should be taken into consideration when presenting descriptive statistics, because the age-crime curve reaches a peak in teenage years and then decreases.[501] Therefore, when looking at the lifetime and last-year prevalence of 14 delinquent acts (*Tables 3* and *4*), it is not surprising that Serbia has the highest rates while Kosovo records the lowest ones.

The prevalence rates of 14 different delinquent acts showed that among juveniles in all studied countries, illegal downloading is the most representative act, followed by graffiti. Depending on the country, the third-most-reported offence is either shoplifting or participating in group fights. In the Balkan cluster, 8.1 % of respondents reported having participated in a group fight, which can be seen as a part of the primary and secondary school children's culture in the Balkans. This is something the programmes dealing with preventing violence in schools should focus on. On the other hand, illegal downloading is seen as being socially acceptable behaviour, caused by the bad economic situation in the region. Therefore, it is apparent that most young offenders reported acts of a rather non-serious nature. More serious offences are reported by less than 6 % of respondents in most of the Balkan countries.

Figure 4 illustrates that Serbia has the highest rates in both minor and serious lifetime and last-year offences. Serbia also has the highest differences between lifetime and last-year offences, which may be due to Serbia having the oldest sample among all

---

500   The exception is Bosnia and Herzegovina which had also participated in the ISRD2 study.
501   *Farrington* 1986, 189.

countries in the region. In contrast, in the case of Kosovo, there are almost no differences between these two categories, probably because of its young sample. This highlights the obvious impact age has on the sample. All serious offences in all Balkan countries were reported by less than 10 % of respondents, except in the case of Serbia. Between 20 % and 30 % of respondents reported minor offences in most countries of the Balkan region; only in Serbia, they were reported by more than 30 %, while in Kosovo, this share was below 15 %. The analyses of different types of crime – be it property crimes or acts of violence or vandalism – suggest that the most frequent types of crime in all countries are vandalism acts. This is mainly because of graffiti. Some cities organize programmes that target graffiti sprayers, but, evidently, there is either a shortage of such programmes or they prove to be rather ineffective. Results also suggested that violence is a serious problem in Serbia and North Macedonia. It is worth noting that North Macedonia has the highest rate of last-year violence among all participating countries. Other countries have almost the same rates of last-year violence, at less than 10 %. Serbia reported the highest rate of property crime, followed by Croatia, while in the other countries, the rates were lower than 10.5 %.

A variety scale was made in order to see how many respondents reported having committed more than one offence. Lifetime offending versatility by country showed that among those who reported having committed a crime, most respondents reported only one offence, with the exception of Serbia. Croatia recorded the highest number of respondents who reported one offence (39.4 %), while other countries recorded rates that were twice as low, i.e., less than 20 %. The case of Serbia points to an alarming situation, as 28.8 % of respondents there reported having committed three or more offences in their lifetime. This suggests that every fourth student in Serbia had committed not only a minor offence but also at least one serious offence. Here, the smallest percentage was found among respondents who reported no offence at all, compared to other separate categories (participants who reported one, two, three, or more offences). It can be concluded that Serbia is facing a problem with serious juvenile crime, which should be tackled by implementing national programmes dealing with this problem at an early stage in life, preferably already in primary schools.

When analysing the juvenile crime prevalence based on gender, it becomes clear that in general, the female population commits fewer criminal offences than the male population. The only exception to this pattern can be seen in the case of graffiti vandalism in Croatia and Bosnia and Herzegovina, where females reported slightly more incidences than males. This is in line with the impression that graffiti (as well as illegal downloading) is not perceived as a crime but as a form of art and creative expression.

The age-crime curve continuously rises from 12 to 17 years of age in cases of property and vandalism. However, the Balkan sample indicates that violence reaches its peak at 16 years of age. After that age, the curve stagnates. The results are almost the same in cases of lifetime and last-year offences, while the only thing that varies is the steepness of the curve. Looking at the age-crime curve by country, the only difference that stands out refers to violent offences in Kosovo. In this case, the peak is at 13 years of age. The curve decreases when respondents reach 15 years of age, contrary to the other Balkan countries.

Another exception in the age-crime curve in the Balkan cluster is visible in the case of property crime in Serbia. Here, the age-crime curve has a more or less constant and very high rate. It reaches its peak at the age of 13 and then again at the age of 17. Therefore, we can say that the age-crime curve does not exist as a curve in Serbia.

Summarizing, there are differences in the crime rates between Balkan countries. The distribution of crime is very clear. Serbia has the highest rates among all observed countries, while Kosovo, which has the lowest crime rates, is situated at the opposite end of the incidence scale. This can be explained primarily by the age differences between the samples and by the validity of the self-report survey, which is a clear product of non-existing empirical studies in the Balkans. The validity of the data depended on the readiness of respondents to answer questions honestly, which, in turn, was possibly influenced by the still looming anxiety towards the authorities left over from past regimes, despite the anonymity of the survey. This is most obvious in the case of Kosovo (see *Figure 1*), which has by far the lowest rates of reported crime in all observed countries. Therefore, the sensitive validity of the data should be taken into consideration in any future self-report research in the Balkan region. However, this research has identified the phenomenology of juvenile crime and has emphasised the most frequent offences in the Balkans. These data foster guidelines for policy-makers to decide on new solutions that are to be implemented.

6.2 Explaining Juvenile Crime in the Balkans

The main idea of this research project was to identify the causes of juvenile crime in the Balkan region. It tested the influence of family, economy, school, and religion on juvenile crime in the region. Analyses were made relying on the informal control theory, which is based on *Hirschi's* social control theory (1969). Its basic premise is that juveniles who develop strong bonds and are closely controlled by authority figures (parents, teachers, priests…) do not want to disappoint them, consequently behaving in a norm-conforming way. Family plays a central role in the lives of juveniles in the Balkans. As a result, family influence was tested from different angles. Two different scales were used for parental control and parental attachment respectively, as well as other family-related variables, such as having dinner with one's parents, parents' serious illnesses, etc. Each of these scales and variables represented a different connection between family and juvenile crime. In *Hirschi's* research, parental attachment was seen as the most important connection, which was not the case in this study. Among all family-related indicators, parental control plays the most important role in juvenile crime in the Balkans, followed by parental attachment. The results show that strong parental control is the primary factor for decreasing juvenile crime in the region. However, parental attachment also plays an important role, though not to such an extent as parental control. Multivariate regression analyses have also shown that the type of family structure – whether it was living with one parent, both parents, or a stepfather/stepmother – also has an impact on juvenile crime. Analyses also suggest that juveniles who have been living through a parent's serious illness or experienced serious conflict between their parents have a higher probability of getting involved in juvenile crime. However, family control proved to have the strongest impact among all the family factors. This finding is in line with the hypothesis that parental control exerts a stronger influence on crime than attachment does for juveniles raised in post-socialist countries, countries with young democracies, and countries that are still in a transitional phase. In conclusion, parental control and monitoring are considered to be two of the main factors for preventing juvenile crime.

The second segment of the analyses focused on examining the economic variables related to juvenile crime in the region. Socio-economic disadvantages is the most controversial correlate of crime. However, this study sought to examine the association between economy and juvenile crime, seeking a foothold in the informal control theory. The bad economic situation in conjunction with high unemployment rates in the Balkan region undoubtedly affects the whole family and therefore juvenile crime in general. Consequently, as part of this research, the analyses focused on the mother and father employment as well as the family funds status. Surprisingly, multivariate regression analyses showed that only the mother's unemployment has a positive impact on juvenile crime. It should be noted that female unemployment rates are very high throughout the Balkans. To put these data in perspective, in 2014, the female unemployment rate in Bosnia and Herzegovina reached 30 %, whereas this applied to only 5 % of the female population in Western European countries, such as Germany. The consequence of such high unemployment rates is that mothers tend to stay at home and take care of raising their children, while fathers rather take care of earning the family income. However, the cultural setting of the region also plays an important role in that it supports the same idea.

Further analyses focused on the impact of school on juvenile crime. The hypothesis was that the higher attachment is to school, the less susceptible one is to juvenile crime. Again, this segment focused on the informal control theory. Juveniles who display strong bonds to school have a high risk of losing these bonds when participating in criminal behaviour. Control theories assume that we all have an urge to commit delinquent acts, but we will resist because someone or something prevents us from doing so. The multivariate regression analyses have shown that in the Balkans, truancy and school attachment have the strongest influence on juvenile crime among all school-related factors. Attachment to school was analysed on four different levels. The most surprising results refer to student opinions on how interesting their classes are and whether they like going to school. In the case of Croatia, more than half of respondents thought that their classes are not interesting so they did not like going to school. Therefore, the high levels of reported truancy could also have resulted from a lack of interesting classes and a generally negative opinion about the schooling system. This should alarm regional policy-makers, who should consider reforming the curricula for primary and secondary education. School disorganization was also measured through four different offences (stealing, fighting, vandalism, and drug use). Vandalism and fighting were the most frequently reported offences in school. In Serbia, more than 30 % of students reported that drug dealing was an issue in their school. Therefore, future school programmes should focus on obviating school vandalism and fighting as well as educating students on the harmful consequences of drug use.

Final analyses were done that aimed at finding a connection between religion and juvenile crime. "Hellfire and Delinquency", a publication by *Hirschi* and *Stark* (1969), changed the path of criminological research on religion. *Hirschi's* social control theory recognises four main elements of religion in connection with crime. Involvement is measured by the frequency of attending religious services, commitment is seen in that an individual has invested time into developing a religious identity, while attachment is examined through one's closeness to religion and the importance of an individual's religious identity. The last element is belief, measured by the individual's identification with a particular religion. The ISRD3 questionnaire offered the possibility to test only two out of four of the above-mentioned elements, namely religion affiliation and religiosity. Study findings suggested that there is a certain connection between juvenile delinquency and the respondent's level of religiosity, while the affiliation to a certain religious group (such as Christians, Muslims, etc.) proved to have no effect as a relevant impact factor. However, religiosity has a low impact on juvenile crime, stressing that higher religiosity results in a proportionally lower rate of juvenile crime. Therefore, with respect to juvenile crime, juvenile affiliation to a particular religion is not important, but juvenile belief in his/her religion is. Summarising this, the study findings show that the informal control theory is valid in the Balkan region, especially regarding the impact of family on juvenile crime.

The main idea of this project was to find causes of juvenile crime in the Balkan region. It tested the influences of family, economy, school, and religion. Analyses were made based on the informal control theory, which in turn is based on *Hirschi's* social control theory (1969). The basic premise was that juveniles who have strong bonds to and experience strong control by authority figures (parents, teachers, priests, etc.) are less susceptible to crime since they do not want to disappoint them and consequently behave in a norm-conforming way. The family plays a highly important role in the lives of juveniles in the Balkans. Therefore, its influence was tested from different perspectives. Two different scales were used (parental control and parental attachment), as well as other family-related variables, such as regularly having dinner with one's parents, serious illness of parents, etc. Each of these scales and variables represented a different connection between one's family and juvenile crime. In *Hirschi's* research, parental attachment was seen as the most important connection, which was not the case in the study at hand. Among all family-related indicators, parental control proved to play the most important role in juvenile crime in the Balkans, followed by parental attachment. The multivariate regression analyses show that different types of family structure, such as living with one parent, both parents, or one's stepfather/stepmother, also have an impact on juvenile crime. Analyses furthermore suggest that juveniles who have experienced a serious illness among their parents or serious conflicts between them have a higher probability to get involved in juvenile crime. However, among all family-related factors, the strongest impact on juvenile crime was found in family control. This finding is in line with the hypothesis that for juveniles raised in post-socialist societies, in countries with young democracies or still being in a transitional phase, parental control exerts a stronger influence on crime than attachment does. Parental control and monitoring thus constitute two of the factors which play a vital role in preventing juvenile crime.

The next step of the analyses examined economy-related variables. Socio-economic disadvantages are the most controversial correlates of crime. However, this study sought to examine the association between the economy and juvenile crime by seeking a foothold in the informal control theory. The bad economic situation in conjunction with high unemployment rates in the Balkan region undoubtedly affects whole families and therefore juvenile crime in general. Thus, in this research, the analyses focused on mother and father employment as well as family funds statuses. Interestingly, multivariate regression analyses show that only maternal unemployment has a positive impact on the juvenile crime. It should be noted in this context that the female unemployment rates are very high in the Balkans, e.g. at 30 % in Bosnia and Herzegovina in 2014, as opposed to Western European countries such as Germany, where only 5 % of females are actively looking for a job. The consequence of such high unemployment rates is that mothers stay at home and take care of raising their children, while the fathers contribute the family income through work. However, the cultural setting in the region also plays an important role by supporting the same idea, i.e., that the mothers are responsible for raising the children, while the fathers are responsible for earning money.

Further analyses of this research focused on the impact of the schools on juvenile crime. The hypothesis was that a high attachment to school results in low juvenile crime. Again, the focus was on the informal control theory. Control theories assume that all humans have an urge to commit delinquent acts, but we will not give in to the temptation because someone or something prevents us from doing so. The multivariate regression analyses show that among all school-related factors, truancy and school attachment have the strongest influence on juvenile crime in the Balkans. Attachment to school was analysed on four different levels. Juveniles with strong bonds to school have a high risk of losing these bonds with participating in crime behaviour. The somewhat disillusioning results for the education system in the participating countries were found among the students' opinions on how interesting their classes are and whether they like going to school. In the case of Croatia, more than half of respondents thought that their classes are not interesting and that they do not enjoy going to school. Therefore, a high presence of reported truancy could also be the result of uninteresting classes and a bad reputation of the schools. This should be alarming for policy-makers, who should consider reforming the curricula for primary and higher education. School disorganization was measured along four different offences (stealing, fighting, vandalism, and drug use). The most frequently reported offences in school were vandalism and fighting. In Serbia, more than 30 % of students reported that drug dealing occurs in their school. Therefore, future school programmes should focus on preventing school vandalism and fighting, as well as educating students about the risks and consequences of drug use.

Final analyses were carried out aiming at finding a connection between religion and juvenile crime. "Hellfire and Delinquency" by *Hirschi* and *Stark* (1969) has changed the path of criminological research on religion. *Hirschi's* social control theory recognizes four main elements of religion in the context of crime. Its involvement was measured through the frequency of attending religious services and commitment in terms of an individual having invested time into developing a religious identity in the past, while attachment was examined through one's closeness to religion and the importance of his/her religious identity. The last element that was examined was belief, measured by the individual's identification with a particular religion. The ISRD3 questionnaire enabled only to test two out of these four elements, i.e. religion affiliation and religiosity. The study findings suggested that certain correlations exist to juvenile delinquency when looking at the respondents' levels of religiosity, while the affiliation to a certain religious group (such as Christians, Muslims, etc.) did not seem to be a relevant impact factor. However, religiosity also has a low impact on juvenile crime: with increasing religiosity comes a lower rate of juvenile crime. Therefore, a juvenile affiliation to a particular religion did not seem to be of relevance, but a juvenile belief in religion did. In summary, the study findings showed that the informal control theory is valid in the Balkan region, especially regarding the impact of an individual's family on juvenile crime.

Chapter 7

Summary

7.1   Overview of the Study

The author conducted the ISRD3 survey in Croatia as a member of the Max Planck Partner Group for 'Balkan Criminology' (MPPG) under the leadership of Assoc. Prof. Dr. *Anna-Maria Getoš Kalac*. The ISRD3 study was conducted in two cities in Croatia, and the author worked as a leader of a student group that was responsible for conducting fieldwork. As part of the ISRD3 project, members of the Croatian team were allowed to use data from other countries that also participated in the project. The author decided to focus her research exclusively on countries from the Balkan region, as it is considered *sui generis*. The research had two aims: to present an overview of juvenile crime in the region and to work out the main influencing factors. In conclusion, the survey focused on measuring the phenomenology and aetiology of juvenile crime in the Balkan region. A juvenile crime scale was drafted to this end and was mainly used as a dependent variable of all statistical models in these analyses.

In this PhD project, the ISRD data served as a base for presenting the phenomenology of juvenile crime in the region. Analyses were carried out for lifetime and last-year prevalence of 14 delinquent acts, different types of crime, minor and serious offences, lifetime offending versatility, as well as gender differences between offenders who reported different types of offences and age-crime curves. Some of these variables were constructed specifically for the purpose of this research. This was crucial for presenting the phenomenology through its categorization not only by different offences but also by different legal categories such as minor and serious offences.

The aetiology of juvenile crime in the Balkans mainly focused on the informal control theory. Therefore, the analyses were based on the following indicators: family, economy, school, and religion. For this purpose, various scales were created in order to measure the indicators' different aspects (i.e., family control scale, religiosity, school attachment scale, etc.). The analyses were based on two constructed levels. The first level provided an overview of all indicators by country and the correlations between different variables. This provided a correlation matrix with the possibility to see which variables have the strongest influence on lifetime juvenile crime. The next step referred to multivariate regression analyses, which represented the second

level of analyses in this doctoral research. This step included variables that proved
to be in a strong correlation with juvenile crime in the correlation matrix. In order to
contain the effects of age in these research findings – and due to the significant age
differences between country samples (i.e., between Kosovo and Serbia) –, Age14
was added as a new variable in all statistical models. After testing all models which
contained different variables and scales, only the main findings were presented in
this research.

Chart 1   Overview of research

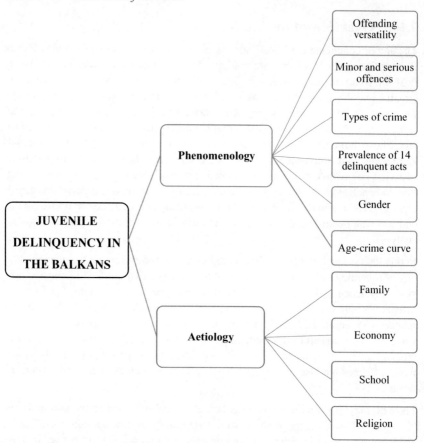

7.2   Main Research Findings

Chart 2 presents the main research findings on juvenile crime in the Balkans. The
analyses showed that Serbia has the highest rates in all delinquent acts, followed
by Croatia. At the other end of the scale, Kosovo had the lowest rates. The main

reported offences are minor ones, with illegal downloading and graffiti being the most-reported offences in all observed countries. Compared to other Balkan countries, Bosnia and Herzegovina as well as Kosovo reported very low rates of shoplifting. Serious offences are very rare in the Balkans, except in the case of Serbia which has at least twice as many minor and serious offences (lifetime) in comparison to other countries in the region. In North Macedonia, the rate of group fighting is higher than in other Balkan countries. When looking at the number of reported crimes per respondent (offending versatility), the data showed differences between the countries. Croatia has the highest percentage of juveniles who reported having committed one offence in their lifetime, whereas these rates for Bosnia and Herzegovina, Kosovo, and North Macedonia are much higher. Contrary to that, Serbia has the highest rate of juveniles who reported three or more offences in their lifetime.

As expected, gender differences also occurred between the reported offences: males reported more crimes than females. However, female respondents in Bosnia and Herzegovina and Croatia reported a higher rate of graffiti vandalism than males. Analyses of the age-crime curve suggest that the rate of crime is on an increase between the ages of 12 and 17 in cases of property offences and vandalism. However, for violence, the rate increases until the age of 16. The lifetime violence age-crime curve is stable beyond this age, while last-year violence decreases among older respondents. In Kosovo, the age-crime curve of violence reaches its peak at the age of 14 and then rapidly decreases. In Serbia, property crime does not follow the age-crime curve of the Balkan cluster. It reaches its peak at the age of 13 and another one at 17.

In conclusion, the Balkan countries show differences not only in the prevalence of juvenile crime but also in the reported types of crime.

When looking for factors that have an influence on juvenile crime in the region, the analyses were based on the informal control theory. This theory was used because of the specific cultural and historical setting in the Balkans. Results showed that parental control is the main influencing factor for juvenile crime in the region. This finding is in line with the informal control theory, which suggests that a stronger family bond results in lower crime rates. Besides parental control, strong parental attachment also plays a role in decreasing juvenile crime, although it is not as strong. The results suggest that with respect to their children's law-abidingness, it might be more important for parents to focus on their supervision and direct control of children rather than on the quality of attachment during a juvenile's infancy. Other family-related factors that were analysed in this doctoral thesis also showed a statistically significant correlation with juvenile crime, but none was as strong as parental control. Mothers' unemployment is the only economy-related variable which proved to have an influence on juvenile crime.

Truancy and attachment to school have the strongest impact on juvenile crime among all school-related indicators. Religion affiliation has no significant impact on juvenile crime, while religiosity does. To conclude, the results suggest that the informal control theory is applicable to juvenile crime in the Balkans.

Chart 2   Overview of the main findings on the juvenile crime phenomenology in the Balkans

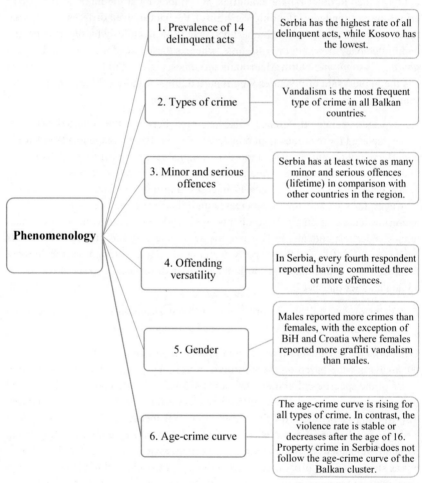

Chart 3   Overview of the main findings in aetiology in the Balkans

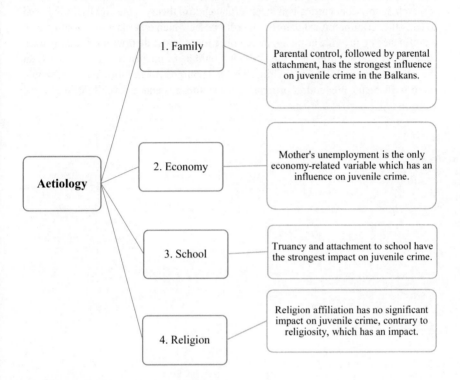

1. Family

Parental control, followed by parental attachment, has the strongest influence on juvenile crime in the Balkans.

Aetiology

2. Economy

Mother's unemployment is the only economy-related variable which has an influence on juvenile crime.

3. School

Truancy and attachment to school have the strongest impact on juvenile crime.

4. Religion

Religion affiliation has no significant impact on juvenile crime, contrary to religiosity, which has an impact.

7.3   Future Fields of Research

This thesis showed that self-report research in the field of juvenile crime in the Balkans is still scarce. Therefore, self-report studies should be included in governmental funding practices more and more. There is also a need to increase the political will to develop juvenile justice policies on "evidence-based" approaches such as self-report surveys. These practices are currently not applied. The region should also be more involved in various cross-national studies. It is important to stress that researchers should pay attention to methodological issues by running a range of reliability and validity tests in order to find a way to bridge the current validity problems of self-report studies in the region. Therefore, Balkan countries should take part in the fourth sweep of the ISRD study. This will give already participating countries the opportunity to see the trends in juvenile crime and enable new members to measure the prevalence and incidence rates of juvenile crime. The main future field of research should focus on the aetiology of juvenile crime in the Balkans. This doctoral research mainly concentrated on the informal control theory. This highlights the need to test other criminological theories in order to see which other factors possibly have an influence on juvenile crime in the region. Most of these theories have mainly been tested in Western Europe and the USA. It would be of interest to see to what extent the results differ in the Balkan setting. The main purpose of all future research should be to draft better prevention programmes in order to reduce juvenile crime in the Balkans.

References

Adler, F. (1975): Sisters in Crime. New York: McGraw-Hill.

Aebi, M.F. (2009): Self-reported delinquency surveys in Europe, in: Zauberman, R. (ed.), Self-reported crime and deviance studies in Europe. Vubpress Brussels University Press, 11–51.

Agnew, R. & Brezina, T. (2012): Juvenile delinquency: Causes and control. New York: Oxford University Press.

Ajduković, M., Rimac, I., Rajter, M. & Sušac, N. (2013): Epidemiološko istraživanje prevalencije i incidencije nasilja nad djecom u obitelji u Hrvatskoj, Annual of Social work, Vol. 19(3), 367–412.

Akers, R.L. (1964): Socio-Economic Status and Delinquency Behaviour: A Retest. The Journal of Research in Crime and Delinquency 1(1), 38–46.

Akers, R.L., Krohn, M.D., Lanza-Kaduce, L. & Radosevich, M. (1979): Social learning and deviant behavior: A specific test of a general theory. American Sociological Review 44, 636–655.

Albrecht, H.-J. (1988): Comparative research on crime and delinquency – the role and relevance of national penal codes and criminal justice systems, in: Klein, M.W. (ed.), Cross-National Research in Self-Reported Crime and Delinquency. NATO ASI series. Series D, Behavioural and social sciences: no. 50, 227–248.

Albrecht, H.-J. & Kilchling, M. (2002): Jugendstrafrecht in Europa. Freiburg i.Br.: Max-Planck-Institut für ausländisches und internationales Strafrecht.

Albrecht, S.L., Chadwick, B.A. & Alcorn, D.S. (1977): Religiosity and deviance: Application of an attitude-behavior contingent consistency model. Journal for the Scientific Study of Religion 16(3), 263–274.

Allardt, E. (1990): Challenges for comparative social research. Acta Sociologica 33, 183–193.

Anderson, L.S., Chiricos, T.G. & Waldo, G.P. (1977): Formal and informal sanctions: A comparison of deterrent effects. Social Problems 25, 103–112.

Andersson, L. (2009): Self-Report Delinquency in Sweden, in: Zauberman, R. (ed.), Self-reported crime and deviance studies in Europe. Brussels: Vubpress Brussels University Press, 11–51.

Armer, M. & Grimshaw, A.D. (1973): Comparative social research: Methodological Problems and Strategies. New York, NY: Wiley.

Arnold, W.R. (1966): Continuities in research: Scaling delinquent behaviour. Social Problems 13, 59–66.

Austin, R.L. (1993): Recent trends in official male and female crime rates: the convergence controversy. Journal of Criminal Justice 21, 457–466.

Bachman, J.G., O'Malley, P.M., Schulenberg, J.E., Johnston, L.D., Bryant, A.L. & Merline, A.C. (2002): The decline of substance use in young adulthood: Changes in social activities, roles, and beliefs. Mahway, NJ: Lawrence Erlbaum.

Baker, C.K., Hishinuma, E.S., Chang, J.Y. & Nixon, D.C. (2010): The relationship among exposure to stressful life events, drug use, and violence perpetration in a sample of Native Hawaiian, Samoan, and Filipino adolescents. Journal of Interpersonal Violence 25, 379–399.

Belfast Youth Development Research Team (2012): The Belfast Youth Development Study: A Longitudinal Study of Adolescent Drug Use, Well-Being and Behaviour Undertaken at the Institute of Child Care Research – A Summary of Published Findings.

Benda, B.B. & Corwyn, R.F. (1997): Religion and delinquency: The relationship after considering family and peer influences. Journal for the Scientific Study of Religion 36, 81–92.

Bennett, R.R. (2009): Comparative criminological and criminal justice research and the data that drive them. International Journal of Comparative and Applied Criminal Justice 33, 171–192.

Biglan, A., Duncan, T.E., Ary, D.V. & Smolkowski, K. (1995): Peer and parental influences on adolescent tobacco use. Journal of Behavioral Medicine 18(4), 315–330.

Bjarnason, T. (1995): Administration mode bias in school survey on alcohol, tobacco and illicit drug use. Addiction 90, 555–559.

Boers, K. & Reinecke, J. (eds.) (2007): Delinquenz im Jugendalter. Erkenntnisse einer Münsteraner Längsschnittstudie. Münster: Waxmann.

Bouffard, L.A. (2009) Age and Crime, in: Miller, J.M. (ed.), 21st century criminology: a reference handbook. Los Angeles: Sage, 28–35.

Bowling, B., Graham, J. & Ross, A. (1994): Self-reported offending among young people in England and Wales, in: Junger-Tas, J. et al. (eds.), Delinquent Behavior Among Young People in the Western World: First Results of the International Self-Report Delinquency Study. Amsterdam: RDC – Ministry of Justice, Kugler Publications, 42–64.

Boyce, W., Torsheim, T., Currie, C. & Zambon, A. (2006): The Family Affluence Scale as a Measure of National Wealth: Validation of an Adolescent Self-Report Measure. Social Indicators Research 78, 473–487.

Brettfeld, K. & Wetzels, P. (2007): Muslime in Deutschland: Integration, Integrationsbarrieren, Religion sowie Einstellungen zu Demokratie, Rechtsstaat und politisch-religiös motivierter Gewalt; Ergebnisse von Befragungen im Rahmen einer multizentrischen Studie in städtischen Lebensräumen. Berlin, Bundesministerium des Inneren.

Broidy, L.M. (1995): Direct supervision and delinquency: Assessing the adequacy of structural proxies. Journal of Criminal Justice Vol. 23(6), 541–554.

Budimlić, M., Maljević, A. & Muratbegović, E. (2010): Bosnia and Herzegovina, in: Junger-Tas, J. et al. (eds.), Juvenile Delinquency in Europe and Beyond. New York: Springer, 341–358.

Burfeind, J. & Bartusch, D.J. (2016): Juvenile delinquency: An integrated approach. London: Routledge.

Burkett, S.R. (1993): Perceived parents' religiosity, friends' drinking, and hellfire: A panel study of adolescent drinking. Review of Religious Research 35, 136–154.

Burkett, S.R. & White, M. (1974): Hellfire and delinquency: Another look. Journal for the Scientific Study of Religion 13, 455–462.

Bužarovska, G. (2014): Criminology and Crime in Macedonia, in: Getoš Kalac, A.-M. et al. (eds.), Mapping the Criminological Landscape of the Balkans. Balkan Criminology Series Volume 1. Berlin: Duncker & Humblot, 245–284.

Cain, M. (1990): Towards transgression: New directions in feminist criminology. International Journal of the Sociology of Law 18, 1–18.

Capak, K. (2016): Europsko istraživanje o pušenju, pijenju i uzimanju droga među učenicima – ESPAD. Hrvatski zavod za javno zdravstvo.

Cernkovich, S.A. & Giordano, P.C. (1987): Family Relationships and Delinquency. Criminology 25, 295–321.

Chapple, C.L., McQuillan, J.A. & Berdahl, T.A. (2005): Gender, social bonds, and delinquency: A comparison of boys' and girls' models. Social Science Research 34, 357–383.

Chesney-Lind, M. (1989): Girls' crime and women's place: Towards a feminist model of female delinquency. Crime and Delinquency 35, 5–29.

Clark, J.P. & Wenninger, E.P. (1962): Socio-economic class and area as correlates of illegal behavior among juveniles. American Sociological Review 27, 826–834.

Cochran, J.K. (1988): The effect of religiosity on secular and ascetic deviance. Sociological Focus 21, 293–306.

Cochran, J.K. & Akers, R.L. (1989): Beyond hellfire: An exploration of the variable effects of religiosity on adolescent marijuana and alcohol use. Journal of Research in Crime and Delinquency 26, 198–225.

Cohen, A.K. (1955): Delinquent boys: the culture of the gang. New York: Free Press.

Coleman, J.S. (1990): Foundations of social theory. Cambridge, MA: Harvard University Press.

Conger, R. (1976): Social control and social learning models of delinquency: A synthesis. Criminology 14, 17–40.

Conger, R.D., Ge, X., Elder Jr., G.H., Lorenz, F.O. & Simons, R.L. (1994): Economic Stress, Coercive Family Process, and Developmental Problems of Adolescents. Child Development 65, 541–561.

Costello, B.J. & Vowell, P.R. (1999): Testing control theory and differential association: a reanalysis of the Richmond Youth Project data. Criminology 37, 815–842.

Council of Europe (1999): European Sourcebook of Crime and Criminal Justice Statistics. Strasbourg: Council of Europe.

Council of Europe (2003): European Sourcebook of Crime and Criminal Justice Statistics. 2nd ed., The Hague: Ministry of Justice, WODC.

Council of Europe (2006): European Sourcebook of Crime and Criminal Justice Statistics. The Hague: Ministry of Justice, WODC.

Council of Europe (2014): European Sourcebook of Crime and Criminal Justice Statistics. 5th ed., Helsinki: HEUNI Publications Series 80.

Currie, C.E., Elton, R.A., Todd, J. & Platt, S. (1997): Indicators of socioeconomic status for adolescents: the WHO Health Behaviour in School-aged Children Survey. Health Education Research 12, 385–397.

Currie, C.E., Roberts, C., Morgan, A., Smith, R., Settertobulte, W. & Samdal, O. (2004): Young people's health in context. Copenhagen, Denmark: WHO Regional Office for Europe.

Currie, E. (1998): Crime and punishment in America. New York: Metropolitan Books.

Dentler, R.A. & Monroe, L.J. (1961): Social correlates of early adolescent theft. American Sociological Review 26, 733–743.

Dishion, T.J., Capaldi, D., Spracklen, K.M. & Li, F. (1995): Peer ecology of male adolescent drug use. Development and Psychopathology 7(4), 803–824.

Dishion, T.J. & McMahon, R.J. (1998): Parental monitoring and the prevention of child and adolescent problem behavior: A conceptual and empirical formulation. Clinical Child and Family Psychology Review 1(1), 61–75.

Dong, B. & Krohn, M.D. (2016): Dual trajectories of gang affiliation and delinquent peer association during adolescence: An examination of long-term offending outcomes. Journal of Youth and Adolescence 45, 746–762.

Dünkel, F., Gebauer, D. & Kestermann, C. (2005): Mare-Balticum-Youth-Survey. Selbstberichtete Delinquenz und Gewalterfahrungen von Jugendlichen im Ostseeraum. Monatsschrift für Kriminologie und Strafrechtsreform 88, 215–239.

Durkheim, E. (1982): The Rules of Sociological Method, edited with an Introduction. Lukes, S., translated Halls, W.D., New York: Free Press, 155–158; https://monoskop.org/images/1/1e/Durkheim_Emile_The_Rules_of_Sociological_Method_ 1982.pdf [15/01/2018].

Eaton, N.R., Krueger, R.F., Johnson, W., McGue, M. & Iacono, W.G. (2009): Parental monitoring, personality, and delinquency: Further support for a reconceptualization of monitoring. Journal of Research in Personality 43, 49–59.

Egli, N.M., Lucia, S. & Berchtold, A. (2012): Integrated vs. differentiated school systems and their impact on delinquency. European Journal of Criminology 9(3), 245–259; https://journals.sagepub.com/doi/abs/10.1177/1477370812438140 [15/ 01/2018].

Elder, J.W. (1976): Comparative cross-national methodology. Annual Review of Sociology 21, 209–230.

Elliott, D.S. & Ageton, S.S. (1980): Reconciling Race and Class Differences in Self-Reported and Official Estimates of Delinquency. American Sociological Review 45(1), 95–110.

Elliott, D.S., Huizinga, D. & Ageton, S.S. (1985): Explaining delinquency and drug use. Beverly Hills: Sage.

Ellis, L. & Walsh, A. (1999): Criminologists' opinions about causes of crime and delinquency. The Criminologist 24(4), 1–6.

Empey, L.T. & Erickson, M.L. (1966): Hidden delinquency and social status. Social Forces 44, 546–554.

Enzmann, D. (2010): Germany, in: Junger-Tas, J. et al. (eds.), Juvenile Delinquency in Europe and Beyond. Results of the Second International Self-Report Delinquency Study. New York: Springer, 47–64.

Enzmann, D. (2017): Die Anwendbarkeit des Crosswise-Modells zur Prüfung kultureller Unterschiede sozial erwünschten Antwortverhaltens: Implikationen für seinen Einsatz in internationalen Studien zu selbstberichteter Delinquenz, in: Eifler, S. & Faulbaum, F. (eds.), Methodische Probleme von Mixed-Mode-Ansätzen in der Umfrageforschung (Schriftenreihe der ASI Arbeitsgemeinschaft Sozialwissenschaftlicher Institute). Wiesbaden: Springer VS, 239–277.

Enzmann, D., Kivivuori, J., Marshall, J.H., Steketee, M., Hough, M. & Killias, M. (2018): A Global Perspective on Young People as Offenders and Victims. First Results from the ISRD3 Study. New York: Springer.

*Enzmann, D., Marshall, I.H., Killias, M., Junger-Tas, J., Steketee, M. &
Gruszczyńska, B.* (2010): Self-reported youth delinquency in Europe and beyond:
First results of the second International Self-Report Delinquency Study in the context of police and victimization data. European Journal of Criminology 7, 159–
183.

Erickson, M.L. & Empey, L.T. (1963): Court records, undetected delinquency, and
decision-making. Journal of Criminal Law, Criminology and Police Science 54,
456–469.

Esbensen, F. & Deschenes, E.P. (1998): A multisite examination of youth gang
membership: Does gender matter? Criminology 36, 799–828.

Esbensen, F., Melde, C., Taylor, T.J. & Peterson, D. (2008): Active parental consent
in school-based research: How much is enough and how do we get it? Evaluation
Review 32(4), 335–362.

Esbensen, F., Miller, M.H., Taylor, T.J., He, N. & Freng, A. (1999): Differential
attrition rates and active parental consent. Evaluation Review 23, 316–325.

ESPAD Group (2016): ESPAD Report 2015: Results from the European School Survey Project on Alcohol and Other Drugs. Luxembourg: Publications Office of the
European Union.

Evans, T.D., Cullen, F.T., Dunaway, R.G. & Burton, V.S. (1995): Religion and crime
reexamined: The impact of religion, secular controls, and social ecology on adult
criminality. Criminology 33(2), 195–224.

Farnworth, M., Thornberry, T.P., Krohn, M.D. & Lizotte, A.J. (1994): Measurement
in the Study of Class and Delinquency: Integrating Theory and Research. Journal
of Research in Crime and Delinquency 31, 32–61.

Farrington, D.P. (1973): Self-reports of deviant behavior: predictive and stable?
Journal of Criminal Law and Criminology 64, 99–110.

Farrington, D.P. (1986): Age and Crime. Crime and Justice 7, 189–250.

Farrington, D.P. (1989): Self-reported and official offending from adolescence to
adulthood, in: Klein, M.W. (ed.), Cross-National Research in Self-Reported
Crime and Delinquency. Dordrecht: Springer Netherlands, 399–423.

Farrington, D.P. (1990): Implications of criminal career research for the prevention
of offending. Journal of Adolescence 13, 93–113.

Farrington, D.P. (1995): The Development of Offending and Antisocial Behaviour
from Childhood: Key Findings from the Cambridge Study in Delinquent Development. Journal of Child Psychology and Psychiatry 36, 929–964.

Farrington, D.P. (2003): Key results from the first 40 years of the Cambridge Study in Delinquent Development, in: Thornberry, T.P. & Krohn, M.D. (eds.), Taking Stock of Delinquency: An Overview of Findings from Contemporary Longitudinal Studies. New York: Kluwer/Plenum, 137–183.

Farrington, D.P. (2015a): Cross-national comparative research on criminal careers, risk factors, crime and punishment. European Journal of Criminology 12(4), 386–399.

Farrington, D.P. (2015b): Prospective longitudinal research on the development of offending. Australian & New Zealand Journal of Criminology 48(3), 314–335.

Fergusson, D., Swain-Campbell, N. & Horwood, J. (2004): How does childhood economic disadvantage lead to crime? Journal of Child Psychology and Psychiatry 45(5), 956–966.

Fernander, A., Wilson, J.F., Staton, M. & Leukefeld, C. (2005): Exploring the type-of-crime hypothesis, religiosity, and spirituality in an adult male prison population. International Journal of Offender Therapy and Comparative Criminology 49, 682–95.

Getoš, A.-M. (2012a): Politische Gewalt auf dem Balkan. Schwerpunkt Terrorismus und Hasskriminalität: Konzepte, Entwicklungen und Analysen. Berlin: Duncker & Humblot.

Getoš, A.-M. (2012b): Mapping the Criminological Landscape of the Balkans. MPICC, Freiburg i. Br.; www.pravo.unizg.hr/criminologia-balcanica [15/05/2018].

Getoš, A.-M. (2014): Crime and Criminology in the Balkans. Criminology in Europe. Newsletter of the European Society of Criminology 13(1), 8–14.

Getoš Kalac, A.-M. (2014): Mapping the Criminological Landscape of the Balkans, in: Getoš Kalac, A.-M. et al. (eds.), Mapping the Criminological Landscape of the Balkans. Balkan Criminology Series Volume 1. Berlin: Duncker & Humblot, 23–56.

Getoš Kalac, A.-M. & Bezić, R. (2017): Criminology, Crime and Criminal Justice in Croatia. European Journal of Criminology 14(2), 242–266.

Getoš Kalac, A-M. & Karlović, R. (2014): Criminology and Crime in Croatia, in: Getoš Kalac, A.-M. et al. (eds.), Mapping the Criminological Landscape of the Balkans. Balkan Criminology Series Volume 1. Berlin: Duncker & Humblot, 139–174.

Gold, M. (1966): Undetected delinquent behavior. Journal of Research in Crime and Delinquency 3, 27–46.

Gold, M. (1970): Delinquent behavior in an American city. Belmont, CA: Brooks/Cole Publishing Company.

Görgen, T. & Rabold, S. (2009): Self-Report Delinquency Surveys in Germany, in: Zauberman, R. (ed.), Self-reported crime and deviance studies in Europe. Brussels: Vubpress Brussels University Press, 77–101.

Gottfredson, M.R. & Hirschi, T. (1990): A general theory of crime. Stanford, CA: Stanford University Press.

Graham, J., Bowling, B. & Smith, D. (1996): Young people and crime. Children and society 10(3), 245–247.

Gruszczynska, B., Lucia, S. & Killias, M. (2012): Juvenile Victimization from an International Perspective, in: Junger-Tas, J. et al. (eds.), The Many Faces of Youth Crime. New York: Springer, 95–117.

Hagan, J. (1989): Structural Criminology. New Brunswick, NJ: Rutgers University Press.

Harland, P., Reijneveld, S.A., Brugman, E. Verloove-Vanhorick, S.P. & Verhulst, F.C. (2002): Family factors and life events as risk factors for behavioural and emotional problems in children. European Child & Adolescent Psychiatry 11(4), 176–184; researchgate.net/publication/journal/1018-8827_European_Child_Adolescent_Psychiatry [15/01/2018].

Hartjen, A.C. & Priyadarsini, S. (2003): Gender, peers, and delinquency: A study of boys and girls in rural France. Youth and Society 34, 387–414.

Harvey E. (1999): Short-Term and Long-Term effects of early parental employment on children of the National Longitudinal Survey of Youth. Developmental Psychology 35, 445–459.

Hawkins, J.D., Catalano, R.F. & Miller, J.Y. (1992): Risk and protective factors for alcohol and other drug problems in adolescence and early adulthood: Implications for substance abuse prevention. Psychological Bulletin 112, 64–105.

Heinrich-Böll-Stiftung (2014): Political analyses and commentary, Southeastern Europe, Vol. 1. Belgrade: Heinrich-Böll-Stiftung Southeastern Europe.

Helmken, D. (2010): Kosovo, in: Dünkel, F. et al. (eds.), Juvenile Justice Systems in Europe: Current Situation and Reform Developments Vol. 2. Mönchengladbach: Forum Verlag Godesberg, 803–832.

Hepburn, J.R. (1976): Testing alternative models of delinquency causation. Journal of Criminal Law and Criminology 67, 450–460.

Hibell, B., Andersson, B., Ahlström, S., Balakireva, O., Kokkevi, A. & Morgan, M. (2004): The 2003 ESPAD Report, in: Alcohol and drug use among students in 35 European countries. Stockholm: The Swedish Council for Information on Alcohol and Drugs.

Hibell, B., Guttormsson, U., Ahlström, S., Balakireva, O., Bjarnason, T., Kokkevi, A. & Kraus, L. (2012): The 2011 ESPAD Report: Substance Use Among Students in 36 European Countries. Stockholm: The Swedish Council for Information on Alcohol and Other Drugs.

Higgins, P.C. & Albrecht, G.L. (1977): Hellfire and delinquency revisited. Social Forces 55, 952–958.

Hikan, S. & Kerr, M. (2000): Parental Monitoring: A Reinterpretation. Child Development 71, 1072–1085.

Hindelang, M.J. (1973): Causes of delinquency: A partial replication and extension. Social Problems 20, 471–487.

Hindelang, M.J., Hirschi, T. & Weiss, J.G. (1979): Correlates of Delinquency: The Illusion of Discrepancy between Self-Report and Official Measures. American Sociological Review Vol. 44(6), 995–1014.

Hindelang M.J., Hirschi T. & Weiss, J.G. (1981): Measuring delinquency. Beverly Hills: Sage.

Hirschi, T. (1969): Causes of delinquency. Berkeley: University of California Press.

Hirschi, T. & Gottredson, M.R. (2001): Self-control theory, in: Paternoster, R. & Bachman, R. (eds.), Explaining criminals and crime. Essays in contemporary criminological theory. Los Angeles: Roxbury Publishing Company, 81–96.

Hirschi, T. & Selvin, H.C. (1967): Delinquency research: an appraisal of analytic methods. New York: The Free Press.

Hirschi, T. & Stark, R. (1969): Hellfire and delinquency. Social Problems 17, 202–213.

Hoeve, M., Stams, G.J.J.M., van der Put, C.E., Dubas, J.S., van der Laan, P.H. & Gerris, J.R.M. (2012): A meta-analysis of attachment to parents and delinquency. Journal of Abnormal Child Psychology 40, 771–785.

Howard, G., Newman, G. & Pridemore, W. (2000): Theory, method, and data in comparative criminology crime and justice 2000. Washington, D.C.: National Institute of Justice.

Huizinga, D., Weiher, A.W., Espiritu, R. & Esbensen, F. (2003): Delinquency and Crime: some Highlights from the Denver Youth Survey, in: Thornberry, T.P. & Krohn, M.D. (eds.), Taking stock of delinquency: an overview of findings from contemporary longitudinal studies. New York: Kluwer Academic/Plenum Publishers, 47–92.

Ispa, J.M., Fine, M.A., Halgunseth, L.C., Harper, S., Robinson, J., Boyce, L. & Brady-Smith, C. (2004): Maternal intrusiveness, maternal warmth, and mother-toddler relationship outcomes: Variations across low-income ethnic and acculturation groups. Child Development 75, 1613–1631.

Jamieson, J., McIvor, G. & Murray, C. (1999): Understanding Offending among Young People. Edinburgh: Stationery Office Books.

Jensen, E. & Erickson, M.L. (1979): The religious factor and delinquency: Another look at the hellfire hypotheses, in: Wuthnow, R. (ed.), The religious dimension. New York: Academic Press, 157–178.

Jensen, G.F. (1973): Inner containment and delinquency. Journal of Criminal Law and Criminology 64, 464–470.

Jensen, G.F., Erickson, M.L. & Gibbs, J.P. (1978): Perceived risk of punishment and self-reported delinquency. Social Forces 57, 57–78.

Jessor, R., van Den Bos, J., Vanderryn, J., Costa, F. & Turbin, M. (1995): Protective factors in adolescent problem behavior: Moderator effects and developmental change. Developmental Psychology 31, 923–933.

Johnson, B.R. & Siegel, M.V. (2008): The great escape: How religion alters the delinquent behavior of high-risk adolescents. ISR Report, Institute for Studies of Religion, Baylor University; http://www.baylorisr.org/wp-content/uploads/ISR_ Great_ Escape.pdf [15/04/2018].

Junger-Tas, J. (2010): The Significance of the International Self-report Delinquency Study (ISRD). European Journal on Criminal Policy and Research 16, 71–87.

Junger-Tas, J. (2012a): Delinquent Behaviour in 30 Countries, in: Junger-Tas, J. et al. (eds.), The Many Faces of Youth Crime. New York: Springer, 69–93.

Junger-Tas, J. (2012b): The Importance of the Family, in: Junger-Tas, J. et al. (eds.), The Many Faces of Youth Crime. New York: Springer, 185–209.

Junger-Tas, J., Enzmann, D., Steketee, M. & Marshall, I.H. (2012): Concluding Observations: The Big Picture, in: Junger-Tas, J. et al. (eds.), The Many Faces of Youth Crime. New York: Springer, 329–353.

Junger-Tas, J. & Marshall, I.H. (1999): The self-report methodology in crime research, in: Tonry, M. (ed.), Crime and Justice: A Review of Research Vol. 25. Chicago: University of Chicago Press, 291–368.

Junger-Tas, J. & Marshall, I.H. (2012): Introduction to the International Self-Report Study of Delinquency (ISRD-2), in: Junger-Tas, J. et al. (eds.), The Many Faces of Youth Crime. New York: Springer, 3–20.

Junger-Tas, J., Marshall, I.H., Enzmann, D., Killias, M., Steketee, M. & Gruszczynska, B. (2010): History and Designee of the ISRD Study, in: Junger-Tas, J. et al. (eds.): Juvenile delinquency in Europe and beyond. Results of the Second International Self-Report Delinquency Study. New York: Springer, 1–11.

Junger-Tas, J., Marshall, I.H., Enzmann, D., Killias, M., Steketee, M. & Gruszczynska, B. (eds.) (2012): The Many Faces of Youth Crime. New York: Springer.

Junger-Tas, J., Marshall, I.H. & Ribeaud, D. (2003): Delinquency in an International perspective: The International self-report Delinquency Study (ISRD). The Hague: Kugler.

Junger-Tas, J., Ribeaud, D. & Cruyff, Maarten J.L.F. (2004): Juvenile Delinquency and Gender. European Journal of Criminology 1, 333–375.

Junger-Tas, J., Terlouw, G. & Klein, M.W. (eds.) (1994): Delinquent Behavior among Young People in the Western World: First Results of the International Self-Report Delinquency Study. Amsterdam: Kugler Publications.

Kaplan, H.B. (1972): Toward a general theory of psychosocial deviance: The case of aggressive behavior. Social Science and Medicine 6, 593–617.

Karstedt, S. (2001): Comparing cultures, comparing crime: Challenges, prospects and problems for a global criminology. Crime, Law and Social Change 36, 285–308.

Kelly, D.H. (1974): Track position and delinquent involvement: A preliminary analysis. Sociology and Social Research 58, 380–386.

Kelly, P.E., Polanin, J.R., Jang, S.J. & Johnson, B.R. (2015): Religion, Delinquency, and Drug Use: A Meta-Analysis. Criminal Justice Review 40(4), 505–523.

Kerr, M. & Stattin, H. (2000): What parents know, how they know it, and several forms of adolescent adjustment: Further support for a reinterpretation of monitoring. Developmental Psychology 36, 366–380.

Kirk, D.S. (2006): Examining the Divergence Across Self-report and Official Data Sources on Inferences About the Adolescent Life-course of Crime. Journal of Quantitative Criminology 22(2), 107–129.

Kivivuori, J. (2007): Delinquent Behaviour in Nordic Capital Cities. Helsinki National Research Institute of Legal Policy, Publication 227. Helsinki.

Kivivuori, J. (2009): Self-Report Delinquency Surveys in Finland, in: Zauberman, R. (ed.), Self-reported crime and deviance studies in Europe. Brussels: Vubpress Brussels University Press, 77–101.

Kivivuori, J. (2011): Discovery of hidden crime. Self-report surveys in criminal policy context. Oxford: Oxford University Press.

Kivivuori J. (2014): History of the Self-Report Delinquency Surveys, in: Bruinsma G. & Weisburd, D. (eds.), Encyclopedia of Criminology and Criminal Justice. New York: Springer, 2309–2319.

Kivivuori, J. & Bernburg, J.G. (2011): Delinquency research in the Nordic countries, in: Tonry, M. & Lappi-Seppälä, T. (eds.), Crime and justice in Scandinavia. Crime and justice: A Review of Research, Vol. 40. Chicago: University of Chicago Press, 405–477.

Kivivuori, J., Salmi, V. & Walser, S. (2013): Supervision mode effects in computerized delinquency surveys at school: Finnish replication of a Swiss experiment. Journal of Experimental Criminology 9, 91–107.

Knudten, R.D. & Knudten, M.S. (1971): Juvenile delinquency, crime and religion. Review of Religious Research 12, 130–152.

Kohn, M.L. (1987): Cross-national research as an analytic strategy. American Sociological Review 52, 713–731.

Koster, F., Goudriaan, H. & van der Schans, C. (2009): Shame and Punishment: An International Comparative Study on the Effects of Religious Affiliation and Religiosity on Attitudes to Offending. European Journal of Criminology 6(6), 481-495.

Krasniqi, L. (2014): Criminology and Crime in Kosovo, in: Getoš Kalac, A.-M. et al. (eds.), Mapping the Criminological Landscape of the Balkans. Balkan Criminology Series Volume 1. Berlin: Duncker & Humblot, 235–244.

Kraus, L. (2015): ESPAD Report 2015: Results from the European School Survey Project on Alcohol and other Drugs. Lisbon: EMCDDA.

Krohn, M.D., Thornberry, T.P., Gibson, C.L. & Baldwin, J.M. (2010): The development and impact of self-report measures of crime and delinquency. Journal of Quantitative Criminology 26(4), 509–525.

Kugler Smith, P., Marshall, I.H. & van Gammeren, M. (2008): An empirical approach to country clustering, in: Aromaa, K. & Heiskanen, M. (eds.), Crime and criminal justice systems in Europe and North America 1995–2004. Helsinki: HEUNI, 169–195.

Larzelere, R. & Patterson, G. (1990): Parental management: mediator of the effect of socioeconomic status on early delinquency. Criminology 28, 301–323.

Layton-MacKenzie, D. & De Li, S. (2002): The impact of formal and informal social controls on the criminal activities of probationers. Journal of Research in Crime and Delinquency 39(3), 243–276.

Li, D.S. (1999): Social control, delinquency, and youth status achievement: A development approach. Sociological Perspectives 42, 305–324.

Litchfield, A.W., Thomas, D.L. & Li, B.D. (1997): Dimensions of religiosity as mediators of the relations between parenting and adolescent deviant behavior. Journal of Adolescent Research 12(2), 199–226.

Loeber, R., Farrington, D.P., Southamer-Loeber, M., Moffitt, T.E., Caspi, A., White, H.R., Wei, E.H. & Beyers, J.M. (2003): The Development of Male Offending: Key Findings from Fourteen Years of The Pittsburgh Youth Study, in: Thornberry, T.P. & Krohn, M.D. (eds.), Taking Stock of Delinquency: An Overview of Findings from Contemporary Longitudinal Studies. New York: Kluwer/Plenum, 93–136.

Loeber, R. & Stouthamer-Loeber, M. (1986): Family factors as correlates and predictors of juvenile conduct problems and delinquency, in: Tonry, M. & Morris, N. (eds.), Crime and justice. Chicago: University of Chicago Press, 29–149.

Lucia, S., Killias, M. & Junger-Tas, J. (2012): The school and its Impact on Delinquency, in: Junger-Tas, J. et al. (eds.), The Many Faces of Youth Crime. New York: Springer, 211–235.

Lynch, J.P. & Addington, L.A. (2015): Crime trends and the elasticity of evil: Has a broadening view of violence affected our statistical indicators? Crime and Justice 44, 297–331.

Maccoby, E.E. & Jacklin, C.N. (1980): Sex differences in aggression: A rejoinder and reprise. Child Development 51, 964–980.

Mack, D.M., Behler, A., Roberts, B. & Rimland, E. (2007): Reaching students with Facebook: Data and best practices. Electronic Journal of Academic and Special Librarianship 8; southernlibrarianship.icaap.org/content/v08n02/mack_d01.html [15/06/2018].

Madge, N. (1983): Families at risk. London: Heinemann.

Maljević, A. & Muratbegović, E (2014): Criminology and Crime in Bosnia and Herzegovina, in: Getoš Kalac, A.-M. et al. (eds.), Mapping the Criminological Landscape of the Balkans. Balkan Criminology Series Volume 1. Berlin: Duncker & Humblot, 99–112.

Maljević, A. (2006): Legal and Actual Treatment of Juveniles Within the Criminal Justice System of Bosnia and Herzegovina, in: Junger-Tas, J. & Decker, S.H. (eds.), International Handbook of Juvenile Justice. New York: Springer, 415–436.

Maljević, A., Janjetović, V.S., Budimlić, M., Jović, N, Miodragović, B. & Vujović, S. (2017): Međunarodna studija o samoprijavljenom prijestupništvu djece u Bosni i Hercegovini: Izvještaj za stručne radnike u oblasti zaštite djece. UNICEF "Pravda za svako dijete".

Mannheim, H., Spencer, J. & Lynch, G. (1957): Magisterial policy in the London juvenile courts. British Journal of Delinquency 8(1), 13–33.

Marsh, R.M. (1967): Comparative Sociology: a codification of cross-societal analysis. New York: Harcourt, Brace & World, 155–187.

Marshall Hean, I. & Enzmann, D. (2012): Methodology and Design of the ISRD-2 Study, in: Junger-Tas, J. (ed.), The Many Faces of Youth Crime. New York: Springer, 21-65.

Marshall, H.I., Enzmann, D., Hough, M., Killias, M., Kivivuori, J. and Steketee, M. (2013): International Self-Report Delinquency Questionnaire 3 (ISRD-3): Background paper to explain ISRD2-ISRD3 changes. ISRD3 Technical Report Series #1; http://www.northeastern.edu/isrd/isrd3/ [01/08/2018].

Marshall, I.H. & Marshall, C.E. (1983): Towards a refinement of purpose in comparative criminological research: Research site selection in focus. International Journal of Comparative and Applied Criminal Justice 7, 84–97.

Marvell, T.B. & Moody Jr., C.E. (1991): Age structure and crime rates: The conflicting evidence. Journal of Quantitative Criminology 7, 237–273.

Masten, A.S. (1994): Resilience in individual development: Successful adaptation despite risk and adversity, in: Wang, M.C. & Gordon, E.W. (eds.), Educational resilience in inner-city America: Challenges and prospects. Hillsdale, NJ: Erlbaum, 3–25.

Matsueda, R.L. & Heimer, K. (1987): Race, family structure and delinquency: A test of differential association and social control theories. American Sociological Review 52, 826–840.

Matthews, V.M. (1968): Differential identification: An empirical note. Social Problems 14, 376–383.

Maxfield, M.G. & Babbie, E.R. (2001): Research Methods for Criminal Justice and Criminology. 3rd ed., Belmont, CA: Wadsworth.

Mazerolle, P. (1998): Gender, general strain, and delinquency: An empirical examination. Justice Quarterly 15(1), 1565–1591.

McVie, S. (2009): Self-Report Delinquency Surveys in Great Britain and Ireland, in: Zauberman, R. (ed.), Self-reported crime and deviance studies in Europe. Brussels: Vubpress Brussels University Press, 155–188.

Metzler, C.W., Biglan, A., Ary, D., Noell, J. & Smolkowski, K. (1993): The relationships among high-risk sexual behavior and other adolescent problem behaviors. Journal of Behavioral Medicine 17, 419–438.

Miller, T. & Vuolo, M. (2018): Examining the Antiascetic Hypothesis Through Social Control Theory: Delinquency, Religion, and Reciprocation Across the Early Life Course. Crime & Delinquency Vol. 64(11), 1–31.

Minkov, M. & Hofstede, G. (2012): Cross-cultural analysis: the science and art of comparing the world's modern societies and their cultures. Thousand Oaks, CA: Sage.

Mishler, W. & Rose, R. (2001): What are the Origins of Political Trust? Testing Institutional and Cultural Theories in Post-Communist Societies. Comparative Political Studies 34(1), 30–62.

Moffitt, T.E., Caspi A., Rutter M., Silva P.A. (2001): Sex differences in antisocial behavior: conduct disorder, delinquency, and violence in the Dunedin longitudinal study. Cambridge: Cambridge University Press.

Muratbegović, E. & Vujović, S. (2016): Ponašanje i navike djece na internetu: stavovi djece, roditelja i nastavnika informatike. Sarajevo, Save the children.

References   167

Naplava, T. & Oberwittler, D. (2002): Methodeneffekte bei der Messung selbstberichteter Delinquenz von männlichen Jugendlichen. Monatsschrift für Kriminologie und Strafrechtsreform 85, 401–423.

Nelken, D. (2009): Comparative criminal justice: Beyond ethnocentrism and relativism. European Journal of Criminology 6, 291–311.

Nelken, D. (2010): Comparative criminal justice: Making sense of difference. Los Angeles: Sage.

Nikolaidis, G., Petroulaki, K., Zarokosta, F., Tsirigoti, A., Hazizaj, A., Cenko, E., Brkic-Smigoc, J., Vajzovic, E., Stancheva, V., Chincheva, S., Ajdukovic, M., Rajter, M., Raleva, M., Trpcevska, Lj., Roth, M., Antal, I., Ispanovic, V., Hanak, N., Olmezoglu-Sofuoglu, Z., Umit-Bal, I., Bianchi, D., Franziska Meinck, F. & Browne, K. (2018): Lifetime and past-year prevalence of children's exposure to violence in 9 Balkan countries: the BECAN study. Child and Adolescent Psychiatry and Mental Health 12, Article 1.

Nikolić-Ristanović, V. (2016): Delinkvencija i viktimizacija maloletnih lica u Srbiji: Rezultati Međunarodne ankete samoprijavljivanjem delinkvencije. Beograd: Prometej.

Nikolić-Ristanović, V. & Stevković, Lj. (2015): Međunarodna anketa samoprijavljivanjem maloletničke delinkvencije: istraživanje delinkventnog ponašanja i viktimizacije maloletnih lica, in: Stevanović, I. (ed.), Maloletnici kao učinioci i žrtve krivičnih dela i prekršaja. Beograd: Institut za kriminološka i sociološka istraživanja, 259-274.

Ninamedia Research (2015): Istraživanje o položaju i potrebama mladih u Srbiji [Research on the position and needs of young people in Serbia]; http://www.mos.gov.rs/dokumenta/omladina/istrazivanja [15/06/2018].

Nisbett, R.E. & Cohen, D. (1996): Culture of honor: the psychology of violence in the south. Boulder, CO: Westview Press.

Nye, F.I. (1958): Family relationship and delinquent behavior. New York: Wiley.

Nye, F.I., Short, J.F. Jr. & Olson, V.J. (1958): Socioeconomic Status and Delinquent Behavior. American Journal of Sociology 63(4), 381–389.

Oba, S. (1908): Unverbesserliche Verbrecher und ihre Behandlung. Berlin: Facsimile Publisher.

Oberwittler, D., Blank, T., Köllisch, T. & Naplava, T. (2001): Soziale Lebenslagen und Delinquenz von Jugendlichen: Ergebnisse der MPI-Schulbefragung 1999 in Freiburg und Köln. Freiburg i. Br.: Max-Plank-Institut für ausländisches und internationales Strafrecht.

Paternoster, R. & Piquero, A. (1995): Reconceptualizing Deterrence: An Empirical Test of Personal and Vicarious Experiences. Journal of Research in Crime and Delinquency 32(3), 251–286.

Patterson, C.J., Griesler, P.C., Vaden, N.A. & Kupersmidt, J.B. (1992): Family economic circumstances, life transitions, and children's peer relations, in: Parke, R.D. & Ladd, G.W. (eds.), Family-peer relationships: Modes of linkage. Hillsdale, NJ: Erlbaum, 385–424.

Patterson, G.R. (1995): Coercion as a basis of early age of onset for arrest, in: McCord, J. (ed.), Coercion and punishment in long-term perspective. Cambridge: Cambridge University Press, 81–105.

Pauwels, L.J.R. & Svensson, R. (2008): How serious is the problem of item nonresponse in delinquency scales and aetiological variables? A cross-national inquiry into two classroom PAPI self-report studies in Antwerp and Halmstad. European Journal of Criminology 5, 289–308.

Pease, K. & Hukkula, K. (eds.) (1990): Criminal justice systems in Europe and North-America. Helsinki: Helsinki Institute for Crime Prevention and Control.

Pedersen, W. & Wichstroem, L. (1995): Patterns of Delinquency in Norwegian Adolescents. British Journal of Criminology 35(4), 543–562.

Petersen, T., Voss, P., Sabel, P. & Grube, N. (2004): Der Fragebogen Karls des Großen. Kölner Zeitschrift für Soziologie und Sozialpsychologie 56(4), 736–745.

Pettersson, T. (1991): Religion and Criminality: Structural Relationships between Church Involvement and Crime Rates in Contemporary Sweden. Journal for the Scientific Study of Religion 29, 279–291.

Petts, R.J. (2009): Family and religious characteristics' influence on delinquency trajectories from adolescence to young adulthood. American Sociological Review 74(3), 465–483.

Pew Research Center (2015): The Future of World Religions: Population Growth Projections; http://assets.pewresearch.org/wp-content/uploads/sites/11/2015/03/PF_15.04.02_ProjectionsFullReport.pdf [01/06/2018].

Pew Research Center (2017): Religious Belief and National Belonging in Central and Eastern Europe; http://www.pewforum.org/2017/05/10/religious-belief-and-national-belonging-in-central-and-eastern-europe/ [01/06/2018].

Pogarsky, G. (2009): Chapter 13: deterrence and decision-making: research questions and theoretical refinements, in: Krohn, M.D. et al. (eds.), Handbook on crime and delinquency. New York: Springer, 241-258.

Pokorny, S.B., Jason, L.A., Schoeny, M.E., Townsend, S.M. & Curie, C.J. (2001): Do participation rates change when active consent procedures replace passive consent. Evaluation Review 25, 567–580.

Polk, K. (1969): Class strain and rebellion among adolescents. Social Problems 17, 214–224.

Porterfield, A.L. (1943): Delinquency and its outcome in court and college. American Journal of Sociology 49, 199–208.

Prezworski, A. & Teune, H. (1970): The logic of comparative social inquiry. New York: Wiley.

Rabow, J. (1966): Delinquent Boys Revisited: A Critique of Albert K. Cohen's Delinquent Boys. Criminology Vol. 4(1), 22–28.

Ragin, C.C. (1987): The comparative method. Moving beyond qualitative and quantitative strategies. Berkeley: University of California Press.

Regnerus, M.D. (2003): Religion and positive adolescent outcomes: A review of research and theory. Review of Religious Research 44, 394–413.

Regnerus, M.D. & Elder, G.H. (2003): Religion and vulnerability among low-risk adolescents. Social Science Research 32, 633–658.

Reisig, M.D., Wolfe, S.E. & Pratt, T.C. (2012): Low self-control and the religiosity-crime relationship. Criminal Justice and Behavior 39, 1172–1191.

Reiss, A.J. Jr. & Rhodes, A.L. (1964): An empirical test of differential association theory. Journal of Research in Crime and Delinquency 1, 5–18.

Riley and Shaw (1985): Parental supervision re-examined. The British Journal of Criminology 27(4), 421–424.

Rimac, I. & Štulhofer, A. (2004): Sociokulturne vrijednosti, gospodarska razvijenost i politička stabilnost kao čimbenici povjerenja u Europsku Uniju, in: Ott, K. (ed.), Pridruživanje Hrvatske Europskoj Uniji. Izazovi institucionalnih prilagodbi, 2. Sv. Institut za javne financije. Zagreb: Zaklada Friedrich Ebert, 287–312.

Robertson, R. (1970): The sociological interpretation of religion. Oxford: Blackwell.

Robinson, S.M. (1936): Can Delinquency Be Measured. New York: Columbia University Press.

Rocque, M., Posick, C. & Hoyle, J. (2016): Age and Crime, in: Jennings, W.G. (ed.), The Encyclopedia of Crime and Punishment. 1st ed., Chichester: Wiley Blackwell, 1-8.

Rodriguez, J.A., Pérez-Santiago, N. & Birkbeck, C. (2015): Surveys as cultural artefacts: Applying the International Self-Report Delinquency Study to Latin American adolescents. European Journal of Criminology 12(4), 420–436.

Rokkan, S. (1968): Comparative research across cultures and nations. The Hague: Mouton.

Roy, P. (1963): Adolescent Roles: Rural-Urban Differentials, in: Nye, F. (ed.), The employed mother in America. Chicago: Rand McNally, 165–181.

Ručević, S. (2008): Metodološki postupci i izazovi primjene samoiskaza i longitudinalnih nacrta u istraživanjima razvoja delikventnog ponašanja. Studijski Centar Socijalnog Rada. Ljetopis Vol. 15(3), 421–443.

Ručević, S., Ajduković, M. & Šincek, D. (2009): Razvoj upitnika samoiskaza rizičnog i delinkventnog ponašanja mladih (SRDP-2007): Kriminologija i socijalna integracija Vol. 17(1), 1-11.

Rutter, M. & Giller, H. (1983): Juvenile delinquency: Trends and Perspectives. Harmondsworth Middlesex: Penguin.

Rutter, M., Giller, H. & Hagell, A. (1998): Antisocial behavior by young people. Cambridge: Cambridge University Press.

Rutter, M., Maughan, B., Mortimore, P. & Ouston, J. (1979): Fifteen thousand hours: secondary schools and effects on children. Cambridge, MA: Harvard University Press.

Salmi, V. (2009): Self-reported juvenile delinquency in Finland 1995–2008. Research Report No. 246. Helsinki: National Research Institute of Legal Policy, 207–216.

Saltzman, L.E., Paternoster, R., Waldo, G.P. & Chiricos, T.G. (1982): Deterrent and experiential effects: the problem of causal order in perceptual deterrence research. Journal of Research in Crime and Delinquency 19, 172–189.

Sampson, R.J. & Laub, J.H. (1993): Crime in the making: pathways and turning points through life. Cambridge, MA: Havard University Press.

Schreck, C.J. & Hirschi, T. (2009): Social Control Theory, in: Miller, J.M. (ed.), 21st Century Criminology: A Reference Handbook. Thousand Oaks, CA: Sage.

Schumann, K.F. (2007): Berufsbildung, Arbeit und Delinquenz: empirische Erkenntnisse und praktische Folgerungen aus einer Bremer Längsschnittstudie, in: Dessecker, A. (ed.), Jugendarbeitslosigkeit und Kriminalität. 2. Aufl., Wiesbaden: Eigenverlag Kriminologische Zentralstelle, Wiesbaden, 43–68.

Sellin, T. (1931): The basis of a crime index. Journal of Criminal Law and Criminology 22, 335–356.

Shoemaker, D.J. (2018): Juvenile delinquency. 3rd edition, Lanham, MD: Rowman & Littlefield.

Short, J.F. (1957): Differential association and delinquency. Social Problems 4, 233–239.

Short, J.F. & Olson, V.J. (1958): Socioeconomic status and delinquent behavior, in: Nye, F.I. (ed.), Family relationship and delinquent behavior. New York: Wiley, 23–33.

Silberman, M. (1976): Toward a theory of criminal deterrence. American Sociological Review 41, 442–461.

Simeunović-Patić, B., Meško, G. & Ignjatović, Đ. (2016): Results from Recent European Research on Youth Violence Prevention: Some Lessons for Serbia. Revija za kriminalistiko in kriminologijo, Ljubljana 67(4), 404–413.

Simon, R.J. (1975): The contemporary woman and crime. Washington D.C.: National Institute of Mental Health.

Škulić, M. (2010): Serbia, in: Dünkel, F. et al. (eds.), Juvenile Justice Systems in Europe: Current Situation and Reform Developments, Vol. 3. Mönchengladbach: Forum Verlag Godesberg, 1195–1244.

Sloane, D. & Potvin, R. (1986): Religion and delinquency: cutting through the maze. Social Forces 65, 87–105.

Slocum, W. & Stone, C.L. (1963): Family culture patterns and delinquent-type behavior. Marriage and Family Living 25, 202–208.

Smith, D.J. & McVie, S. (2003): Theory and Method in the Edinburgh Study of Youth Transitions and Crime. The British Journal of Criminology Vol. 43(1), 169–195.

Stanfield, R. (1966): The interaction of family variables and gang variables in the aetiology of delinquency. Social Problems 13, 411–417.

Stark, R. (1984): Religion and conformity: Reaffirming a sociology of religion. Sociological Analysis 45, 273–282.

Stark, R., Kent, L. & Doyle, D.P. (1982): Religion and delinquency: The ecology of a lost relationship. Journal of Research in Crime and Delinquency 19, 4–24.

Steffensmeier, D.J., Allan, E.A., Harer, M.D. & Streifel, C. (1989): Age and the distribution of crime. American Journal of Sociology 94, 803–831.

Steketee, M. (2012): Substance Use of Young People in 30 Countries, in: Junger-Tas, J. et al. (eds.), The Many Faces of Youth Crime. New York: Springer, 117–143.

Steketee, M., Jonkman, H., Berten, H. & Vettenburget, N. (2013): Alcohol use Among Adolescents in Europe: Environmental Research and Preventive Actions. Utrecht: Verwey-Jonker Instituut.

Stevković, Lj. & Nikolic-Ristanovic, V. (2015): International Self-Report Delinquency Study (ISRD3) in Serbia: Technical report. Translation, schools contacts, school-system-related aspects, and field data collection.

Stevković, Lj. & Nikolić-Ristanović, V. (2016): Istraživanje maloletničke delinkvencije u Srbiji primenom Međunarodne ankete samoprijavljivanjem (ISRD3)-metodološki okvir, in: Nikolić-Ristanović, V. (ed.), Delinkvencija i viktimizacija maloletnih lica u Srbiji: Rezultati Međunarodne ankete samoprijavljivanjem delinkvencije. Beograd: Prometej, 7–14.

Stice, E., & Barrera, M. (1995): A Longitudinal Examination of the Reciprocal Relations Between Perceived Parenting and Adolescents' Substance Use and Externalizing Behaviors. Developmental Psychology 31(2), 322–334.

Stone, A.A., Christine A. Bachrach, C.A., Jobe, J.B., Kurtzman, H.S. & Cain, V.S. (2000): The Science of Self-report: Implications for Research and Practice. Mahwah, NJ: Lawrence, Erlbaum associates.

Storvoll, E.E., Wichstrøm, L., Kolstad, A. & Pape, H. (2002): Structure of conduct problems in adolescence. Scandinavian Journal of Psychology 43, 81–91.

Sumter, M., Wood, F., Whitaker, I. & Berger-Hill, D. (2018): Religion and Crime Studies: Assessing What Has Been Learned. Religions 9, 193–209.

Sundhaussen, H. (1999): Europa balcanica. Der Balkan als historischer Raum Europas. Geschichte und Gesellschaft 25, 626–653.

Sundhaussen, H. (2014): The Balkan Peninsula: A Historical Region *Sui Generis*, in: Getoš Kalac, A.-M. et al. (eds.), Mapping the Criminological Landscape of the Balkans. Balkan Criminology Series Volume 1. Berlin: Duncker & Humblot, 3–22.

Sutherland, E. (1934): Principles of criminology. 2nd ed., Chicago: J.B. Lippincott.

Sweeten, G. (2012): Scaling Criminal Offending. Journal of Quantitative Criminology 28, 533–557.

Thornberry, T.P. & Krohn, M. (2000): The Self-Report Method for Measuring Delinquency and Crime. Measurement and Analysis of Crime and Justice, Vol. 4. Washington, D.C.: National Institute of Justice.

Thornberry, T.P. & Krohn, M. (2003): Comparison of Self-Report and Official Data for Measuring Crime, in: Pepper, J.V. & Patrie, C.V. (eds.), Measurement Problems in Criminal Justice Research: Workshop Summary, National Research Council. Washington, D.C.: The National Academies Press, 43–94.

Thornberry, T.P., Lizotte, A.J., Krohn, M.D., Smith, C.A. & Porter, P.K. (2003): Causes and Consequences of Delinquency: Findings from the Rochester Youth Development Study, in: Thornberry, T.P. & Krohn, M.D. (eds.), Taking Stock of Delinquency: An Overview of Findings from Contemporary Longitudinal Studies. New York: Kluwer/Plenum, 11-46.

Tibbets, S.G. & Hemmens, C. (2015): Criminological theory: A Text/Reader. Thousand Oaks, CA: Sage.

Tittle, C.R., & Welch, M.R. (1982): Religiosity and deviance: Toward a contingency theory of constraining effects. Social Forces 61, 653–682.

Toby, J. (1957): Social disorganization and stake in conformity: Complementary factors in the predatory behavior of hoodlums. Journal of Criminal Law, Criminology and Police Science 48, 12–17.

Trzun, Z. (2012): Kriza povjerenja u institucije: istraživanje povjerenja u vojsku. Polemos 15(1), 33–54.

Uecker, J.E., Regnerus, M.D. & Vaaler, M.L. (2007): Losing my religion: The social sources of religious decline in early adulthood. Social Forces 85, 1667–1692.

Ulmer, J.T., Desmond, S.A., Jang, S.J. & Johnson, B.R. (2010): Teenage religiosity and changes in marijuana use during the transition to adulthood. Interdisciplinary Journal of Research on Religion 6, article 3, 1–19.

Van de Vijver, F. & Tanzer, N.K. (2004): Bias and equivalence in cross-cultural assessment: An overview. European Review of Applied Psychology 54, 119–135.

Van der Laan, A.M. & Blom, M. (2006): Jeugdelinquentie. Risico's en bescherming: Bevindingen uit de WODC monitor zelfgerapporteerde jeugdcriminaliteit 2005. Den Haag: Boom Juridische Uitgevers.

Van Dijk, J.J.M. (2010): Revisiting the 'dark number of crime', in: Herzog-Evans, M. (ed.), Transnational Criminology Manual No. 2. Nijmegen: Wolf Legal Publishers (WLP).

Van Dijk, J.J.M., van Kesteren, J. & Smit, P. (2007): Criminal Victimization in International Perspective: Key Findings from the 2004–2005 ICVS and EUICS. Den Haag: Boom Juridische Uitgevers.

Vander Ven, T.M., Cullen, F.T., Carrozza, M.A. & Wright, J.P. (2001): Home alone: The Impact of Maternal Employment on Delinquency. Social Problems 48(2), 236–257.

Vaz, E. (1966): Self-reported juvenile delinquency and social status. Canadian Journal of Corrections 8, 20–27.

Vetere, E. & Newman, G. (1977): International crime statistics: An overview from a comparative perspective. Abstracts on Criminology and Penology 17, 251–604.

Villmow, B. & Stephan, E. (unter Mitarbeit von *Harald Arnold*) (1983): Jugendkriminalität in einer Gemeinde. Eine Analyse erfragter Delinquenz und Viktimisierung sowie amtlicher Registrierung. Freiburg i. Br.: Max-Plank-Institut für ausländisches und internationales Strafrecht.

Viner, R.M. & Taylor, B. (2007): Adult outcomes of binge drinking in adolescence: findings from a UK national birth cohort. Journal of Epidemiology and Community Health 61, 902–907.

Voss, H. (1964): Differential association and reported delinquent behavior: A replication. Social Problems 11, 78–85.

Voss, H. (1966): Socio-economic status and reported delinquent behavior. Social Problems 13, 314–324.

Waldo, G.P. & Chiricos, T.G. (1972): Perceived penal sanction and self-reported criminality: A neglected approach to deterrence research. Social Problems 19, 522–540.

Walser, S. & Killias, M. (2012): Who should supervise students during self-report interviews? A controlled experiment on response behaviour in online questionnaires. Journal of Experimental Criminology 8, 17–28.

Wells, L.E. (1978): Theories of deviance and the self-concept. Social Psychology 41, 189–204.

Wells, L.E. & Rankin, J.H. (1988): Direct parental controls and delinquency. Criminology 26, 263–285.

White, V., Hill, D.J. & Effendi, Y. (2004): How does active parental consent influence the findings of drug-use surveys in schools? Evaluation Review 28, 246–260.

Wikström, P.-O.H. & Butterworth, D.A. (2006): Adolescent crime: Individual differences and lifestyles. Collumpton: Willan.

Wikström, P.-O.H., Oberwittler, D., Treiber, K. & Hardie, B. (2012): Breaking Rules: The Social and Situational Dynamics of Young People's Urban Crime. Oxford: Oxford University Press.

Williams, F. & McShane, M. (2010): Criminological theory. 5th ed., Upper Saddle River, NJ: Prentice Hall.

Williams, K.S. (2012): Textbook on Criminology. Oxford: Oxford University Press.

Wilmers, N. (2002): Jugendliche in Deutschland zur Jahrtausendwende, gefährlich oder gefährdet? Ergebnisse wiederholter, repräsentativer Dunkelfelduntersuchungen zu Gewalt und Kriminalität im Leben junger Menschen 1998–2000. Baden-Baden: Nomos.

Winterdyk, J. & Kilchling, M. (2014): Creating a Sustainable Criminological Landscape: Building Capacity and Networking the Balkans, in: Getoš Kalac, A.-M. et al. (eds.), Mapping the Criminological Landscape of the Balkans. Balkan Criminology Series Volume 1. Berlin: Duncker & Humblot, 57–74.

World Travel & Tourism Council (2015): Travel & Tourism: Economic Impact 2015 World. London: World Travel & Tourism Council.

Wright, B.R., Caspi, A., Moffitt, T.E. & Silva, P.A. (1999): Low self-control, social bonds, and crime: social causation, social selection, or both? Criminology 37(3), 479–514.

Yu, J.-W., Tian, G.-L. & Tang, M.-L. (2008): Two new models for survey sampling with sensitive characteristics: Design and analysis. Metrika 67, 251–263.

Zhang, S., Benson, T. & Deng, X. (2000): A Test-retest Reliability Assessment of the International Self-report Delinquency Instrument. Journal of Criminal Justice 28, 283–295.

Zvekić, U. (1996): The International Crime (Victim) Survey: Issues of Comparative Advantages and Disadvantages. International Criminal Justice Review 6, 1–21.

Zvekić, U. (1998): Criminal Victimisation in Countries in Transition. Rome: UNICRI.

Online Reports

Balkan Criminology official homepage (n/a): ISRD3 Croatia – International Self-Report Delinquency Study; https://www.balkan-criminology.eu/projects/isrd3-croatia-international-self-report-delinquency-study/ [01/08/2018].

Croatian Bureau of Statistics (2014): Stopa registrirane nezaposlenosti; dzs.hr/Hrv/system/first_resu lts.htm [01/06/2018].

European Union (2018): Candidate countries and potential candidates; http://ec.eur opa.eu/environment/enlarg/candidates.htm [01/08/2018].

European Union (2018): Conditions for membership; https://ec.europa.eu/neighbour hood-enlargement/policy/conditions-membership_en [01/08/2018].

EUROSTAT (2014): Statistika zaposlenosti; http://ec.europa.eu/eurostat/statistics-explained/index.php/Employment_statistics/hr#Stope_zaposlenosti_prema_spol u.2C_dobi_i_razini_obrazovanja [14/06/2018].

EUROSTAT (2018): Estimated average age of young people leaving the parental household by sex; https://data.europa.eu/euodp/en/data/dataset/Lagl5xPW8qsjM BcrPi9iQ [01/08/2018].

Helsinki Committee for Human Rights of the Republic of Macedonia (2015): Analysis of the Situation with Hate Speech in the Republic of Macedonia; http://www.mhc.org.mk/system/uploads/redactor_asscts/documents/1058/Hate_Speech_web _eng.PDF [01/08/2018].

ESPAD (2015): EASPAD Report 2015; http://www.espad.org/report/methodology/espad-2015 [01/04/2018].

International Self-Report Delinquency Study (n/a): ISRD3 https://web.northeastern.edu/isrd/isrd3/ [01/05/2018].

Law No. 05/L-020 on Gender Equality (2015); https://gzk.rks-gov.net/ActDetail.aspx?ActID=2457 [01/06/2018].

OECD (2018): International Migration Outlook 2018. OECD Publishing, Paris; https://doi.org/10.1787/migr_outlook-2018-en. [01/06/2018].

OSCE Mission in Kosovo (2015): Information Guide on Women and Men's Access to Property and Housing Rights in Kosovo. Organization for Security and Co-operation in Europe; https://www.osce.org/kosovo/197371 [01/02/2018].

OSCE Mission in Kosovo (2018): A Men's Perspective on Gender Equality in Kosovo. Organization for Security and Co-operation in Europe; https://www.osce.org/mission-in-kosovo/382507?download = true [12/08/2018].

Regulation (EC) No 110/2008 of the European Parliament and of the Council; https://eur-lex.europa.eu/legal-content/EN/TXT/PDF/?uri = CELEX:32008R0110&from = HR [02/06/2018].

Regulation on Rules of Procedure of the Ombudsperson Institution (02/2016); https://gzk.rks-gov.net/ActDetail.aspx?ActID = 12504 [15/07/2018].

The Ministry of Science and Education in Croatia (n/a): Nacionalni kurikulum Republike Hrvatske za predškolski, osnovnoškolski i srednjoškolski odgoj i obrazovanje; https://mzo.gov.hr/istaknute-teme/odgoj-i-obrazovanje/nacionalni-kurikulum/125 [01/07/2018].

World Bank (2014): South East Europe Regular Economic Report No. 6: Brittle Recovery. Washington, D.C.; https://openknowledge.worldbank.org/bitstream/handle/10986/19021/879620NWP0P1470R60WEB0V20Box385214B.pdf?sequence = 1&isAllowed = y [14/06/2018].

World Bank (2016): International Telecommunication Union, World Telecommunication / ICT Development Report and database Individuals using the Internet (% of population); https://data.worldbank.org/indicator/IT.NET.USER.ZS?end = 2016&locations = HR-MK&start = 1990&view = chart [02/06/2018].

World Bank (2018): Unemployment, female (% of female labor force) (modeled ILO estimate); http://data.worldbank.org/indicator/SL.UEM.TOTL.FE.ZS [01/07/2018].

World Bank Group (2015): South East Europe Regular Economic Report No. 8: Growth Recovers, Risks Heighten. Macroeconomics & Fiscal Management. Washington, D.C.; https://openknowledge.worldbank.org/bitstream/handle/10986/23684/Growth0recovers00risks0heighten.pdf?sequence = 1&isAllowed = y [14/06/2018].

Appendix

Questionnaire[502]

Questionnaire ISRD-3

(10/2012)

Hello,

This questionnaire is about you and your friends. We are interested in getting to know more about your life, school, what you do in your free time and about the problems you might have. The questions are about your personal experience and your opinions, but you are free to answer them or not.

Of course, the questionnaire is anonymous: your name is not on it, your parents or your teachers won't see your answers. Even our research team will not know who has given what answer. Once you have finished, the questionnaires will be transferred [In the online version, insert: automatically and anonymously] to the University of ....

If there are any questions you don't understand, please ask the assistant who has come to your school to help you [In the online version or in countries where teachers are the only persons, the students can ask – replace by: teacher in your class to help you (but don't let her/him see your answers!)]. Don't think too much about answering the questions, just answer them spontaneously.

Thank you very much for taking part!

Before you start, please enter the number which will be shown to you into the fields below:

ID: ⊔ ⊔ ⊔   ⊔ ⊔   ⊔   ⊔ ⊔ ⊔   ⊔ ⊔

---

502   Original fonts, page breaks, and colour scheme of instruction fields adjusted to the book layout.

Some questions about yourself

1.1) Are you male or female?

    ○   male

    ○   female

1.2) How old are you?

    _____ years (enter your age)

1.3) Which country were you born in?

(Please tick only ONE box!)

    ○   in this country

    ☐   Italy [this and the next 4 categories: country-specific sequence!]

    ☐   Kosovo

    ☐   Portugal

    ☐   Germany

    ☐   Turkey

    ☐   in another country (write in): _____

1.4) Which country was your (natural) mother born in?

(Please tick only ONE box!)

    ☐   she was born in this country

    ☐   Italy [this and the next 4 categories: country-specific sequence!]

    ☐   Kosovo

    ☐   Portugal

    ☐   Germany

    ☐   Turkey

    ☐   in another country (write in): _____

    ☐   I don't know

1.5) Which country was your (natural) father born in?

(Please tick only ONE box!)

    ☐   he was born in this country

    ☐   Italy [this and the next 4 categories: country-specific sequence!]

    ☐   Kosovo

    ☐   Portugal

    ☐   Germany

    ☐   Turkey

    ☐   in another country (write in): _____

    ☐   I don't know

1.6)   Which people are involved in bringing you up?

☐   Father and mother (or stepfather/stepmother)
☐   One parent only (father or mother)
☐   Other situation (specify): _____

1.7)   What language do you MOST OFTEN speak with the people you live with?

☐   [dominant language 1 of country]
☐   [dominant language 2 of country – can be extended to more than 2 languages]
☐   My native language, (write in) _____

1.8)   What is your religion or which religious community do you belong to?

(Please tick only ONE box!)

☐   I do not belong to a religion / a religious community
☐   Catholic Christianity [from here on, country-specific sequence!]
☐   Protestant Christianity
☐   Orthodox Christianity [In India/Indonesia: replace this by Hinduism]
☐   Sunni Islam
☐   Shi'ite Islam
☐   Judaism
☐   another religion / religious community (write in):
          _____

1.9)   How important to you (personally) is religion in your everyday life?

very important	quite important	a bit important	a bit unimportant	quite unimportant	totally unimportant
☐	☐	☐	☐	☐	☐

1.10) What is your [category – each country will use its own organizing dimensions!] [To which of the following groups do you belong]?

Tick ONE box

☐   [category 1]
☐   [category 2]
☐   [category 3]
☐   None of the above, but _____

1.11) Is your FATHER (or the man in your home) unemployed?

Tick ONE box

☐   Yes, he is unemployed.

☐   No, he is working.

☐   Other (is retired, has long-term illness, looks after the home, is a student, ...)

1.12) Is your MOTHER (or the woman in your home) unemployed?

Tick ONE box

☐   Yes, she is unemployed.

☐   No, she is working.

☐   Other (is retired, has long-term illness, looks after the home, is a student, ...)

1.13) Where does your family get its income from?

Tick ALL that apply

❏   They receive unemployment or social welfare benefits [each country has to translate "social welfare" into an equivalent, appropriate category!]

❏   Earnings, wages, or property of my parents

❏   Other (write in): _____

1.14) How well-off is your family, compared to others?

In comparison to most other families that I know we are ...

much worse off	worse off	somewhat worse off	the same	somewhat better off	better off	much better off
❏	❏	❏	❏	❏	❏	❏

1.15) If you compare yourself with other people of your age: do you have more, the same, or less money (pocket money + presents + own earnings, etc.) to spend?

much less	less	somewhat less	the same	somewhat more	more	much more
❏	❏	❏	❏	❏	❏	❏

About your family

Note: Some of the following questions ask about your parents. If mostly foster parents, step-parents or others brought you up, answer for them. For example, if you have both a stepfather and a natural father, answer for the one that is the most important in bringing you up.

2.1) How well do you get along with your parents?

Tick one box for each line, indicating how much you agree or disagree

	totally agree	rather agree	neither nor	rather disagree	totally disagree	there is no such person
I get along just fine with my father (stepfather)	❑	❑	❑	❑	❑	❑
I get along just fine with my mother (stepmother)	❑	❑	❑	❑	❑	❑
I can easily get emotional support and care from my parents	❑	❑	❑	❑	❑	
I would feel very bad about disappointing my parents	❑	❑	❑	❑	❑	

2.2) How many <u>days a week</u> do you usually eat an evening meal with your parent(s)?

Tick ONE box

☐   Never

☐   Once a week

☐   Twice a week

☐   Three times a week

☐   Four times a week

☐   Five times a week

☐   Six times a week

☐   Daily

2.3) How often do the following statements apply to you?

Tick one box for each line

	almost always	often	some-times	seldom	almost never
My parents know *where I am* when I go out.	❑	❑	❑	❑	❑
My parents know *what I am doing* when I go out.	❑	❑	❑	❑	❑
My parents know *what friends I am with* when I go out.	❑	❑	❑	❑	❑
If I have been out, my parents ask me what I did, where I went, and who I spent time with.	❑	❑	❑	❑	❑
If I go out in the evening, my parents tell me when I have to be back home.	❑	❑	❑	❑	❑
If I am out and it gets late, I have to call my parents and let them know.	❑	❑	❑	❑	❑
My parents check if I have done my homework.	❑	❑	❑	❑	❑
My parents check that I only watch films/DVDs allowed for my age group.	❑	❑	❑	❑	❑
I tell my parents who I spend time with.	❑	❑	❑	❑	❑
I tell my parents how I spend my money.	❑	❑	❑	❑	❑
I tell my parents where I am most afternoons after school.	❑	❑	❑	❑	❑
I tell my parents what I do with my free time.	❑	❑	❑	❑	❑

2.4) Have you ever experienced any of the following serious events?

Tick one box for each line

	No	Yes
Death of your father or mother.	❑	❑
Very serious illness of one of your parents or someone else close to you.	❑	❑
One of your parents having problems with alcohol or drugs.	❑	❑
Physical fights between your parents.	❑	❑
Repeated serious conflicts between your parents.	❑	❑
Divorce or separation of your parents.	❑	❑

About your school

3.1) How strongly do you agree or disagree with the following statements about your school?

Tick one box for each line

	I fully agree	I somewhat agree	I somewhat disagree	I fully disagree
If I had to move, I would miss my school.	❑	❑	❑	❑
Most mornings I like going to school.	❑	❑	❑	❑
I like my school.	❑	❑	❑	❑
Our classes are interesting.	❑	❑	❑	❑
There is a lot of stealing in my school.	❑	❑	❑	❑
There is a lot of fighting in my school.	❑	❑	❑	❑
Many things are broken or vandalized in my school.	❑	❑	❑	❑
There is a lot of drug use in my school.	❑	❑	❑	❑

3.2) If you had to move to another city, how much would you miss your favourite teacher?

I would miss my teacher ... (Tick one box)

not at all	not much	only a bit	somewhat	quite a lot	very much
❑	❑	❑	❑	❑	❑

3.3) How important is it to you how your favourite teacher thinks about you?

totally unimportant	quite unimportant	a bit unimportant	a bit important	quite important	very important
❑	❑	❑	❑	❑	❑

3.4) Have you ever stayed away from school for at least a whole day without a proper reason in the <u>last 12 months</u>? If yes, how often?

☐   No, never.

☐   yes, ____ times (*enter frequency*)

3.5) How well do you do at school?

☐   Excellent, I'm probably one of the best in my class(es)

☐   Well above average

☐   Above average

☐   Average

☐   Below average

☐   Well below average

☐   Poor, I'm probably one of the worst in my class(es)

3.6) Have you ever been held back, that is, did you ever have to <u>repeat a year (grade)</u>?

☐   No, never.

☐   yes, ____ times (*enter frequency*)

3.7) What do you think you will do when you finish compulsory school (when you reach the age when you can leave school if you choose)?

Tick ONE box

☐   I will (continue) going to school to preparie for higher education

☐   I will (continue to) attend a school where I can learn a trade

☐   I will start an apprenticeship

☐   I will look for a job to earn money

☐   Other, _____

☐   I don't know yet.

Some bad things that may have happened to you

4.1.   Try to remember: Did any of the following things ever happen to you? If so, was it reported to the police?

| a) | Someone wanted you to give them money or something else (like a watch, shoes, mobile phone) and threatened you if you refused? |

Has this ever happened to you?

☐   no   *If no, continue with question b)*

☐   yes   How often has this happened to you in the last 12 months? _____ times

How many of these incidents were reported to the police?   _____ incidents

| b) | Someone hit you violently or hurt you – so much that you needed to see a doctor? |

Has this ever happened to you?

☐   no   *If no, continue with question c)*

☐   yes   How often has this happened to you in the last 12 months? _____ times

How many of these incidents were reported to the police?   _____ incidents

| c) | Something was stolen from you (such as a book, money, mobile phone, sports equipment, bicycle...)? |

Has this ever happened to you?

☐   no   *If no, continue with question d)*

☐   yes   How often has this happened to you in the last 12 months? ____ times

How many of these incidents were reported to the police?   ____ incidents

| d) | Someone threatened you with violence or committed physical violence against you *because* of your religion, the language you speak, the colour of your skin, your social or ethnic background, or for similar reasons? |

Has this ever happened to you?

☐   no   *If no, continue with question e)*

☐   yes   How often has this happened to you in the last 12 months? ____ times

How many of these incidents were reported to the police?   ____ incidents

| e) | Has anyone made fun of you or teased you seriously in a hurtful way through e-mail, instant messaging, in a chat room, on a website, or through a text message sent to your mobile phone? |

Has this ever happened to you?

    ☐   no   *If no, continue with question f).*

    ☐   yes   How often has this happened to you in the last 12 months? ____ times

                    How many of these incidents were reported to the police? ____ incidents

f)   Has your mother or father (or your stepmother or stepfather) ever hit, slapped or shoved you (Include also times when this was a punishment for something you had done)?

Has this ever happened to you?

    ☐   no   *If no, continue with question g)*

    ☐   yes   How often has this happened to you in the last 12 months? ____ times

g)   Has your mother or father (or your stepmother or stepfather) ever hit you with an object, punched or kicked you forcefully or beaten you up (Include also times when this was a punishment for something you had done)?

Has this ever happened to you?

    ☐   no   *If no, continue with the next section.*

    ☐   yes   How often has this happened to you in the last 12 months? ____ times

About leisure time and your peers

5.1)   How many times a week do you usually go out in the evening [translators: night], such as going to a party, going to somebody's house, or hanging out in the street?

        ☐   Never, I don't go out in the evening [translators: night]

        ☐   Once a week

        ☐   Twice a week

        ☐   Three times a week

        ☐   Four times a week

        ☐   Five times a week

        ☐   Six times a week

        ☐   Daily

5.2)   When you go out on a weekend evening [translators: night], what time do you normally get back home?

☐   I don't go out in the evening [translators: night] at weekends

☐   Generally, I am back home at ____ : ____ (enter *hour : minutes*)

5.3)   Who do you spend MOST of your free time with?

Please tick only ONE box!

☐   On my own.

☐   With my family.

☐   With 1–3 friends.

☐   With a larger group of friends (4 and more).

5.4)   Think back over the LAST SIX MONTHS: Would you say that most of the time you have been happy?

Most of the time I have been ... [Tick ONE box that best applies]:

☺   ☹

very happy	happy	a bit more happy than unhappy	a bit more unhappy than happy	unhappy	very unhappy
☐	☐	☐	☐	☐	☐

5.5)   How many of your friends have at least one parent of foreign origin? [country-specific: ... (see Translator's Guide to Q1.10 and Q5.5!)]

☐   None at all

☐   A few

☐   Many of them

☐   All of them

5.6)   What kind of things do you usually do in your leisure time?

	never	sometimes	often
I go to coffee bars or pop concerts.	☐	☐	☐
I do something creative (theatre, music, drawing, writing, reading books).	☐	☐	☐
I am engaged in fights with others.	☐	☐	☐
I do sports, athletics, or exercise.	☐	☐	☐
I study for school or do homework.	☐	☐	☐
I hang out in shopping centres, streets, parks, or the neighbourhood just for fun.	☐	☐	☐
I do something illegal to have fun.	☐	☐	☐
I drink beer/alcohol or take drugs.	☐	☐	☐
I frighten and annoy people just for fun.	☐	☐	☐

5.7)   Some people have a friend or a group of friends they spend time with, doing things together or just hanging out. Do you have a friend or a group of friends like that?

      ☐   No => *skip questions 5.8–5.9 and continue with question 5.10*

      ☐   Yes

5.8)   If you had to move to another city, how much would you miss your friend or group of friends?

I would miss my friend or my group of friends ... (Tick one box)

not at all	not much	only a bit	somewhat	quite a lot	very much
☐	☐	☐	☐	☐	☐

5.9)   How important is it to you what your friend or group of friends think(s) about you?

Tick one box

totally unimportant	quite unimportant	a bit unimportant	a bit important	quite important	very important
☐	☐	☐	☐	☐	☐

5.10) Young people sometimes engage in illegal activities. <u>How many friends</u> do you know who have done any of the following?

	(either check "no" or fill in the number)	(check)	(your best guess)
a)	I have friends who used soft or hard drugs like weed, hash, ecstasy, speed, heroin or coke.	☐ no	yes, ___ friends
b)	I have friends who have stolen things from a shop or department store.	☐ no	yes, ___ friends
c)	I have friends who have entered a building without permission to steal something.	☐ no	yes, ___ friends
d)	I have friends who have threatened somebody with a weapon or beaten someone up, just to get their money or other things.	☐ no	yes, ___ friends
e)	I have friends who have beaten someone up or hurt someone badly with something like a stick or a knife.	☐ no	yes, ___ friends

What do you think about the following?

6.1) How wrong do you think is it for someone of your age to do the following?

Tick one box for each line

	very wrong	wrong	a little wrong	not wrong at all
Lie, disobey, or talk back to adults such as parents and teachers.	☐	☐	☐	☐
Knowingly insult someone because of his/her religion, skin colour, or ethnic background.	☐	☐	☐	☐
Purposefully damage or destroy property that does not belong to you.	☐	☐	☐	☐
Illegally download films or music from the internet.	☐	☐	☐	☐
Steal something small like a chocolate bar from a shop.	☐	☐	☐	☐
Break into a building to steal something.	☐	☐	☐	☐
Hit someone with the idea of hurting that person.	☐	☐	☐	☐
Use a weapon or force to get money or things from other people.	☐	☐	☐	☐

6.2)   Imagine you were caught shoplifting, would you feel ashamed if ...

	no, not at all	yes, a little	yes, very much
a) your *best friend* found out about it?	❏	❏	❏
b) your *teacher* found out about it?	❏	❏	❏
c) your *parents* found out about it?	❏	❏	❏

6.3)   Imagine you were caught physically hurting another person, would you feel ashamed if ...

	no, not at all	yes, a little	yes, very much
a) your *best friend* found out about it?	❏	❏	❏
b) your *teacher* found out about it?	❏	❏	❏
c) your *parents* found out about it?	❏	❏	❏

6.4)   Imagine you were arrested by the police for committing a crime, would you feel ashamed if ...

	no, not at all	yes, a little	yes, very much
a) your *best friend* found out about it?	❏	❏	❏
b) your *teacher* found out about it?	❏	❏	❏
c) your *parents* found out about it?	❏	❏	❏

6.5)   How much do you agree or disagree with the following statements?

Tick one box for each line

	fully agree	somewhat agree	somewhat disagree	fully disagree
I act on the spur of the moment without stopping to think.	❏	❏	❏	❏
I do whatever brings me pleasure here and now, even at the cost of some future goal.	❏	❏	❏	❏
I'm more concerned with what happens to me in the short run than in the long run.	❏	❏	❏	❏
I like to test myself every now and then by doing something a little risky.	❏	❏	❏	❏
Sometimes, I will take a risk just for the fun of it.	❏	❏	❏	❏
Excitement and adventure are more important to me than security.	❏	❏	❏	❏
I try to look out for myself first, even if it means making things difficult for other people.	❏	❏	❏	❏
If things I do upset people, it's their problem, not mine.	❏	❏	❏	❏
I will try to get the things I want even when I know it's causing problems for other people.	❏	❏	❏	❏

6.6)   Did you ever have an accident that was so serious you had to see a doctor, such as during sports or a traffic accident (not just a simple cut)?

☐   No

☐   Once

☐   _____ times (*enter number*)

Next, we will ask you some questions about your neighbourhood. Neighbourhood is the area within a short walking distance (say a couple of minutes) from your home. That is the street you live in and the streets, houses, shops, parks, and other areas close to your home. When asked about your neighbours, think about the people living in this area.

6.7)   How much do you agree or disagree with the following statements about your neighbourhood?

Tick one box for each line

	fully agree	somewhat agree	somewhat disagree	fully disagree
Many of my neighbours know me.	☐	☐	☐	☐
People in my neighbourhood often do things together.	☐	☐	☐	☐
There is a lot of crime in my neighbourhood.	☐	☐	☐	☐
There is a lot of drug selling in my neighbourhood.	☐	☐	☐	☐
There is a lot of fighting in my neighbourhood.	☐	☐	☐	☐
There are a lot of empty and abandoned buildings in my neighbourhood.	☐	☐	☐	☐
There is a lot of graffiti in my neighbourhood.	☐	☐	☐	☐
People around here are willing to help their neighbours.	☐	☐	☐	☐
This is a close-knit neighbourhood.	☐	☐	☐	☐
People in this neighbourhood can be trusted.	☐	☐	☐	☐
People in this neighbourhood generally get along well with each other.	☐	☐	☐	☐

About things young people sometimes do

7.1)   Young people sometimes do things that are forbidden, for example damaging or stealing another person's property. Some hit and hurt others on purpose (we don't mean situations in which young people play-fight with each other just for fun). <u>What about you?</u> Have you ever done any of the following, and if so, how often within the last 12 months?

Please remember that nobody, not your family nor your teachers nor the police nor anybody else will be told what you have told us. You can be sure that what you tell us will remain secret.

Have you ever in your life ...   *... how often in the last 12 months?*

... painted on a wall, train, subway or bus (graffiti)?	◯ ◯ (No) (Yes)	*If you ticked "yes":* How often in the last *12 months?* ___ times
... damaged something on purpose, such as a bus shelter, a window, a car or a seat in the bus or train?	◯ ◯ (No) (Yes)	*If you ticked "yes":* How often in the last *12 months?* ___ times
... stolen something from a shop or department store?	◯ ◯ (No) (Yes)	*If you ticked "yes":* How often in the last *12 months?* ___ times
... broken into a building to steal something?	◯ ◯ (No) (Yes)	*If you ticked "yes":* How often in the last *12 months?* ___ times
... stolen a bicycle?	◯ ◯ (No) (Yes)	*If you ticked "yes":* How often in the last *12 months?* ___ times
... stolen a motorbike or car?	◯ ◯ (No) (Yes)	*If you ticked "yes":* How often in the last *12 months?* ___ times
... stolen something off or from a car?	◯ ◯ (No) (Yes)	*If you ticked "yes":* How often in the last *12 months?* ___ times
... used a weapon, force or threat of force to get money or things from someone?	◯ ◯ (No) (Yes)	*If you ticked "yes":* How often in the last *12 months?* ___ times
... stolen something from a person without force or threat?	◯ ◯ (No) (Yes)	*If you ticked "yes":* How often in the last *12 months?* ___ times
... carried a weapon, such as a stick, knife, gun, or chain?	◯ ◯ (No) (Yes)	*If you ticked "yes":* How often in the last *12 months?* ___ times
... taken part in a group fight in a football stadium, on the street or in another public place?	◯ ◯ (No) (Yes)	*If you ticked "yes":* How often in the last *12 months?* ___ times

... beaten someone up or hurt some-one with a stick or knife so badly that the person was injured?	○ ○ (No) (Yes)	*If you ticked "yes":* How often in the last *12 months?* ___ times
... illegally downloaded music or films from the internet?	○ ○ (No) (Yes)	*If you ticked "yes":* How often in the last *12 months?* ___ times
... sold any drugs or helped someone sell drugs?	○ ○ (No) (Yes)	*If you ticked "yes":* How often in the last *12 months?* ___ times
[optional!] ... hurt an animal on purpose?	○ ○ (No) (Yes)	*If you ticked "yes":* How often in the last *12 months?* ___ times

7.2)   Have you ever had <u>contact with the police</u> because you <u>yourself</u> did something illegal, like one of the things listed above?

○   No

○   Yes, I have had contact with the police because I did something illegal.

    ✎ <u>If yes</u>   How often in the last 12 months? ____ times (*enter frequency*)

a)

b)   The last time because of which offence?

             It was because _____

c)   What happened the last time you had contact with the police?

Tick all that apply

❑   My parents were notified about the incident.

❑   The school / My teacher was notified.

❑   I was sent to the court or a prosecutor.

❑   I was given a warning by the court/prosecutor/police.

❑   I was punished by the court or a prosecutor.

❑   I was punished by my parents.

❑   Nothing happened.

❑   Something else happened: _____

Next are questions about alcohol and drugs. When we ask about occasions, this can be a party, a normal day, or a special situation. Please answer as thoughtfully and frankly as possible!

8.1   a)   Have you ever drunk alcohol?

O   No, never (if no, continue with question 8.2)

O   Yes

b)   Think back over the LAST 30 DAYS. On how many occasions (if any) have you had any of the following to drink?

If never, fill in 0!

Beer or alcopops   _____ occasions

Wine   _____ occasions

Strong spirits [e.g. whisky, gin, vodka, ...]   _____ occasions

c)   Think back again over the LAST 30 DAYS. How many times (if any) have you had FIVE OR MORE DRINKS on one occasion? (A "drink" is a can, glass or 0.33 l bottle of beer, a glass of wine, or a 2 cl glass of spirits)

O   never

O   once

O   twice

O   3–4 times

O   5–9 times

O   10–19 times

O   20 times or more

8.2)   Have you ever used cannabis (cannabis / marijuana / hash)?

O   No, never (if no, continue with question 8.3)

O   Yes

↳ If yes, on how many occasions during the last 30 days?

_____ occasions (if never, fill in 0!)

8.3)   Have you ever used Relevin?

O   No, never (if no, continue with question 8.4)

O   Yes

8.4) Have you ever used XTC, LSD, speed, amphetamines or similar drugs?

   O   No, never (if no, continue with question 8.5)

   O   Yes

        ↳ If yes, on how many occasions during the last 12 months?

           _____ occasions (if never, fill in 0!)

8.5) Have you ever used heroin, cocaine, or crack?

   O   No, never (if no, continue with question 8.6)

   O   Yes

        ↳ If yes, on how many occasions during the last 12 months?

           _____ occasions (if never, fill in 0!)

8.6) Imagine you had used cannabis (cannabis / marijuana / hash), do you think that you would have said so in this questionnaire?

Tick ONE box

   O   I have already said that I have used it

   O   Definitely yes

   O   Probably yes

   O   Probably not

   O   Definitely not

What would other people think …

Next are two imaginary situations. Perhaps you have never been in such situations. We would like to know what other people would think IF you ever did something like this.

Imagine: *You own a two-year-old mobile phone. You convince a classmate that this old model is great without saying that the new model that is much better and cheaper. You are able to sell your classmate your old mobile phone for a price that allows you to buy yourself the brand-new model.*

9.1 IF you did this: How would the following people feel about it?

Tick one box for each line	would admire me for it		neither … nor		would criticize me for it
My best friend	☐	☐	☐	☐	☐
The other people in my class	☐	☐	☐	☐	☐
My mother (or stepmother)	☐	☐	☐	☐	☐
My father (or stepfather)	☐	☐	☐	☐	☐
My favourite teacher	☐	☐	☐	☐	☐
Other people of my age in my neighbourhood	☐	☐	☐	☐	☐

9.2　Can you imagine actually doing this?

not at all	probably not	undecided	probably yes	yes, surely
❏	❏	❏	❏	❏

Imagine: *In a big store, you see something which you always wanted but couldn't afford (e.g. smart trainers, expensive tee shirt, CD, or perfume). You take it home without paying.*

9.3　IF you did this: How would the following people feel about this?

Tick one box for each line	would admire me for it ☺	☺	neither ... nor ☺	☹	would criti- cize me for it ☹
My best friend	❏	❏	❏	❏	❏
The other people in my class	❏	❏	❏	❏	❏
My mother (or stepmother)	❏	❏	❏	❏	❏
My father (or stepfather)	❏	❏	❏	❏	❏
My favourite teacher	❏	❏	❏	❏	❏
Other people of my age in my neighbourhood	❏	❏	❏	❏	❏

9.4　Can you imagine actually doing this if you were certain of not getting caught?

not at all	probably not	undecided	probably yes	yes, surely
❏	❏	❏	❏	❏

The following questions ask what you think about the police. Normally, such questions are meant for adults, and probably you have never thought about this before. But we feel that young people like you also have an opinion and can also answer questions like these.

10.1) When victims report crimes to the police, do you think the police treat people of different races, different ethnic groups, or of foreign origin equally?

Tick ONE box

❏　　Yes, everyone is treated equally.

❏　　No, some groups are treated worse.

　　　Which groups? _____ (*write in*)

10.2) If a violent crime or a burglary happened near where you live and the police were called, how quickly do you think they would arrive at the scene?

Tick one box between 0 and 10

very slowly										very quickly
0	1	2	3	4	5	6	7	8	9	10
❑	❑	❑	❑	❑	❑	❑	❑	❑	❑	❑

10.3) Would you say the police generally treat young people with respect?

(almost) never	sometimes	often	(almost) always
❑	❑	❑	❑

10.4) How often, would you say, the police make fair decisions when dealing with young people?

(almost) never	sometimes	often	(almost) always
❑	❑	❑	❑

10.5) How often would you say the police explain their decisions and actions to young people?

(almost) never	sometimes	often	(almost) always
❑	❑	❑	❑

10.6) How you think about your duty towards the police: To what extent is it your duty to do what the police tell you, even if you don't understand or agree with the reasons?

Tick one box between 0 and 10

Not at all my duty										Totally my duty
0	1	2	3	4	5	6	7	8	9	10
❑	❑	❑	❑	❑	❑	❑	❑	❑	❑	❑

10.7) To what extent do you agree or disagree with the following statements about the police?

Tick one box for each line

	agree strongly	agree	neither agree nor disagree	disagree	disagree strongly
The police generally have the same sense of right and wrong as I do.	❑	❑	❑	❑	❑
The police are appreciative of how young people think.	❑	❑	❑	❑	❑
I generally support how the police usually act.	❑	❑	❑	❑	❑

10.8) Do you think the police take bribes, and if yes, often?

Tick one box between 0 and 10

never										always
0	1	2	3	4	5	6	7	8	9	10
❑	❑	❑	❑	❑	❑	❑	❑	❑	❑	❑

Module 11: Optional

In the following, there are some questions about your group of friends.

11.1) Some people have a certain group of friends that they spend time with, doing things together or just hanging out. Do you have a group of friends like that?

Please tick only ONE box!

O   Yes

O   No

↳ *If no*, skip questions 11.2 to 11.8 and go to the last question on page [200]

11.2) Which of the following best describes the ages of people in your group?

Tick ONE box

O   under twelve

O   twelve to fifteen

O   sixteen to eighteen

O   nineteen to twenty-five

O   above twenty-five

11.3) Does this group spend a lot of time together in public places like parks, the street, shopping areas, or the neighbourhood?

O No

O Yes

11.4) How long has this group existed for?

Tick ONE box

O less than three months

O three monts to less than one year

O one to four years

O five to ten years

O eleven to twenty years

O more than twenty years

11.5) Is doing illegal things (against the law) accepted by or okay for your group?

O No

O Yes

11.6) Do people in your group actually do illegal things (against the law) together?

O No

O Yes

11.7) Do you consider your group of friends to be a gang?

O No

O Yes

11.8) Are they all boys or all girls, or is it a mixed group?

O We are all boys.

O We are all girls.

O It is a mixed group.

Your last answer in this questionnaire *(Grade 9 only)*

Please read the following instruction carefully:

Next, we apply a novel questioning technique to provide additional protection of your privacy. We will ask you now <u>two questions,</u> but you will give us <u>only one answer.</u>

Please think first about how you would honestly answer each of the two questions (either with *Yes* or with *No*) but do not write these answers down:

Question 1:   *Is your mother's birthday in January, February, or March?*

    (if you really don't know, make a most likely guess)

Question 2:   *Did you commit one of the following criminal offenses in the last 12 months?*

    (shoplifting, robbery, assault resulting in an injury, or burglary)

Now, please mark option (A) or option (B) depending on your answers:

– If your answer to both questions is the same (<u>both</u> *YES* or <u>both</u> *NO*) tick option (A)

– If your answers to both questions are different (<u>one</u> *YES* and <u>one</u> *NO*) tick option (B)

(Your privacy remains protected because we do not know your answers to the separate questions. With the help of statistical procedures, however, we can compute to how many people <u>overall</u> the second question applies.)

What are your answers to the two questions?

   Tick ONE box

   ○   (A) *NO* to <u>both</u> questions or *YES* to <u>both</u> questions

   ○   (B) *YES* to <u>one</u> of the questions and *NO* to the other

Thank you for your cooperation!

BALKAN
CRIMINOLOGY

Anna-Maria Getoš Kalac
Hans-Jörg Albrecht
Michael Kilchling (eds.)

Mapping the Criminological
Landscape of the Balkans

A Survey on Criminology and Crime with an
Expedition into the Criminal Landscape of the
Balkans

Research Series of the Max Planck
Institute for Foreign and International
Criminal Law

Publications of the Max Planck
Partner Group for Balkan Criminology
Edited by Hans-Jörg Albrecht
& Anna-Maria Getoš Kalac

Volume BC 1

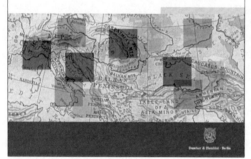

BALKAN
CRIMINOLOC

Sunčana Roksandić Vidlička

Prosecuting Serious
Economic Crimes as
International Crimes

A New Mandate for the ICC?

Research Series of the Max Planck
Institute for Foreign and International
Criminal Law

Publications of the Max Planck
Partner Group for Balkan Criminology
Edited by Hans-Jörg Albrecht
& Anna-Maria Getoš Kalac

Volume BC 2

BALKAN
CRIMINOLOGY

Lucija Sokanović

Fraud in
Criminal Law

A Normative and Criminological Analysis of
Fraudulent Crime in Croatia and the Regional Context

Research Series of the Max Planck
Institute for Foreign and International
Criminal Law

Publications of the Max Planck
Partner Group for Balkan Criminology
Edited by Hans-Jörg Albrecht
& Anna-Maria Getoš Kalac

Volume BC 4

BALKAN
CRIMINOLOG

Filip Vojta

Imprisonment for
International Crimes

An Interdisciplinary Analysis of the
ICTY Sentence Enforcement Practice

Research Series of the Max Planck
Institute for Foreign and International
Criminal Law

Publications of the Max Planck
Partner Group for Balkan Criminology
Edited by Hans-Jörg Albrecht
& Anna-Maria Getoš Kalac

Volume BC 5